THE MINISTRY OF THE CELEBRATION OF THE SACRAMENTS

VOL. I
SACRAMENTS OF INITIATION AND UNION

CELEBRATION OF BAPTISM
CELEBRATION OF CONFIRMATION
CELEBRATION OF THE EUCHARIST

VOL. II
SACRAMENTS OF RECONCILIATION

CELEBRATION OF PENANCE
CELEBRATION OF ANOINTING OF THE SICK

VOL. III
SACRAMENTS OF COMMUNITY RENEWAL

CELEBRATION OF HOLY ORDERS
CELEBRATION OF MATRIMONY

THE MINISTRY OF
THE CELEBRATION OF THE SACRAMENTS

Sacraments of Community Renewal

Nicholas Halligan, O.P.

Volume III
Holy Orders, Matrimony

ALBA · HOUSE NEW · YORK

SOCIETY OF ST. PAUL, 2187 VICTORY BLVD., STATEN ISLAND, NEW YORK 10314

Library of Congress Cataloging in Publication Data

Halligan, Francis Nicholas, 1917-
  The sacrament of community renewal: holy orders,
matrimony.
  (His The ministry of the celebration of the
sacraments, v. 3)

  Includes bibliographical references.
  1. Ordination-Catholic Church. 2. Marriage—
Catholic Church. I. Title. II. Series.
BX2200.H25 vol. 3 [BX2240] 264' .02'008s
[265' .4] 74-3209
ISBN 0-8189-0288-4 (v. 3)

Nihil Obstat:

Very Rev. Joseph C. Taylor, O.P., S.T.M., Ph.D.
Very Rev. William B. Ryan, O.P., S.T.M., J.C.D.

Imprimi Potest:

Very Rev. Terrence Quinn, O.P., S.T.L., Provincial

Nihil Obstat:

Very Rev. Joseph C. Taylor, O.P.
Censor Deputatus

Imprimatur:

Patrick Cardinal O'Boyle
Archbishop of Washington
August 28, 1972

The Nihil Obstat and Imprimatur
are a declaration that a book or pamphlet is considered
to be free from doctrinal or moral error. It is not implied that
those who have granted the Nihil Obstat and Imprimatur agree
with the contents, opinions or statements expressed.

Designed, printed and bound in the United States of
America by the Fathers and Brothers of the Society of St. Paul,
2187 Victory Boulevard, Staten Island, New York, 10314,
as part of their communications apostolate.

1 2 3 4 5 6 7 8 9 (Current Printing: first digit).

Foreword

Word and sacrament in the Church of Christ are not separated but intimately united in their distinctiveness. The ministry of the word leads to the ministry of the sacraments, and the sacraments themselves are celebrated in the word. The pastoral ministry in the Church is charged with conveying to all those who respond to the invitation of the grace of Christ the unfathomable and salutary riches of both word and sacrament. The present volumes are limited to the consideration of the ministry of the sacraments and their authentic celebration.

The ministry of the sacraments is an "ad-ministration," that is, a ministering *to* the People of God. What the legitimate minister brings to them are the graces of the sacraments and the benefits of the Sacrifice of the Mass, as sacrament and sacrifice have been handed down and understood in the Church and regulated by her authority. It is a worship ministry in which the minister by ordination or deputation offers homage in the name of all. It is an authentic ministry when it is exercised in union with the bishops under the Chief Pastor and thus in accordance with and expressive of their teaching and directives.

The minister who is earnest in fulfilling his ministry with fidelity and pastoral responsibility is responsive to the guidance and direction of the Church in whose name he functions. The burden of these volumes is to provide the minister and aspirants to the ministry with authorized norms whereby they may be safely guided in practice in the ministry of the celebration of the sacraments.

Although proper theological exploration and canonical interpretation continue to exercise their helpful roles in the understanding of sacramnt and worship life in the Church, the acceptable celebration of this ministry in the pastoral care of souls has been clearly and sufficiently delineated by competent authority in the Church during the period of renewal inaugurated by the recent Council. The text of these volumes, then, as the citations indicate, proposes to make this evident from the full use of the relevant documents and pertinent directives.

The sacramental ministry is considered in the celebration first, of the sacraments of initiation and union: Baptism, Confirmation, Eucharist; second, of the sacraments of reconciliation: Penance, the Anointing of the Sick; third, of the sacraments of community renewal: Holy Orders, Matrimony.

THE SACRAMENTS OF COMMUNITY RENEWAL

Foreword

Orders and Matrimony are sacraments of Christian continuation. Sacred or ordained ministers through the handing down of the power of Christ over his Eucharistic and Mystical Body perpetuate and apply in each generation the priesthood of Christ, the fruits of which are for all men for all time. Thus the sanctity of the People of God is maintained and fostered by the sacred and ordained ministry, for those of the faithful who are consecrated by Holy Orders are approved to feed the Church in Christ's name with the Word and the grace of God.[1]

By the sacrament of Matrimony couples mirror the union of Christ and his Church, the community of the People of God with Christ the Head. The community which marriage constitutes and which by the sacrament is made a holy community, provides children, normally the fruit of mutual love. Thus the Christian parents in each generation provide the progeny which the salvific grace of

---

1. Vatican II, Const. **Lumen Gentium,** n. 11.

Christ, through the sacramental ministrations of the sacred ministers, constitutes sons of God and joint heirs with Christ of heaven.[2] The union of husband and wife, itself sacramentalized, is conditioned to continue in its own way, within the common priesthood of the People of God, the apostolate of bringing souls to God, which at the same time is the more direct activity of the ordained priesthood.

Thus, these two sacraments, each in a different but related way, exercise spiritual paternity. They are social sacraments instituted by Christ to insure throughout time the continuation of the Christian community or society. They are sacraments of community renewal.

2. "For from the wedlock of Christians there comes the family, in which new citizens of human society are born. By the grace of the Holy Spirit received in Baptism these are made children of God, thus perpetuating the People of God throughout the centuries." (**ibid.**)

TABLE OF CONTENTS

FOREWORD v

THE CELEBRATION OF HOLY ORDERS

I. Holy Orders, a Shared Sacrament 3
II. Role of the Sacrament of Orders 4
III. Minister of the Celebration of Orders and the Ministries 6
    A. Orders 6
    B. Ministries 8
IV. Candidates for the Ministries 8
    A. General Norms 8
    B. Lector 10
    C. Acolyte 11
V. Candidates for the Diaconate 11
    A. General Norms 11
    B. Transitional Diaconate 15
    C. Permanent Diaconate 16
    D. Celebration of the Conferral of Diaconate 16
VI. Candidates for the Priesthood 17
    A. General Norms 17
    B. Celebration of the Conferral of the Priesthood 18
    C. Capable Candidates 18
    D. Qualified Candidates 19
        1. Divine Vocation 20
            a. the call 20
            b. the right intention 21
        2. Suitability 22
            a. physical and psychical 23
            b. intellectual 25
            c. moral 25
        3. Canonical Age 29
        4. Confirmation 30
        5. State of Grace 30
        6. Interstices 30
        7. Retreat 30
    E. Title of Ordination 31
    F. Record of Ordination 32

VII. Irregularities 32
    A. Norms 32
    B. Individual Irregularities 35
        1. Arising from defect 35
        2. Arising from delict 37
VIII. Impediments 38
    A. Norms 38
    B. Individual Impediments 38
        1. Catholic children of non-Catholics 38
        2. Married men 39
        3. Clerics in forbidden activity 39
        4. Slaves 39
        5. Subjects of military service 39
        6. Neophytes 40
        7. The disreputable 40

THE CELEBRATION OF MATRIMONY

  I. Marriage, a Sacrament of Community 41
 II. Basic Elements in the Structure of Marriage 43
    A. Elements essential to all marriages 43
    B. Sacramental marriage 47
III. Types of Marriage 49
    A. Valid 49
    B. Invalid 50
    C. Public 52
    D. Secret 52
 IV. Properties of Marriage 52
    A. Unity 53
    B. Indissolubility 54
  V. Contract of Marriage 57
 VI. Matrimonial Consent 58
    A. Qualities 59
        1. internal 59
        2. mutual 59
        3. free 59
        4. deliberate and simultaneous 59

      5. of the present 60
      6. externally expressed 60
        a. requisites 60
        b. interpreter 60
        c. proxy 60
   B. Obstacles 61
      1. want of use of reason 61
      2. ignorance 62
      3. error 63
      4. force or fear 65
      5. pretence or simulation 67
      6. condition 67
VII. Ordinary Juridical Form of Marriage 71
   A. Valid form 72
      1. Pastor 72
        a. designation 72
        b. conditions or qualifications 73
        c. common error 74
      2. Delegated priest or deacon 75
        a. delegation 75
        b. conditions or qualifications 75
        c. subdelegation 77
      3. Other witnesses 77
   B. Those bound by the form for validity 78
   C. Those not bound by the form for validity 80
   D. Dispensation from the ordinary valid form
      of marriage 80
   E. Those bound by a rite 81
   F. Dispensation to marry in another rite 83
   G. Lawful assistance at the celebration of marriage 83
      1. Pastor 83
      2. Delegated priest 85
      3. Other witnesses 85
VIII. Extraordinary Juridical Form of Marriage 86
   A. Danger of Death 86
      1. Norm 86
      2. Validity 86

3. Lawfulness 87
B. Outside the Danger of Death 87
    1. Norm 87
    2. Validity 87
    3. Lawfulness 88
C. Marriage of Conscience 88
IX. Liturgical Form of Marriage 89
X. Time and Place of Celebration 91
XI. Registration of Marriage 92
    A. Marriage register 92
    B. Baptismal register 93
    C. Civil register 93
XII. Banns of Marriage 94
    A. Obligation 94
    B. Form 94
    C. Time 94
    D. Place 95
    E. Omission 95
    F. Dispensation 96
    G. Interval 96
    H. Existence of Impediments 97
        1. Obligation of disclosure 97
        2. Continuance of the banns 97
XIII. Pre-marital Investigation 98
    A. General Norms 98
    B. Pastor in investigation 99
    C. Questionary 100
        1. Oath and identification 100
        2. Residence 101
        3. Baptism 101
        4. Confirmation 102
        5. Confession and Communion 102
        6. Unworthy Catholics 102
        7. Minors 103
    D. *Nihil obstat* 104
    E. Documentation 105
    F. Pre-marital instruction 107

XIV. Impediments to Marriage 108
   A. Authority over marriage 108
   B. Circumstance of impediment 109
   C. Division of impediments 110
      1. origin 110
      2. effect 110
      3. extension 110
      4. duration 110
      5. dispensation 110
      6. grade 111
      7. knowledge 111
      8. proof 112
   D. Impedient impediments 113
      1. Simple vows 113
         a. notions 113
         b. vow of virginity 113
         c. vow of chastity 114
         d. vow of celibacy 114
         e. Vow to receive sacred orders 114
         f. vow to embrace the religious state 115
      2. Legal relationship 115
      3. Mixed religion 115
         a. impediment 115
         b. subject 116
         c. dispensation 116
   E. Diriment impediments 118
      1. Want of age 118
         a. impediment 118
         b. subject 119
         c. cessation 120
      2. Impotency 120
         a. male reproductive organism 120
         b. female reproductive organism 122
         c. impotency and sterility 124
         d. types of impotency 124
         e. canonical impediment of impotency 125
         f. obligations 127

3. Marriage bond 128
   a. impediment 128
   b. conditions 128
   c. obligations 130
   d. penalties 130
4. Disparity of worship 131
   a. impediment 131
   b. conditions 131
   c. dispensation 132
5. Sacred orders 132
   a. impediment 132
   b. dispensation 133
   c. penalties 133
6. Solemn vows 133
   a. impediment 133
   b. dispensation 133
   c. penalties 134
7. Abduction 134
   a. impediment 134
   b. conditions 135
   c. dispensation 135
   d. penalties 135
8. Crime 135
   a. impediment 136
   b. dispensation 137
   c. dispensation 138
9. Consanguinity 138
   a. notion of blood relationship 138
   b. impediment 140
   c. dispensation 141
   d. penalties 142
10. Affinity 142
    a. notion of in-law-ship 142
    b. impediment 143
    c. dispensation 143
    d. penalties 144
11. Public propriety 144

a. impediment 144
b. dispensation 145
12. Spiritual relationship 145
a. impediment 145
b. dispensation 146
13. Legal relationship or adoption 146
XV. Matrimonial dispensations 146
A. Notions 146
B. Competent authority to dispense 147
C. Taxes and expenses 147
D. Causes or reasons 148
E. Procedure 151
F. Case of Death 152
1. law 152
2. pastor 152
a. valid exercise 152
b. lawful exercise 154
3. assisting priest of c. 1098, 2° 154
4. confessor 155
G. Case of urgency 156
1. law 156
2. pastor 157
a. valid exercise 157
b. lawful exercise 158
3. assisting priest of c. 1098, 2° and the confessor .. 158
XVI. Validation of an invalid marriage 158
A. Simple validation 158
1. presence of a removable diriment impediment .. 158
2. lack of consent 160
3. defect of form 160
B. Radical sanation 161
1. nature and effects 161
2. required conditions 161
3. competent authority 163
C. Cautions 163
XVII. Dissolution of the marriage bond 166
A. Sacramental and consummated marriage 166

B. Sacramental but unconsummated marriage 167
   1. fact 167
   2. solemn religious profession 167
   3. papal dispensation 168
      a. power 168
      b. proof of non-consummation 169
      c. causes 170
      d. cautions 170
C. Pauline privilege cases 171
   1. privilege 171
   2. conditions 172
      a. conversion 172
      b. departure 173
      c. interpellations 174
   3. use of the privilege 176
   4. effect of the privilege 176
   5. cautions 177
D. Petrine privilege cases 178
   1. Apostolic Constitutions 179
   2. doubtful cases 181
   3. other natural bond cases 182
   4. requirements 183
XVIII. Separation of spouses 184
   A. Notion of separation 184
   B. Perpetual separation 185
      1. cause 185
      2. requities 185
      3. authority 186
      4. effect 186
   C. Temporary separation 187
      1. causes 187
      2. authority 187
      3. effect 188
   D. Cautions 188
XIX. Civil divorce and marriage 189
XX. Legitimation of offspring 190
   A. Notion of legitimation 190

B. Law 191
XXI. Conjugal act: right and obligation 192
A. Right 192
B. Obligation to render the debt 193
C. Obligation to request the debt 194
D. Limitations 194
E. Lawfulness 196
   1. conjugal act itself 196
   2. the intention of the spouse 196
   3. circumstances 197
   4. accessory acts 198
   5. cautions 200
XXII. Conjugal act: abuses 201
A. Artificial insemination 201
   1. Notion 201
   2. Morality 202
B. Copula dimidiata 202
   1. Notion 202
   2. Morality 203
C. Amplexus reservatus 203
   1. Notion 203
   2. Morality 204
D. Canugal onanism: natural onanism 204
   1. Notion 204
   2. Morality 208
      a. malice 208
      b. cooperation 209
      c. confessional treatment 210
XXIII. Conjugal act: periodic continence and
regulation of birth 212
A. Periodic continence 212
   1. Physical aspect 212
   2. Moral aspect 212
B. Regulation of births 214
XXIV. Duties of Spouses 215
A. To each other 215
B. To their children 216

THE MINISTRY OF THE CELEBRATION OF THE SACRAMENTS

THE CELEBRATION OF HOLY ORDERS

I. *Holy Orders, a Shared Sacrament*

The sacrament of Holy Orders is a shared sacrament, fully possessed by the Bishops, and in a limited way by the priests or presbyters, and less so by the deacons.[3] Bishops are the principal dispensers of the mysteries of God,[4] the high priests of the flock, from whom the life of Christ in his faithful is in some way derived and dependent.[5] Through those who were appointed Bishops by the Apostles, and through their successors down to our own time, the apostolic tradition is manifested and preserved throughout the world. Bishops, exercising the office of pastor and teachers as one who serves,[6] have taken up the service of the community, presiding in place of God over the flock whose shepherds they are, as teachers of doctrine, priests of sacred worship, and officers of good order,[7] in order to continue throughout the ages the work of Christ the eternal Pastor.[8] In the Bishops, for whom priests or presbyters are assistants, our Lord Jesus Christ, the supreme High Priest, is present in the midst of those who believe.[9]

Priests or presbyters do not possess the highest degree of the priesthood; they are dependent on the Bishops in the exercise of their power. Nevertheless, they are united with the Bishops in sacerdotal dignity.[10] By the sacrament of Orders priests are configured to Christ the Priest so that, as ministers of the Head and coworkers of the episcopal order, they can build up and establish his whole Body which is the Church.[11] In virtue of this sacrament, as partakers on the level of their ministry of the function of Christ the

---

3. **Ibid.,** n. 28.
4. Decree, **Christus Dominus,** n. 15.
5. Const. **Sacrosanctum Concilium,** n. 41.
6. **Christus Dominus,** n. 16.
7. **Lumen Gentium,** n. 20.
8. **Christus Dominus,** n. 2.
9. **Lumen Gentium,** n. 21.
10. **Ibid.,** n. 28.
11. Decree, **Presbyterorum Ordinis,** n. 12.

sole Mediator,[12] priests of the New Testament exercise the most excellent and necessary office of father and teacher among the People of God and for them.[13] Their ministry, which takes its start from the Gospel message, derives its power and force from the sacrifice of Christ.[14] The purpose which priests pursue by their ministry and life is the glory of God the Father as it is to be achieved in Christ, namely, that men knowingly, freely, and gratefully accept what God has achieved perfectly through Christ, and manifest it in their whole lives.[15] By their vocation and ordination priests of the New Testament are truly set apart in a certain sense within the midst of God's People. But this is so, not that they may be separated from this people or from any man but that they may be totally dedicated to the work for which the Lord has raised them up.[16]

Deacons, at the lower level of the hierarchy, are ordained not for the priesthood but for a ministry of service. Strengthened by sacramental grace and in communion with the Bishop and his group of priests, they serve the People of God in the ministry of the liturgy, of the word, and of charity.[17]

II. *Role of the Sacrament of Orders*

Order in general is the disposition, arrangement or coordination of many things among themselves in the manner of superior and inferior. It also stands for grade or dignity; thus as regards the clergy it means hierarchical order or sacred hierarchy. The sacrament, called in English "Holy Orders," confers a spiritual power for the purpose of governing the faithful and of providing a ministry of divine worship.[18] The power of Orders or the sacerdotal power

12. **Lumen Gentium**, n. 28.
13. **Presbyterorum Ordinis**, n. 9.
14. **Ibid.**, nn. 2, 6.
15. **Ibid.**, n. 2.
16. **Ibid.**, n. 3.
17. **Lumen Gentium**, n. 29.
18. "The sacrament of Orders is the seal of the Church, whereby spiritual power is conferred on the person ordained"; (**Summa Theol., Suppl.**, q. 34, a. 2) it is the sacrament of hierarchical sanctification. "Ordination" is the sacred action by which this spiritual power is conferred. (Cf. cc. 948; 950; 197).

regards the Eucharistic Body of Christ (and all the other sacraments and connected things inasmuch as they are ordered to the Eucharist) ; the power of jurisdiction regards the Mystical Body of Christ or the Church through ruling, governing, and directing the Christian people toward eternal happiness.

It is of faith that Holy Orders is a true sacrament instituted by Christ,[19] and that it imprints an indelible character in the soul distinct from that of Baptism and Confirmation.[20] Thus by divine institution there is an essential distinction between clergy and laity, the ministerial priesthood and the common priesthood.[21] By a necessity of the sacrament itself, Holy Orders presupposes Baptism, and by a necessity of precept, Confirmation.

Because of the indelible character, the sacrament of Holy Orders is not repeatable. Although it may accidentally give first grace, as a sacrament of the living Holy Orders confers an increase in sanctifying grace, and in an eminent degree, since it is the most worthy sacrament after the Eucharist, to which it is immediately related. Infused at the same time is the sacramental grace proper to it. "The worthy exercise of Orders requires not any kind of goodness but excellent goodness, in order that as they who receive Orders are set above the people in the degree of Order, so may they be above them by the merit of holiness. Hence they are required to have the grace that suffices to make them worthy members of Christ's people, but when they receive Orders they are given a yet greater gift of grace, whereby they are rendered apt for greater things."[22]

---

19. Florence, Denz.-Schön. 1326; Trent, Denz.-Schön. 1766; 1771; 1773; Vatican II, **Presbyterorum Ordinis**, n. 2: "Therefore, while it indeed presupposes the sacraments of Christian initiation, the sacerdotal office of priests is conferred by that special sacrament through which priests, by the anointing of the Holy Spirit, are marked with a special character and are so configured to Christ the Priest that they can act in the person of Christ our Head."
20. Trent, Denz.-Schön. 1609; 1767; 1774.
21. c. 107; cf. Trent, Denz.-Schön. 1767-1770; Const. **Lumen Gentium**, n. 10: "Though they differ from one another in essence and not only in degree, the common priesthood of the faithful and the ministerial or hierarchical priesthood are nonetheless interrelated. Each of them in its own special way is a participation in the one priesthood of Christ."
22. **Summa Theol., Suppl.,** q. 35, a. 1, ad. 3. Pius XII, Ency. **Mediator**

It is of faith that the episcopacy, priesthood, and diaconate are of divine institution[23]; it is certainly of faith that the priesthood is a sacrament.[24] It is commonly taught as theologically certain that the episcopacy (considered as a distinct order from the priesthood) and the diaconate are sacraments.

III. Minister of the Celebration of Orders and the Ministries

A. Orders

Every consecrated Bishop and only such is the ordinary minister of valid ordination to Holy Orders, i.e., diaconate and priesthood.[25] It makes no difference for validity even if the Bishop is heretical, schismatic, excommunicated, degraded, etc.[26]

The lawful ordinary minister of the priesthood and the diaconate is the proper Bishop, or the Bishop delegated by him with lawful

Dei (20 nov. 1947): "This sacrament confers, not merely a particular grace that is proper to this state of life and function, but also an indelible 'character,' which conforms the sacred ministers to Jesus Christ the Priest, and renders them competent to carry out the lawful religious acts whereby men are sanctified and due glory is rendered to God, in accordance with the divinely appointed ordinances." Pius XI, Ency. **Ad catholici sacerdotii** (20 dec. 1935), Denz.-Schön. 3755: "Along with the character and the exalted powers of which we have been speaking, the priest receives a new and special grace with special helps. If he does his part faithfully by cooperating with the divine promptings of grace, these aids will enable him to carry out the duties of his office worthily and courageously; they will make it possible for him to bear the very heavy responsibilities. . . ." Cf. Florence, Denz.-Schön. 1326.

23. Trent, Denz.-Schön. 1776.
24. **Ibid.**, Denz.-Schön. 957; 959; 960; 1764; 1766-1767. Cf. also Pius XII, Const. **Sacramentum Ordinis,** 30 nov. 1947, Denz.-Schön. 3857-3858.
25. c. 951; Florence, Denz.-Schön. 1326; Trent, **ibid.,** 1768; 1777. This includes vicars and prefects apostolic, and abbots and prelates **nullius** possessing episcopal character (c. 957, 1).
26. Anglican ordinations were declared invalid (Leo XIII. Const. **Apostolicae curae,** 13 sept. 1896) because the Anglican rite lacked the essential form, did not express the Catholic teaching on sacrifice and priesthood, and lacked the intention of conferring a properly priestly power. Ordinations conferred by dissident Oriental bishops, Jansenists, and Old Catholics, are generally valid, because of a validly consecrated hierarchy (cf. Pius IX, Ency. **Etsi multa,** 21 nov. 1873).

dimissorial letters.[27] The proper Bishop for the ordination of *seculars* is that bishop only who is the Bishop of the diocese in which the candidate possesses a domicile, if it is the diocese also of his origin, or if not, provided the candidate takes an oath of a cleric already incardinated in the diocese, or of one destined in the future to serve in another diocese.[28] The proper Bishop for the ordination of *religious* (and thus to whom the religious superior is obliged to send dimissorial letters) is the Bishop of the place in which is located the religious house to which the candidate is assigned,[29] unless the religious Institute has an indult from the Holy See to present subjects to any Bishop.

One who is not the proper Bishop may lawfully ordain the subject of another on the receipt of lawful dimissorial letters from the Bishop of the one to be ordained, as long as the letters are genuine and accompanied by any requisite testimonies.[30] Dimissorial letters (*litterae dimissoriae*) are those by which a superior releases (*dimittere*) or sends his own subject to another Bishop with the faculty of receiving orders from him. They differ from testimonial letters by which is given merely an authentic attestation of birth, age, character, doctrine, etc., of the one to be ordained. As long as they retain jurisdiction in the territory entrusted to them, the proper Bishop, the vicar general with special mandate, the administrator of the diocese may issue dimissorial letters for *seculars;* likewise vicars and prefects apostolic and abbots and prelates *nullius,* even though without episcopal character.[31]

Religious who are exempt can be lawfully ordained by no Bishop without the dimissorial letters of their own proper major superior.[32]

27. cc. 955-956. To choose an individual who is to ascend to the priestly ministry is an act of jurisdiction and thus can be lawfully exercised only on one's subject.
28. cc. 955-956; 969, 2; Paul VI motu proprio **Sacrum Diaconatus Ordinem**, 18 iun. 1967, 18; motu proprio **Ad pascendum**, 15 aug. 1972, IX. A quasi-domicile is not sufficient. Lacking domicile, a candidate acquires the bishop of the place where he is staying as his proper bishop, taking the oath of intention to remain permanently (PCI 17 aug. 1919).
29. c. 965.
30. c. 962.
31. c. 958.
32. c. 964, 2o.

Religious who are not exempt are governed regarding dimissorials by the norm for seculars, unless the religious Institute enjoys a special Apostolic indult.[33] The religious superior may send dimissorial letters to another Bishop only if the diocesan Bishop grants permission, or he is of a different rite from that of the candidate, or he is absent, or not prepared to ordain at the next lawful date, or if the diocese lacks a head with episcopal character.[34] The religious superior should not send a subject to another religious house or deliberately postpone issuing dimissorials thereby infringing on the right of the diocesan Bishop.[35]

B. *Ministries*

The Ordinary (the Bishop and, in clerical institutes of perfection, the major superior) has the right to accept the petition of candidates or aspirants for the ministries.[36] The ministries are conferred by the aforementioned Ordinary according to the proper liturgical rite.[37]

A Bishop (or major superior) who installs in a ministry a candidate who is not his own proper subject should first receive the permission of the proper Ordinary of that candidate.

IV. *Candidates for the Ministries*

A. *General Norms*

Certain ministries or offices, established by the Church, have been entrusted to the performance of the faithful for the purpose of suitably giving worship to God and for offering service to the People of God according to their needs. Such ministries have entailed duties of a liturgical and charitable nature deemed suitable to varying circumstances. The Latin Church at present retains the

---

33. **Ibid.**, 4o. This includes also quasi-religious institutes (S.C. Rel. 1 dec. 1931). A special indult is restricted to the issuance of dimissorials for sacred orders.
34. c. 966, 1.
35. c. 967.
36. Paul VI, motu proprio **Ministeria quaedam**, 15 aug. 1972, VIII, a.
37. **Ibid.**, IX.

ministries or offices of lector and acolyte, since they are especially connected with the ministries of the Word and of the Altar. The institution of other ministries may be requested of the Apostolic See by episcopal conferences.[38] Lector and acolyte are reserved to men.[39]

For admission to the ministries the candidate should freely make out, in the form of a personal letter, and signed, a petition to the Ordinary (the Bishop and, in clerical institutes of perfection, the major superior) who has the right to accept the petition. The Ordinary should then issue a formal certificate to the candidate as a record of the liturgical institution. A diocesan (and religious) register should be kept in which are inscribed the names of the lectors and acolytes, together with the place, date, and minister of institution.[40]

A suitable age, to be determined by the episcopal conference, is required for installation in the ministries. In the U.S.A. the minimum age is established at eighteen. The Bishop may dispense from this in individual cases, e.g., for one who completes high school at a somewhat earlier age. This age should be an assurance of sufficient maturity. In the case of those who may later be candidates for Orders, or of those in pre-theological studies, it will be the occasion for a prior ministry.[41]

Special qualities, to be determined by the episcopal conference, are required, together with a firm will to give faithful service to God and to the Christian people. Thus no one should be installed in either ministry without a period of thorough preparation in all aspects of the respective ministry. In the U.S.A., this period, as well as the program of formation, should be determined by the Ordinary. It should generally be from three to six months long, so that both the specific requirements of the respective ministry and the necessary leadership qualities may be ascertained and developed.[42]

Intervals, determined by the Holy See or the episcopal conference, are to be observed between the conferring of the ministries of lector and acolyte whenever more than one ministry is conferred on the

38. **Ibid., init.**
39. **Ibid., VII.**
40. **Ibid.,** VIII, a; NCCB, 15 nov. 1972; cf. c. 1010.
41. **Ministeria quaedam,** VIII b; NCCB, **ibid.**
42. **Ministeria quaedam,** VIII b,c; NCCB, **ibid.**

same person. In the U.S.A., a person already installed in one ministry, who later desires institution in the other, should first have already actually exercised the first ministry over a period of at least six months, in order to safeguard the authenticity of the respective ministries.[43]

A person instituted in a ministry for his own diocese (or religious institute) may exercise that ministry in his own diocese in accordance with the diocesan regulations and the rights of the local pastor (or religious superior). For the same person to function in that ministry but in a diocese (or religious institute) not his own, he needs the permission of that diocese in accordance with the regulations of that diocese and the rights of the local pastor (or religious superior).

The conferring of ministries does not imply the right to sustenance or salary from the Church.[44]

B. *Lector*

The lector is appointed for a function proper to him, that of reading the Word of God in the liturgical assembly. Accordingly, he is to read the lessons from Sacred Scripture, except for the Gospel, in the Mass and other sacred celebrations. He is to recite the psalm between the readings when there is no psalmist. He is to present the intentions for the prayer of the faithful in the absence of a deacon or cantor. He is to direct the singing and the participation of the faithful. He is to instruct the faithful for the worthy reception of the sacraments. He can also, insofar as necessary, take care of preparing other faithful who by a temporary appointment are to read the Sacred Scripture in liturgical celebrations.[45]

---

43. NCCB, **ibid.**
44. **Ministeria quaedam,** XII
45. **Ibid.,** V: "That he may more fittingly and perfectly fulfill these functions, let him meditate assiduously on Sacred Scripture. Let the lector be aware of the office he has undertaken and make every effort and employ suitable means to acquire that increasingly warm and living love and knowledge of the Scriptures that will make him a more perfect disciple of the Lord."

C. *Acolyte*

The acolyte is appointed in order to aid the deacon and to minister to the priest. It is therefore his duty to attend to the service of the altar and to assist the deacon and the priest in liturgical celebrations, especially in the celebration of Mass. He is also to distribute Holy Communion as an extraordinary minister when the ministers spoken of in canon 845 of the Code of Canon Law are not available or are prevented by ill health, age, or another pastoral ministry from performing this function, or when the number of those approaching the Sacred Table is so great that the celebration of Mass would be unduly prolonged.

In the same extraordinary circumstances he can be entrusted with publicly exposing the Blessed Sacrament for adoration by the faithful and afterwards replacing it, but not with blessing the people. He can also, to the extent needed, take care of instructing other faithful who by temporary assignment assist the priest or deacon in liturgical celebrations by carrying the missal, cross, candles, etc., or by performing other such duties.[46]

V. *Candidates for the Diaconate*

A. *General Norms*

For the nurturing and constant growth of the People of God, Christ the Lord instituted in the Church a variety of ministries which work for the good of the whole body. Thus from the Apostolic age the diaconate has had a clearly outstanding position among these

---

46. **Ibid.**, VI: "He will perform these functions the more worthily if he participates in the Holy Eucharist with increasingly fervent piety, receives nourishment from it, and deepens his knowledge of it. Destined as he is in a special way for the service of the altar, the acolyte should learn all matters concerning public divine worship and strive to grasp their inner spiritual meaning; in that way he will be able each day to offer himself entirely to God, be an example to all by his seriousness and reverence in the sacred building, and have a sincere love for the Mystical Body of Christ, the People of God, especially the weak and the sick."

ministries, and it has always been held in great honor by the Church.[47] Deacons have been instituted at a lower level of the hierarchy and upon them hands are imposed unto a ministry of service. Strengthened by sacramental grace, in communion with the bishop and his presbyterium, they serve the People of God in the ministry of the liturgy, of the Word, and of charity.[48] The diaconate, as a hierarchic order, is ennobled with an indelible character and a special grace of its own so that those who are called to it can serve the mysteries of Christ and of the Church in a stable fashion.[49]

One who aspires to the diaconate (transitional or permanent) or the priesthood publicly manifests his will to offer himself to God and the Church so that he may exercise a sacred order. The Church, accepting this offering, selects and calls him to prepare himself to receive a sacred order, and in this way he is properly numbered among candidates for the diaconate or priesthood. Thus it is especially fitting that the ministries of lector and acolyte be entrusted to them and be exercised for a fitting time. For the Church considers it to be very opportune that both by study and by gradual exercise of the ministry of the Word and of the Altar candidates for sacred orders should through intimate contact understand and reflect upon the double aspect of the priestly office. Thus it comes about that the authenticity of the ministry shines out with the greatest effectiveness. In this way the candidates accede to sacred orders fully aware of their vocation, fervent in spirit, serving the Lord, constant in prayer and aware of the needs of the faithful. Dispensation from the reception of the ministries on the part of such candidates is reserved to the Holy See.[50]

Entrance into the clerical state and incardination into a diocese are brought about by ordination to the diaconate.[51]

For entrance into the diaconate through the rite of admission the free petition of the candidate, made out in the form of a personal

---

47. Paul VI, motu proprio **Ad pascendum**, 15 aug. 1972.
48. **Ibid.**
49. Paul VI, motu proprio **Sacrum Diaconatus Ordinem**, 18 iun. 1967.
50. **Ad pascendum**, espec. II.
51. **Ibid., IX; Sacrum Diaconatus Ordinem**, 18. For the title of ordination, the oath of service is taken before ordination to the diaconate, in accordance with cc. 979-981.

letter, signed, is presented to his Ordinary (the Bishop, and in clerical institutes of perfection, the major superior). By the latter's written acceptance of the petition (which may be in the form of a certificate to express the fact of acceptance and to be a record of the liturgical celebration) the selection by the Church is brought about. Professed members of clerical congregations who seek the priesthood are not bound to the rite of admission; thus the certificate of acceptance should be appropriately adapted.[52]

Those can be accepted who give signs of an authentic vocation and, endowed with good moral qualities and free from mental and physical defects, wish to dedicate their lives to the service of the Church for the glory of God and the good of souls.[53]

The liturgical rite of admission to the diaconate is performed by the Ordinary of the candidate (Bishop or major superior).[54]

Permission should be sought from the proper Ordinary in the case of a candidate who is not the proper subject of the Ordinary performing the rite. The names of those admitted to candidacy should be inscribed in a diocesan (or religious) register and a formal certificate issued. Upon ordination as deacons notification should be sent to the pastor of the place of Baptism for inscription in the baptismal register.[55]

The intervals established by the Holy See or by the episcopal conference between the conferring, during the course of theological studies, of the ministry of acolyte and the order of deacon are to be observed.[56] In the U.S.A. the required interval between the conferring of the ministry of acolyte (or, according to circumstances, the conferring of the second ministry) and ordination to the diaconate is to be such as to provide a lengthy period for the actual and authentic exercise of the ministry in question. Otherwise, a dispensation

---

52. **Ad pascendum**, I, a-b; NCCB 15 nov. 1972.
53. **Ad pascendum**, I, b. In virtue of the acceptance the candidate must care for his vocation in a special way and foster it. He also acquires the right to the necessary spiritual assistance by which he can develop his vocation and submit unconditionally to the will of God (**ibid.**, I, c).
54. **Ibid.**, III.
55. cc. 470, 2; 1011.
56. **Ad pascendum**, IV

from the Apostolic See should be sought to proceed without delay to ordination to the diaconate.[57]

Before ordination candidates for the diaconate are to give to their Ordinary (Bishop or major superior) a declaration made out and signed in their own hand by which they testify that they are about to receive the sacred order freely and of their own accord.[58] Moreover, before ordination to the diaconate candidates for the priesthood and unmarried deacons are to make a public commitment or special consecration of *celibacy* before God and the Church, for the sake of the kingdom of God, according to the prescribed rite, to which also religious are bound. Celibacy assumed in this way is a diriment impediment to entering marriage.[59]

The *function* of the deacon, to the extent that he has been authorized by the local Ordinary, is the following:[60]

1) To carry out, with Bishop and priest, all the roles in liturgical rites which the ritual books attribute to him;

2) To administer Baptism solemnly and to supply the ceremonies that have been omitted at Baptism in the case of an infant or adult;

3) To have custody of the Eucharist, to distribute it to himself and to others, and to impart Benediction of the Blessed Sacrament to the people with the pyx;

4) To assist at and bless marriages in the name of the Church when there is no priest present, with delegation from the Bishop or pastor, so long as everything else commanded in the Code of Canon Law is observed (cc. 1095, 2; 1096) and with no infringement on Canon 1098, in which case what is said of a priest is to be understood of a deacon as well; this pertains both to the transitional and the permanent deacon;[61]

57. NCCB, **loc. cit.**
58. **Ad pascendum,** V.
59. **Ibid.,** VI. A married deacon who has lost his wife cannot enter a new marriage (**ibid.**).
60. **Sacrum Diaconatus Ordinem,** n. 22. A deacon aspiring to the priesthood enjoys the same functions (Pont. Com. Decr. Conc. Vat. II Interpret., 26 mart. 1968).
61. "when there is no priest present" is not a requirement for the validity of the delegation of the deacon to assist at a marriage (Pont. Com. Decr. Conc. Vat. II Interpret., 4 apr. 1969). More-

5) To administer sacramentals, and to preside at funeral and burial rites;

6) To read the Scriptures to the faithful and to teach and preach to the people;

7) To preside over the offices of religious worship and prayer services when there is no priest present;

8) To direct Bible services when there is no priest present;

9) To do charitable, administrative, and welfare work in the name of the hierarchy;

10) To legitimately guide outlying communities of Christians in the name of the pastor and the Bishop;

11) To foster and aid the lay apostolate.

The deacon is to carry out these offices in complete communion with the bishop and his presbyterium, which means under the authority of the Bishop and the priests who preside over the care of souls in that place.[62]

B. *Transitional Diaconate*

Those who aspire to the transitional diaconate must have completed at least their twentieth year and have begun their course of theological studies.[63] Deacons called to the priesthood are not to be ordained until they have completed the course of studies prescribed by the norms of the Apostolic See.[64] These deacons, moreover, are bound by their sacred ordination by the obligation of celebrating the liturgy of the hours.[65]

over, a deacon who is attached to a parish **stabiliter et legitime** may be granted delegation or permission to assist at marriages within that parish. For this purpose he is comparable to the **vicarii cooperatores** of c. 1096, 1 (ibid., 19 iul. 1970).

62. **Sacrum Diaconatus Ordinem**, n. 23. Deacons should have a part in pastoral councils, insofar as this is possible (**ibid.**, n. 24).
63. **Ad pascendum**, I b. The local Ordinary may dispense for a just cause from defect of age for ordinands provided it does not exceed six complete months (motu proprio **Pastorale Munus**, I, 15).
64. **Ibid., VII a.**
65. **Ibid., VIII a.**

C. *Permanent Diaconate*

The permanent diaconate is not to be conferred before the age of twenty-five, or even later, if the episcopal conference so chooses.[66] The period of preparation for the diaconate should run at least three years and be in accord with the prescriptions of the Apostolic See and the episcopal conference.[67] Unmarried candidates for the diaconate are bound to the public commitment to celibacy.[68]

Men of more mature age (thirty-five years old), whether celibate or married, can be called to the permanent diaconate. A Bishop has the faculty to dispense a married candidate from want of the required age within one year.[69] These more mature candidates should have enjoyed a long-time reputation for exemplary Christian life, and, in the case of the married, also for being good heads of the family. The consent and proper attitude of the wives must be evident.

Appropriate studies and training as prescribed must precede ordination to the diaconate.[70] Decent support for a deacon, and also for his family if he is married, should be regulated by the episcopal conference,[71] which also determines the part of the liturgy of the hours that they should recite daily.[72]

Institution of the permanent diaconate among religious (including other institutions professing the life of the evangelical counsels) is a right reserved to the Apostolic See. The diaconate is exercised by a religious under the authority of the local Ordinary and of the proper religious superior.[73]

D. *Celebration of the Conferral of the Diaconate*

The diaconate may be conferred outside the cathedral church and

66. **Sacrum Diaconatus Ordinem**, n. 5.
67. **Ibid.**, nn. 6-10; **Ad pascendum**, VII b.
68. Cf. note 59 above.
69. **Sacrum Diaconatus Ordinem**, nn. 11-12; Pont. Com. Decr. Conc. Vat. II Interpret., 19 iul. 1970.
70. **Sacrum Diaconatus Ordinem**, nn. 11-15; cf. NCCB, **Permanent Deacons in the U.S. Guidelines on their Ministry and Formation,** 5 aug. 1971.
71. **Sacrum Diaconatus Ordinem**, nn. 19-21; cf. NCCB, **loc., cit.**
72. **Ad pascendum**, VIII b.
73. **Sacrum Diaconatus Ordinem**, nn. 32-35.

outside the canonical times, and even on ferial days, if pastoral considerations so suggest.[74]

The essential rite in the conferral of the diaconate consists of the imposition of hands by the Bishop and the consecratory prayer pronounced by him. Thus the requisite material in the celebration of the sacrament is the imposition of hands by the Bishop which is done in silence on each of the ordinands before the consecratory prayer. The formula of the sacrament is the words of the prayer of consecration, in which the words pertaining to the essence of the sacrament and the validity of the action are: "Lord, we pray, send forth upon them the Holy Spirit so that by the grace of your seven gifts they may be strengthened by him to carry out faithfully the work of the ministry."[75]

The proper insignia of the deacon is the stole, which is worn on the left shoulder and crossed to the right, and to a lesser extent the dalmatic.

VI. *Candidates for the Priesthood*

A. *General Norms*

Priests or presbyters, in virtue of the ordination they have received and the mission entrusted to them by the Bishops, are ordained to serve Christ their Master, Priest, and King, and to share in his ministry.[76] Thus they are given the sacred power of Orders to offer sacrifice, forgive sin, and in the name of Christ publicly to exercise the office of priesthood in the community. The priestly office, joined as it is to that of the Bishop, shares the authority by which Christ himself builds up, sanctifies, and rules this Mystical Body. That is why those ordained to the priesthood require, in addition to the basic sacraments which made them Christians, a special sacrament through which, anointed by the Holy Spirit, they are signed with a specific character and are configured to Christ the Priest and are

74. Paul VI, motu proprio **Pastorale Munus**, 30 nov. 1963, I, 18; cf. cc. 1006, 1009.
75. Paul VI, Const. Apost. **Pontificalis Romani**, 18 iun. 1968; cf. also Pius XII, Const. Apost. **Sacramentum Ordinis**, 30 nov. 1948.
76. Vatican II, decree **Presbyterorum Ordinis**, n. 1.

thus able to act in the person of Christ our Head.[77]

Through the Apostles Christ ordained Bishops to be successors and sharers in his same consecration and calling. The Bishops, in their turn, pass on the functions of their ministry in a lesser degree to priests, who are fellow workers with the Bishops in carrying out the apostolic mission entrusted to them by Christ our Lord. The whole object of the ministry and life of priests is, therefore, to give glory to God the Father through Christ our Lord. Whether praying and worshiping, preaching, offering Mass, administering the other sacraments, or doing any other pastoral work, priests are working for the greater glory of God and the divine sanctification of men.[78]

B. *Celebration of Conferral of the Priesthood*

The priesthood may be conferred outside the cathedral church and outside the canonical times, and even on ferial days, if pastoral considerations so suggest.[79]

The essential rite in the conferral of the priesthood consists of the imposition of hands by the Bishop and the consecratory prayer pronounced by him. Thus the requisite material in the celebration of the sacrament is the imposition of hands by the Bishop which is done in silence on each of the ordinands before the consecratory prayer. The formula of the sacrament is the words of the prayer of consecration, in which the words pertaining to the essence of the sacrament and the validity of the action are: "We ask you, all-powerful Father, give these servants of yours the dignity of the presbyterate. Renew the Spirit of holiness within them. By your divine gift may they attain the second order in the hierarchy and exemplify right conduct in their lives."[80]

The proper insignia of the priest is the stole, which is worn over both shoulders and is not crossed, and to a lesser extent the chasuble.

C. *Capable Candidates*

Only a male who is baptized and has at least the habitual intention

77. **Ibid.,** n. 2.
78. **Ibid.**
79. Cf. note 74 above.
80. Cf. note 75 above.

of receiving the sacrament of Holy Orders is a *capable* subject of *valid* ordination.[81] If there is prudent doubt as to the sex of the candidate, e.g., in the rare instances of a hermaphrodite or pseudo-hermaphrodite, the candidate must be barred from ordination; if ordination has been conferred, recourse must be had to the Ordinary and a competent physician and the individual barred from the ministry in the meantime.

An intention, which is at least habitual and explicit, is required in those who are adults or who have attained the use of reason. Because of the importance and the obligations of the clerical state, an intention which is at least virtual is urged. Those who are ordained when asleep or unconscious, drunk, or insane, receive valid ordination inasmuch as the requisite intention is present or not. Baptized infants are validly ordained, but on the completion of their sixteenth year they may choose or reject the obligations of the clerical state (principally celibacy and the divine office); in the latter choice, they are permitted to live as a layman.[82]

A cleric who has received a sacred order under the influence of grave fear (or of grave deceit, and which have not removed the requisite intention or the use of reason) and has not, after the coercion has ceased, ratified the ordination at least tacitly by the exercise of the functions of the respective order with the intention in so doing of submitting to the obligations imposed by it, shall be reduced to the lay state by a sentence of an ecclesiastical judge after proof of the coercion and the absence of ratification; and this reduction frees the cleric from the obligations of celibacy and the divine office.[83] It is commonly taught that one who deceitfully (*ficte*) approaches the reception of sacred orders is invalidly ordained, i.e., one who outwardly allows the external rite to be completed on him but inwardly dissents or refuses to receive the Sacrament or what the Church does by this rite.

D. *Qualified Candidates*

For the *lawful* reception of sacred orders many other conditions

81. Cf. c. 968; also **Summa Theol., Suppl.,** q. 39, a. 1.
82. Cf. Benedict XIV, Const. **Eo quamvis,** 4 mart. 1745; Instr. **Anno vertente,** 19 iul. 1750; cf. also c. 214, 1.
83. Cf. cc. 214; 1993-1998.

are required of the candidate to be a *qualified* subject. These refer both to the ordinand himself and to the ordination.[84] Thus the candidate must be endowed, in the opinion of his proper Ordinary, with the qualities required by the canons and free from irregularities and impediments; in other words: a divine vocation, suitability, absence of legitimate impediments.[85]

1. *Divine vocation*

a. *the call*

The sacrament of Orders invests a man with priestly and hierarchical functions to be exercised in the Christian society of the Church. Admission to sacred orders is subject to the authority of the Church through its competent representatives, who, in calling candidates to assist the Bishops in the discharge of their duties as actual pastors of the Christian society, select and accept them according to certain norms required by the nature of the sacrament and the ends and needs of the Church, and also of a particular religious institute in the case of religious candidates.[86] This is the external or public call, the so-called ecclesiastical or canonical vocation to Orders. These norms or requirements at the same time are signs of the presence of a divine interior vocation, which they presuppose or guarantee, make known and complete.[87] Thus the Church cooperates

84. Cf. c. 968, 1.
85. Cf. cc. 538; 868; 973, 3.
86. For religious candidates cf. Pius XII, Const. Apost. **Sedes Sapientiae**, 31 maii. 1956, **General Statutes** S. C. Rel., 7 iul. 1956, Tit. Vi, art. 31, 2, 1.
87. Paul VI, Allocutio **Il nostro desiderio**, 5 maii 1965: "The voice of God that calls is expressed in two different ways, wondrous and converging: the one interior, that of grace, that of the Holy Spirit, the inexpressible way of that interior charm exercised by the silent and powerful voice of the Lord in the unsearchable depths of the human soul; the other exterior, human, perceivable, social, juridical, concrete, that of the qualified minister of God, that of the apostle, that of the hierarchy, the indispensable instrument instituted and willed by Christ, as the vehicle charged with translating into perceptible language the message of the divine word and command."

with God who by his special grace interiorly calls the candidate to the service of the Master in Holy Orders. Both a divine interior vocation and the external call of the Church are required of the candidate of Holy Orders.[88]

Vocation to the clerical state is thus an act of divine providence whereby God selects some above others for his priesthood and prepares them with suitable gifts for the worthy exercise of priestly duties. For this reason, and because this sacrament has been instituted not so much for the recipient as for the common good of the faithful, one who is conscious of a lack of vocation or who has made insufficient inquiry or who is in serious doubt about his vocation is liable to serious sin in approaching the reception of sacred orders. Moreover, it is likewise sinful to remain in the clerical state in face of an obvious mistake in choice of life, as long as the individual can legitimately leave. The principal signs of a clerical vocation are a right intention, probity of life, and suitability (knowledge and health).

b. *the right intention*

The right intention essential to vocation is the supernatural motive or desire, free, firm and constant, to procure the glory of God and the salvation of souls; it is a certain supernatural propensity to embrace the clerical life. It is man's response to God's special grace and the primary sign of a divine vocation.[89] The

88. **Letter from the Secretariate of State on the Nature of Priestly Vocation**, 2 iul. 1912: "1. No one ever has any right to ordination antecedently to the free choice of the Bishop; 2. On the part of the candidate, the requirement which has to be examined, and which is called **priestly vocation**, by no means consists, at least necessarily and as a general rule, in a certain interior attraction of the subject, or in invitations of the Holy Spirit, to enter the ecclesiastical state; 3. On the contrary, in order that the candidate may be rightly called by the Bishop, nothing more is required of him than a right intention and fitness; this fitness consists in qualities of nature and grace, proved by uprightness of life and sufficiency of knowledge, as will give solid grounds for hope that he will be able to discharge properly the functions of the priesthood and fulfill its obligations in a holy manner." Cf. also Pius XII, **Sedes Sapientiae**.

89. Pius XII, **Exhortation to All the Clergy "Menti Nostrae,"** 23 sept.

stronger the supernatural motivation of the will, the clearer will be the divine vocation and fitness of the candidate. The intention requisite in the candidate for sacred orders is the determination to go on to the priesthood, which is the contemporary meaning of the requirement: *animus clericandi*.[90] Thus, to have the intention of not persevering in the clerical state or of not going on for the priesthood is usually not without some sin, if not necessarily serious sin. One who, otherwise properly equiped, feels himself less suited for the clerical state, or who has a less worthy primary purpose in embracing the clerical state, e.g., to improve his condition in life, is not often without at least slight sin; it is, however, possible that such a person may in time, under grace, acquire the right intention. If the doubt of the candidate arises about his vocation, due to his uncertainty as to suitable qualities of mind and body on his part, he should not go on to Orders if the doubt cannot be dispelled according to the norms of prudence. If the doubt exists because evil habits exist, which have not yet been overcome or rooted out, he must be considered as not possessing a vocation and not allowed to go on for Orders.

2. *Suitability*

Besides the right intention necessary in the aspirant for the priesthood, there must also be present "those qualities of mind and body which make him fit for that state in life,"[91] i.e., the candidate must possess a suitability for a life of dedicated service to God, a fitness for bearing the burdens and tasks of the priesthood—"a fitness based on qualities of nature and of grace, proved by uprightness of life and sufficiency of knowledge."[92] "A Bishop should not confer sacred

1950: "It is always necessary, however, to examine every candidate for the priesthood with great care, and especially to find out what is his intention and what are the reasons for his decision to become a priest."; cf. also S.C. Rel. Instr., 2 feb. 1961; Pius XII, Ency. **Ad Catholici Sacerdotii**, 20 dec. 1935; S. C. Rel. Instr., 1 dec. 1931; S.C. Rel. Instr., 27 dec. 1930.

90. Cf. c. 973, 1.
91. Pius XI, ency. **Ad Catholici Sacerdotii**.
92. **Letter from the Secretariate of State**, cf. note 88 above. This fitness, then, consists of positive qualities regarding especially

orders upon anyone unless he is *morally* certain by reason of *positive* proof that the candidate is canonically fit; otherwise he not only sins most grievously but also runs the risk of sharing in the sins of others."[93] Both the divine vocation and the suitability of the aspirant are not conferred but are rather presupposed by his admission by the Bishop to Orders. This admission is not of itself a certain sign of either, as the Bishop (or those presenting the candidate to him) may be mistaken. A prudent and founded doubt of fitness in the candidate indicates a lack of requisite qualities and thus he should be rejected. The Bishop, of course, ultimately depends wholly or in great part upon the estimation of fitness made by those engaged in the formation of seminarians, whether secular or religious. It is important, then, to use every effort to certify that an exterior appearance of suitability bespeaks an interior reality. It is not enough merely to be aware of nothing bad about the candidate, but there must be a moral certitude of his uprightness of character relative to the sublimity of the degree of orders desired.[94] Suitability includes the whole man with his complexity of faculties and qualities—physical and psychological, intellectual, moral—which fitness should become more evident as the candidate progresses through the period of preparation.[95]

a. *physical and psychical*

More is required today for the candidate for the priesthood than an absence of bodily defects. He must be completely fit physically

the interior worthiness of the candidate relating to his maturity in the faith, in morals, prudence, and knowledge commensurate with the stage of his approach to sacred orders; and of negative qualities referring to the absence of impediments and the exterior worthiness proper to the divine ministry.

93. c. 973, 3. In a **Reserved Communication** the S.C. Sem. (1 iul. 1955) stated that very often unworthy subjects are promoted to Orders because of insufficient severity and lack of uniformity of criteria in judging the worthiness of such aspirants.

94. St. Pius X, ency. **Pieni L'Animo**, 28 iul. 1906: "To make easy the admission of candidates to Holy Orders undoubtedly leads to an increase in the numbers of priests, but it does not proportionately increase grounds for rejoicing thereafter."

95. Cf. two circular letters to the Bishops of the S.C. Sem., 5 iun. 1959 and 27 sept. 1960.

and able to handle the tasks and responsibilities of the present-day priesthood (as well as the special burdens of the religious life, in the case of the religious priesthood).[96] It should be recognized that not only illness or debility, e.g., incipient deafness or blindness, renders a candidate physically unfit, but also that some past bouts with disease may have left in their train constitutional or even psychical disorders (experts note, for example, especially tuberculosis, epilepsy, encephalitis). Other weaknesses may be handed down directly or indirectly from parents or grandparents to the aspirant, e.g., tuberculosis, venereal disease, alcoholism.

The Church has always been conscious of the likelihood of transmission of incontinency in the case of those who are illegitimate; a cautious circumspection is recommended even in the admission of those for whom the obtaining of a dispensation is otherwise in order. Cases of pronounced stuttering or stammering should be carefully reviewed, since they are deterrents to the ministry and often indicate a deeper psychological problem.

No candidate should seek Orders, or be accepted for or promoted to Orders of whose balanced psychological attitude, sound judgment, and common sense there is not positive proof. Those who give indication of mental illness, nervous disease or psychological disturbance, or traits of vices or mental instability evident in parents or family, should be given special attention, even including expert medical aid and advice. A clear inability or unlikelihood, or a positive doubt of a candidate's fitness or compatibility to carry the burdens of sacred ordination, especially celibacy, with honor to the clerical state is a hindrance to the pursuit of a clerical vocation. It is important to discern the early stages of any psychological abnormality so that the unsuitable may be eliminated or at least detained before advancing further toward orders. A sense of responsibility proportioned to the degree of approach to orders should be characteristic of every candidate.[97]

96. Cf. Pius XII, **Allocution to the Students of the North American College,** 14 oct. 1953.
97. The importance of this investigation and examination was reemphasized by the S.C. Sac., 27 dec. 1955, in a circular letter to Local Ordinaries which includes specific norms regarding physical, psychological, and moral qualities requisite in a priestly

b. *intellectual*

Intellectual ability and knowledge are indispensable for the priesthood. The specific fundamental knowledge required of candidates for promotion to diaconate and the priesthood is regulated by law.[98] Responsible authorities in the formation and the acceptance of such candidates are bound to expect and insure—and can be satisfied with—at least competence in these matters. Local Ordinaries, however, may require more of their own subjects; religious institutes likewise may require a greater or more varied preparation and achievement consonant with their work and purpose. Moreover, a fuller and wider intellectual formation and performance is required of clerical candidates in the modern age.

c. *moral*

"Clerics are bound to lead a more saintly interior and exterior life than the laity, and to give them the example by excelling in virtue and righteous conduct."[99] "Holiness of life and sound doctrine are, therefore, the two conditions which must be regarded as essential for the promotion of clerics." [100] Holiness is not the goal of the priesthood but the preparation for it. A standard of holiness for the priestly office exceeds even that of the religious state.[101] The seminarian, both secular and religious, should have at least the positive beginnings of the virtues eventually expected in the priesthood. Such suitableness must become more manifest as the candidate aspires to one step after another to the priesthood; seminary training is designed to develop such virtues. The Church in requiring these exterior

vocation. Regarding psychoanalytic examinations or investigations before the reception of sacred orders and regarding psychopathic cases, cf. S. Off. Monitum, 15 iul. 1961; S.C. Rel. Instr., 2 feb. 1961.

98. Cf. S.C. Inst. Cath., 16 mart. 1970, **Ratio Fundamentalis Institutionis Sacerdotalis;** NCCB, **The Program of Priestly Formation,** 18 ian. 1971. Cf. note 70 above, NCCB.
99. c. 124.
100. St. Pius X, **Sacrorum Antistitum,** 1 sept. 1910.
101. Cf. **Summa Theol.,** II-II, q. 184, a. 6; q. 189, a. 1 ad. 3.

qualities or evidences of virtue is principally concerned with their interior possession, in which holiness primarily resides.[102] Although all the virtues are present with the state of grace, some especially befit the priest and are to be expected to be manifest in the candidate for Orders as signs of vocation; piety or an earnest striving to use the means of perfection, detachment from worldly goods, obedience and docility, zeal and humility, strength and charity, modesty and chastity.

The Church's appreciation of the sublimity of the priesthood of the New Testament quite soon made obligatory "what the Gospels and Apostolic preaching had already shown to be something like a natural requirement"[103]—*perfect chastity*. The Church, by her ancient law of *celibacy*, often reaffirmed, in recognition of the supreme becomingness of chastity or modesty and purity in the priest, has consistently striven to maintain the highest standards of chastity in the clergy. The priest is called upon to live not an ordinary life but an heroic life of virtue; consequently the great concern of the Apostolic See also in these days for the proper fitness and preparation in clerical candidates in the matter of chastity.[104] Among the gifts of grace and of nature of which there must be positive proof[105] in order to recognize a divine vocation for the priesthood, chastity must be singled out as the *"sine qua non* condition."[106] The chastity must be proven

102. Pius XII, **Menti Nostrae:** "What We have written of priests We likewise insist on here: clerical students must be absolutely convinced that they are bound to strive with all their might to acquire those adornments of the soul, the virtues, and when they have acquired them, to preserve them and zealously develop them."
103. Pius XI, ency. **Ad Catholici Sacerdotii.**
104. Paul VI, ency. **Sacerdotalis Caelibatus,** 24 iun. 1967; **Letter to the Secretary of State, (Le dichiarazioni)**, 2 feb. 1970, reaffirming the tradition of priestly celibacy; Vatican II, **Presbyterorum Ordinis,** n. 16; **Optatam Totius,** n. 10; **Lumen Gentium,** n. 42; S.C. Instr. Cath., **Ratio Fundamentalis Institutionis Sacerdotalis,** 16 mart. 1970, n. 48.
105. c. 973, 3.
106. S.C. Rel., Instr., 2 feb. 1961, n. 29: "Among the proofs and signs of a divine vocation the virtue of chastity is required as absolutely necessary"; S. C. Sem., **Reserved Communication,** 1 iul. 1955; S.C. Sem., **Circular Letter to Local Ordinaries,** 27 dec. 1955.

or tried, in that there must be positive evidence of its presence and not merely an absence of deviations; consequently, the seminarian must be a person of proven purity, solidly possessed, profoundly appreciated and zealously cherished. The severe attitude which the Church takes in this matter is manifest in her exhortations and directives regarding the admission of candidates to the seminary and their promotion to Orders. Competent authorities in the external forum, as well as spiritual directors and confessors in the internal forum, should be guided by the mind of the Church in judging with respect to purity the divine vocation and the suitableness of the aspirant. In a doubt of the suitability of the candidate or in even a probability of a crime committed by him, he (even if a finally professed religious) must be barred from Orders.[107]

The following norms direct the attitude that should be taken in the matter of clerical chastity.[108] By the time the seminarian begins his theology course, he must have put in order all matters relating to chastity, and thus have acquired the habit of chastity. There should be moral certainty arising from this period preceding the entrance into theology that the candidate will persevere in this purity, under God; otherwise, he should be eliminated from the path of the priesthood. On the other hand, he must be excluded from the priesthood if, for *at least* one whole year preceding the beginning of theology, he has not kept himself free from all serious external sins, and especially with another person. Only in an *exceptional* case could a further year of trial be permitted, when a period of crisis was verified or prolonged, depending on the age or special conditions of temperament of the youth, who otherwise appeared gifted with sincere piety and solid virtue, and provided a definitive judgment can be made in the case within the first year of theology.[109] In order that such purity might be clearly possessed before entering theology, no candidate should be received into the seminary who has not overcome the temptations and the disturbances against chastity or does

---

107. Cf. also cc. 970; 2222, 2.
108. Cf. note 106 above; these documents consider all aspects of priestly preparation in this matter.
109. E.g., if a seminarian has committed no sin of unchastity (alone) for many years, and in this year commits one or two of this type, he may be granted a further period of trial.

not show more than merely negative dispositions, or who appears to be given to strong sensuality or sentimentality. A seminarian, no matter at what point in his career, must be excluded from the clerical ranks, without any indulgence or granting of further trials, if he has committed a serious sin with a person of the opposite sex or even with a companion.

Because of the nature of the matter involved, and because unchastity can be more easily hidden than other habits, spiritual directors and *confessors* bear a heavy responsibility in securing the moral firmness of clerical candidates in the area of chastity. The confessor who proceeds here with great caution safeguards the cause of the Church, the good of the faithful, and of the cleric himself. Experience has clearly demonstrated the unfortunate and even tragic results that have ensued in the cases of those in whom chastity has not been well secured and who nevertheless have assumed the clerical state and the priesthood itself. If a candidate cannot remain chaste, he has no vocation. The expectation of the necessary graces from God is insufficient without a required period of trial or proof of positive chastity. The confessor cannot afford to be lax or gentle, even on the eve of ordination, as severity in these cases, even including denial of absolution, is not out of order. Experience also shows here that it is wiser to risk judgment on the side of strictness than of indulgence. The period of probation usually refers to solitary sin, as rarely will there be ordination in cases of sexual sins with others. The period of probation must be *at least* six months (and *at least* a full year, if the time is just previous to entering theology). Virtue cannot be judged to be sufficiently recovered without an adequately prolonged period of testing, since sexual impulses and temptations may enjoy extended periods of latency before an unexpected awakening; good intentions alone are not enough. It is an injustice to allow a candidate to remain on in the seminary or religious novitiate or institute when relapses continue to reappear. It becomes more difficult to withdraw as time goes on, and the candidate, fearing rejection, may then live continently for some time before ordination and subsequently fall back into old habits. Although there cannot be realized such a certainty that the candidate will not relapse, since everyone is always prone to sin, yet the period of probation does give a sufficiently founded hope of his maintaining chastity henceforward, since purity now appears to be solidly possessed, appreciated and cherished.

A clerical candidate who is an habitual sinner, and who is sincerely contrite and firmly resolves amendment, can be absolved by the confessor. However, the latter must refuse absolution to such an habitual sinner who nevertheless intends to take Orders and refuses to submit to a required period of probation, even though he is otherwise disposed for absolution.[110] Besides the state of grace, the lawful reception of Orders demands *outstanding* and *habitual* goodness of life, which is not commonly acquired immediately. Thus, such a clerical penitent would be rash in his resolve and unworthy of sacramental absolution, since he does not have the purpose of fulfilling all the grave precepts and of avoiding all serious sins. An extraordinary confessor, or an occasional confessor to whom the seminarian or aspirant is free to approach, must not deviate from these norms, after he had made a careful inquiry into the candidate's condition of soul and the previous advice he has received from his ordinary confessor or other priests. Nor should he be swayed from insisting upon the period of probation by the tears or other signs of fervent penance or resolution of the penitent; extraordinary signs are sufficient to demonstrate present dispositions but do not guarantee a future proving of chastity. Shame or disgrace feared because of withdrawal from the clerical life does not excuse, as some other pretext for leaving may be alleged, e.g,. more mature consideration, and the spiritual good accomplished outweighs the difficulty. The penitent should also be warned to inform the priest in a subsequent confession of the denial of absolution and the reasons justifying it. It should be noted that addiction to intoxicating drink and to narcotics in clerical candidates should be treated with the same norms as with the habit of impurity.

3. *Canonical age*

The priesthood is not to be conferred before the completion of

110. The distinction between the intemperate and the incontinent sinner is of practical value in judging the dispositions of penitents, but not in judging the suitableness of the ordinand to continue on in the clerical life.

the twenty-fourth year.[111] The local Ordinary may dispense for a just cause from defect of age for ordinands provided it does not exceed six complete months.[112]

4. Confirmation

It befits the sacrament of Holy Orders as a complement of the other sacraments that the other perfections of grace and the gifts infused by the Holy Spirit be already possessed. Those who are bound to the divine ministry by ordination ought to be strong in the faith themselves, and as leaders of others be themselves soldiers of Christ. Thus the sacrament of Confirmation is required for the lawful reception of Holy Orders.[113] The precept, however, does not seem to be grave.

5. State of grace

As a sacrament of the living Holy Orders must be received in the state of grace. This obligation is also serious with respect to the reception of Communion required in the rite of ordination.[114]

6. Interstices

Interstices are the fitting intervals to be kept between the reception of one order and another, so that there might be a period of trial and preparation before promotion to the next order, as well as time for each order to be exercised.

A deacon should possess his order for three months before receiving priestly ordination, unless in the judgment of the bishop the need or profit of the Church indicates otherwise.[115]

7. Retreat

Candidates for sacred orders are to make a retreat of six full days.

---

111. c. 976, 1.
112. Motu proprio, **Pastorale Munus,** 29 nov. 1963, I, 15.
113. c. 974, 1, 1º.
114. c. 1005.
115. c. 978, 2.

In the case of those who within six months are to receive more than one sacred order, the Ordinary can reduce the period of retreat required for the diaconate, but not below three full days. If after the completion of the retreat sacred ordination is postponed for any reason beyond a period of six months, the retreat is to be repeated; if for a shorter period, the Ordinary is to determine whether or not it is to be repeated.[116]

E. *Title of ordination*

No one can be lawfully ordained to sacred orders without a canonical title.[117] The obligation of a title reflects the Church's caution in providing that a cleric receive a fitting and permanent sustenance. If one title is lost, another must be provided or provision for proper livelihood secured. The canonical title for *secular clerics* is the title of benefice, and, if that is not available, the title of patrimony or of pension. Since in the U.S.A. the only benefices are parishes, there can be no title of benefices. In place of these titles the cleric is ordained under the title of service of the diocese, and in places subject to the Sacred Congregation for the Propagation of the Faith by the title of the mission, provided, however, that the candidate takes an oath to dedicate himself to the perpetual service of the diocese or the mission under the authority of the prevailing local Ordinary. He must then be fittingly provided as to support by the Ordinary.[118] Entrance into religion is not excluded by the oath of service of the diocese,[119] but it usually is in that of the mission, except with permission of the Holy See.

For *religious* of solemn vows the canonical title is their solemn religious profession or, as it is called, the title of poverty. Such religious clerics are supported, as it were, by alms, by their religious institute. Some religious of simple vows enjoy the privilege of this title, e.g., Jesuits, Redemptorists. For religious of perpetual vows it is the title of the common table, of the congregation, or any similar title as provided in the constitutions. They thus have the right to be

116. c. 1001.
117. c. 974, 1, 7o; cf. also note 51 above.
118. cc. 979-981.
119. Cf. c. 542.

supported from the common table or the goods of the Institute. Other religious, even in respect to the title of ordination, are governed by the norms for seculars.[120] Often these, as well as societies living in common without vows, enjoy the privilege of the title of common table or of the congregation.

F. *Record of ordination*

After ordination is completed the names of all those ordained and of the ordaining minister, as well as the place and date of ordination, are to be entered into a special book carefully guarded in the curia of the place in which the ordination occurred, together with all pertinent documents. An authentic certificate of the ordination is to be given every candidate ordained; if the legitimately ordaining Bishop was not his own, the candidate is to show this certificate to his own Bishop for recording.[121] The local Ordinary in the case of seculars, or the major superior granting dimissorials for religious, is to send a notification of the promotion to the diaconate of every single candidate to the pastor of the parish in which Baptism was conferred so that the latter might record it in his baptismal register.[122]

VII. *Irregularities*

A. *Norms*

An irregularity is a canonical impediment or disqualification of its nature perpetual which prohibits primarily and directly the reception of Orders (diaconate, priesthood, episcopacy) and secondarily and indirectly the exercise of Orders. Only those capable of receiving Orders can contract an irregularity. The purpose is to safeguard the dignity of the clerical state and office, reverence and becomingness in the sacred ministry, and to avoid offense to the laity, by excluding those unqualified to serve the altar. An irregularity is not a penalty (either medicinal or vindictive) but a disqualification; it binds gravely. An irregularity does not invalidate the reception or exercise

120. c. 982.
121. Cf. cc. 1010.
122. Cf. c. 1011.

of Orders but makes them unlawful.[123] The reception of the other sacraments or of sacramentals is not prohibited, nor the exercise of other ecclesiastical acts or of jurisdiction, but only what is connected with the exercise of the power of Orders.

An irregularity may arise from a defect (*ex defectu*), e.g., blindness, which disqualifies, or from a delict or crime (*ex delicto*), e.g., voluntary homicide, which renders the exercise of the ministry unbecoming. The irregularity may be total or partial in effect in the degree that it prohibits the reception of all Orders or of the next Order, or the exercise of every Order or office or only some, e.g., a crippled priest may be barred from celebrating Mass but not from hearing confessions. The irregularity may arise before or after ordination, and be either public or occult.[124] Irregularities and impediments are multiplied if more than one cause of them exists, but not from the repetition of the same cause, with exception of voluntary homicide.[125]

An irregularity arising from a defect does not indicate or presuppose a fault, as in the case arising from a delict. The latter requires that there be a sin which is serious, certain, and externally manifested, whether publicly or occultly.[126] A merely attempted delict effects an irregularity only when so specified in the law. Whatever removes the seriousness of responsibility or the crime prevents the incurrence of the irregularity, e.g., invincible ignorance. However, ignorance of irregularities, whether of those arising from a delict or of those arising from a defect, or ignorance of the impediments, does not excuse from them.[127] Thus no ignorance excuses from incurrence of an irregularity arising from a defect. It is most commonly held that ignorance of the irregularity itself does not excuse, if the grave delict itself was culpably committed.

An irregularity can be removed or ceases only by dispensation.[128]

---

123. c. 968. A new irregularity is not incurred when one who is irregular nevertheless receives or exercises an order (cf. c. 985, 7°.
124. Cf. cc. 1037; 1047.
125. c. 989.
126. c. 986.
127. c. 988.
128. Excepting illegitimacy which can be removed by solemn profession, and, in the case of an impediment, by the cessation of the fact on which it is based.

The Holy See can dispense from all irregularities and impediments: Sacred Penitentiary in the internal forum, in the external forum the Sacred Congregations of the Sacraments, of Religious, of the Oriental Church, of the Propagation of the Faith for seculars, religious, Eastern rites, and mission subjects respectively. Ordinaries (including those in clerical exempt institutes) may personally or through a delegate dispense their subjects from all irregularities arising from an *occult delict,* with the exception of voluntary homicide and abortion, and any other that has been brought to the judicial forum.[129] The same power is given to every confessor for more urgent occult cases in which it is impossible to reach the Ordinary and imminent danger exists of serious harm or infamy, but only to permit the penitent the lawful exercise of Orders already received.[130] The confessor may exercise this faculty even in the internal extrasacramental forum, [131] as long as at the same time he enjoys jurisdiction to hear the confession of that person. Regulars acting as confessors enjoy the additional privilege of dispensing in order to allow the reception of further Orders.

Bishops may dispense those already ordained from every kind of irregularity either from delict or from defect so that they may celebrate Mass and receive and retain ecclesiastical benefices. This faculty requires that no scandal derive from its use and that the ministry of the altar be duly performed. Excepted from this faculty are the irregularities of c. 985, nn. 3 and 4 (attempted marriage, voluntary homicide, procured abortion). If there is the question of the crime of heresy or schism, an abjuration in the hands of him who absolves must precede the dispensation.[132]

Bishops may not dispense from any irregularity which has been brought into the judicial forum. Moreover, they may not dispense, as to *receiving* Orders, a) from the irregularity *ex defectu* in the case of adulterine or sacrilegious offspring, bodily defects, epileptics, and the mentally deranged; b) from the public irregularity *ex delicto* of those who have completely apostasized from the faith or have gone

129. c. 990, 1.
130. **Ibid.,** 2.
131. c. 202, 2.
132. Motu proprio, **Pastorale Munus,** I, 17.

over to heresy or schism; c) from the public irregularity *ex delicto* of those who have had the audacity to attempt marriage or to place the merely civil act of marriage while they themselves were either validly married or bound by sacred Orders or religious vows, even simple and temporary, or with a woman who was either bound by such vows or validly married; d) from the irregularity *ex delicto*, either public or occult, of those who have committed voluntary homocide or procured the abortion of a human fetus effectively, and all cooperators. Bishops may not dispense, as regards the *exercise of an order* already received, from irregularities, mentioned in c. 985. 3°, in public cases only; and 4°, also in occult cases, unless recourse to the Sacred Penitentiary is impossible, but without prejudice to the obligation of the person dispensed to have recourse to the Sacred Penitentiary as soon as possible.[133]

If a dispensation is general, it will be effective for all irregularities that may have been omitted in good faith (excepting voluntary homicide, abortion and those before a judicial tribunal), but not for any deliberately omitted.[134] A limited or special dispensation does not include any irregularities not mentioned, even inculpably. Under pain of invalidity the number of delicts must be mentioned in seeking a dispensation from the irregularity arising from vountary homicide.[135] A general dispensation for Orders is valid for all major Orders;[136] A dispensation granted in the internal non-sacra-mental forum is to be put into writing and the evidence of it recorded in the secret register of the curia.[137] In practice this latter may be too burdensome or almost impossible.

B. *Individual irregularities*

1. *Arising from defect*[138]

a. *Illegitimacy* (*ex defectu natalium*), whether it is public

---

133. Motu proprio, **De Episcoporum Muneribus**, 15 iun. 1966, IX, 8-10.
134. c. 991, 1.
135. **Ibid.**, 2.
136. **Ibid.**, 3.
137. **Ibid.**, 4.
138. c. 984.

or occult, unless legitimation has taken place[139] or solemn vows taken.

b. *Bodily defects (ex defectu corporis)* which prevent the ministry of the altar from being exercised either safely because of weakness or becomingly because of deformity. To prohibit the exercise of an Order lawfully received, however, a more serious defect is required, and those acts which can be properly performed are not forbidden because of it. Such disqualifications are: mutilation, as the absence of a thumb or index finger, hand, arm, foot, leg, both eyes; weakness, as blindness, complete deafness, dumbness, excessive stammering, lameness requiring a cane; deformity, as genuine dwarfs or giants, the noseless, the excessively hunchbacked, or any affliction which has the effect upon onlookers of disgust and abhorrence or amusement and ridicule.

c. *Mental defects (ex defectu animi)* which are epilepsy, insanity or diabolic possession, whether past or present. But if these defects became present after the reception of Orders and if they are shown now beyond a doubt to have been cured, the Ordinary may again allow his subjects to exercise the Orders received.

d. *Bigamy (ex defectu sacramenti)* or the fact of having contracted successively two or more valid marriages. A plurality of marriages does not perfectly represent the union of Christ to one spouse, namely, the Church.

e. *Infamy of law (ex defectu famae)*, which is the bad reputation which the law itself expressly attaches to an individual.[140]

f. *Capital judgment (ex defectu lenitatis)*, which includes only those who, as judges, have imposed the death sentence. This lack of gentleness is the unfittingness that one representing Christ, gentle and clement, should have inflicted death on another, however just. The irregularity is incurred by a just sentence, since an unjust

---

139. Cf. c. 1116; PCI 13 iul. 1930 states that sons legitimated by the subsequent marriage of their parents are regarded as legitimate for the purpose of admission to the seminary, unless the parental marital impediment was age or disparity of worship (PCI 6 dec. 1930). Legitimation of offspring of an adulterous or sacrilegious union is not usually granted unless under stringent conditions.

140. Cf. cc. 2293, 2; 2294, 1; 2295; 2314, 1, 3o; 2320; 2343, 1, 2o, 2, 2o; 2351, 2; 2356.

sentence is the basis for the irregularity arising from the crime of voluntary homicide.

    g. *Capital execution* (*ex defectu lenitatis*), which includes only those who have assumed the position of executioner and the voluntary and immediate assistants of the same in the execution of a sentence of death.

2. *Arising from delict*[141]

    a. *Apostasy, heresy, schism.* The delinquent need not have belonged to a sect. The irregularity refers to past or present separation or apostasy from the Catholic Church.

    b. *Baptism by a non-Catholic.* Those who, outside of a case of extreme necessity or as allowed in certain circumstances by the Church, in any way allow Baptism to be conferred on them by a non-Catholic. It is an abuse of the sacrament of Baptism.

    c. *Attempted marriage.* Those who have dared to attempt marriage or to perform only the civil act of giving marital consent, while they were bound by a matrimonial bond, by sacred Orders or by (public) religious vows, even though these latter are only simple and temporary, or with a woman who is bound by these vows or by a valid marital bond. This is an abuse of the sacrament of marriage.

    d. *Homicide and abortion.* Those who have committed voluntary homicide or who have effectively procured the abortion of a human fetus, as well as all who cooperate in these delicts. The homicide must be a seriously culpable and formally an unjust taking of another's life. It must be voluntary and directly productive of the result and probably not merely voluntary indirectly or in cause. This will also include craniotomy, etc. The abortion must be the ejection of an immature fetus, which actually takes place as a consequence of the action taken to effect it. All formal and positive cooperators in either delict, without whose cooperation the delict would not have been committed,[142] incur this irregularity. In a case of doubtful incurrence, it is expedient to seek a dispensation *ad cautelam*.

    e. *Mutilation and attempted suicide.* Those who mutilate

---

141. c. 985.
142. Cf. c. 2209.

themselves or others, or who attempt to take their own life. The muti-lation is commonly considered to be one by which is removed a member of the body which enjoys a function of its own distinct from that of other members of the body, e.g., hand, foot, eye, testicles. There must be a serious fault and not a necessary and lawful opera-tion. It seems that the suicide attempt is to be understood as one that was frustrated in its effect by some agency outside the will of the sinner, e.g., a physician.

f. *Medicine or surgery.* Those who as clerics practice medi-cine or surgery when it is forbidden them, if death results from their act. Those who do *not* have an Apostolic indult to *practice* medicine or surgery[143] incur this irregularity if *death* occurs as an *effect* of this practice, even though they are otherwise competent and skilled.

g. *Abuse of a sacred order.* Those who, lacking the requisite Order or restrained from the exercise of it by a canonical penalty, either local or personal, medicinal or vindictive, perform an action of sacred Orders. The usurpation of an Order incurring the irregu-larity obtains when there is the placing of an act of Orders (and not of jurisdiction), by one who lacks this Order. It must be a solemn act in serious matter done with grave responsibility.

VIII. *Impediments*[144]

A. *Norms*

The impediments are temporary disqualifications, and while they exist they impede the reception and exercise of Orders, (diaconate, priesthood, episcopacy). They may cease by dispensation or by the lapse of time or removal of the cause. They have the same effect as irregularities. The basis for them is considered to be lack of faith, lack of freedom, and lack of good reputation.

B. *Individual impediments*

1. *Catholic children of non-Catholics*

The impediment is incurred even if only one parent is non-Cath-

---

143. Cf. c. 139, 2.
144. c. 987, 1o-7o.

olic and even though the mixed marriage was contracted with a dispensation and the promises made; but it does not affect the grandchildren of the non-Catholic.[145] The illegitimate incur the impediment. With the death or conversion of the non-Catholic parent, the impediment ceases. The local Ordinary may dispense from this impediment which bars sons of non-Catholics for as long as the parents remain in their error.[146]

2. *Married men*

The impediment exists as long as the wife is living and the bond of the marriage has not been lawfully dissolved. The Holy See does dispense under certain conditions so that a married man might enter a secular or religious seminary and leave his wife.[147] Civil arrangements may be indicated in this case.

3. *Clerics in forbidden activity*

Those who are charged with an office or an administrative burden forbidden to clerics, which carries with it the obligation of an accounting, until they have resigned the office and the administrative responsibility, have rendered their account, and are free of responsibility of it. These are activities which are especially forbidden in c. 139, 2, 3.

4. *Slaves*

Those who are slaves in the strict sense of the term, until they have obtained their freedom.

5. *Subjects of military service*

Those who are bound by civil law to a period of ordinary military

145. PCI 14 iul. 1922.
146. Motu proprio **Pastorale Munus**, I, 16.
147. The local Ordinary may not dispense (motu proprio **De Episcoporum Muneribus,** IX, 9e).

service and who have not yet served it. This includes also those not yet called due to lack of proper age or because they have been declared temporarily unfit.[148] This would not include the extraordinary service during war time, nor the service of chaplains.

6. *Neophytes.*

They are those who have recently received *absolute* Baptism in the Church as adults. They are impeded from Orders until in the judgment of the Ordinary they have been sufficiently tried. Those converted from heresy or schism fall under the irregularity.

7. *The disreputable*

Those who are infamous in fact, as long as in the judgment of the Ordinary the ill-repute continues. Infamy of fact is contracted when, because of a crime or immoral conduct, one has lost his reputation in the opinion of upright and reliable Catholics, which is left up to the judgment of the Ordinary.[149]

148. PCI 2-3 iun. 1918.
149. c. 2293, 3.

CELEBRATION OF MATRIMONY

I. *Marriage, a Sacrament of Community*

The Creator of all things established the conjugal partnership as the beginning and basis of human society and by his grace has made it a great sacrament in Christ and in the Church. Christian couples are cooperators in grace and witnesses of faith to each other, their children, and other members of the household.[1]

The intimate community character of married life and love, established by the Creator and deriving its structure from his laws, is based on the conjugal pact, an irrevocable personal consent. From this act, by which the parties give and receive each other, there arises an institution which by divine ordinance is stable, even in the eyes of society. This bond, which is sacred for the good of the married parties, the children, and society itself, does not depend on men's choice; God, who made marriage, endowed it with its various values and purposes. All these are of the highest importance for the continuance of the human race, for the personal progress and eternal welfare of the members of families, for the dignity, stability, peace, and prosperity of the family itself and of human society as a whole. By their natural character the institutions of marriage and married love are ordained for the procreation and bringing up of children; they reach their peak or crown in these activities. Man and woman, who by the conjugal pact are no longer two but one, help minister to each other in an intimate linking of their persons and activities. They experience the real meaning of their union and achieve it more every day. As a mutual gift of two persons, this intimate union and the good of the children impose total fidelity on the spouses and argue for an unbreakable oneness between them.[2]

The union of man and woman differs radically from every other human association. It constitutes a truly singular reality, the married couple, grounded on the mutual gift of self to one another. Irrevocable indissolubility is the seal on this unity, stamped on the free,

---

1. Vatican II, Decree **Apostolicam Actuositatem**, n. 11.
2. **Ibid.**, Const. **Gaudium et Spes**, n. 48.

mutual commitment of two free persons who now are no longer two but one flesh. Their unity takes on a social and juridical form through marriage and is manifested by a community of life which finds fruitful expression in their bodily self-giving. When spouses marry they express a desire to belong to each other for life, and to this end they contract an objective bond whose laws and requirements, far from involving servitude, are a guarantee, a protection, and a real support.[3]

In the great work of renewing all things in Christ, marriage too is renewed and purified: it becomes a new reality, a sacrament of the New Covenant.[4] Thus Christian spouses, in virtue of the sacrament of matrimony, signify and partake of the mystery of that unity and fruitful love which exists between Christ and his Church. The spouses thereby help each other to attain holiness in their married life and by means of the rearing and education of their children. And so, in their state and way of life they have their own special gift among the People of God.[5]

The true teaching on marriage, and on Christian marriage in particular, is a part of Christian doctrine. Consequently, it must be known by all the faithful according to their capacities, opportunities, and circumstances of life and state. The obligation is *certainly serious* for priests, no matter what form their ministry takes, whether their exercise of office is in the pastoral or parochial area or happens to be limited mostly to the forum of conscience. Priests are constituted the guides and instructors, in accordance with the Church's magisterium on marriage, of the faithful for whom matrimony is something quite real, necessary, and of considerable duration. The priest must know not only the theoretical teaching on matrimony but also have a handy grasp of the discipline and practice of the Church today. The latter must change and be adapted to fit the constant movement of human life, and at times of human perversity. Thus, regarding the positive laws and the instructions of the Church, the priest cannot be content with the knowledge once acquired in this field but, consonant with the obligation of continuing education of the clergy,[6]

3. Paul VI, Address **Tout d'Abord,** 4 maii 1970.
4. **Ibid.**
5. Vatican II, Const. **Lumen Gentium,** n. 11.
6. **Ibid.,** Decree **Presbyterorum Ordinis,** n. 19.

he must use all ordinary diligence and prudence to keep abreast of the mind of the Church as expressed from time to time and competently reported.

II. *Basic Elements in the Structure of Marriage*

A. *Elements Essential to all Marriages*

Matrimony[7] as an office of nature was instituted by God by a positive ordination when, after the creation of Adam, he formed Eve as a companion and helper and blessed their partnership.[8] Implicitly it was instituted by God in the creation of man and woman. God, in creating them to his own image and likeness, showed at the same time that he wished them to be different in sex and apt to generate offspring, that hence through their matrimonial union of mutual love and help the human race might be propagated. Moreover, to fulfill the purpose of creation and to attain the perfection of his nature, the offspring must for many years be nourished and religiously reared, for which nature requires the cooperation of man and woman. And God wished that this stable partnership should be achieved in a way consonant with an intellectual and free nature, i.e., by mutual and free consent.

Thus matrimony is a special design of God and its essentials have been established by him and not by man. It must be accepted as divinely designed and made; it may not be changed or altered to adapt it to man's whims and wishes. Since it is of natural institution, matrimony truly exists among the non-baptized, and natural

---

7. "The word 'matrimony' (**matrimonium—matris munus**) is derived from the fact that the principal object which a female should propose to herself in marriage is to become a mother; or from the fact that to a mother it belongs to conceive, bring forth, and to train her offspring. It is also called wedlock (**conjugium**—yoking together) from joining together, because a lawful wife is united to her husband, as it were, by a common yoke. It is called nuptials (**nubere, nuptiae**—to veil oneself), because, as St. Ambrose observes, the bride veiled her face through modesty—a custom which would also seem to imply that she was to be subject and obedient to her husband" (**Catechism of the Council of Trent**).
8. Cf. Gn 1:27; 2:3, 18; Mt 19:3-6; Mk 10:2-9; Trent, Denz-Schön. 1797-1799.

reason inclines to it.[9] Thus it is in itself lawful, good, and praiseworthy,[10] because of God its author and inasmuch as it is ordained to the purposes he established.

Although matrimony is good and even necessary for the human race, the precept or obligation of contracting it falls upon the race as a whole and not upon each individual,[11] unless accidently, e.g., to avoid incontinence,[12] to repair an injury, or to fulfill a promise. Each one is free to choose his state of life; no human authority is able *absolutely* to forbid marriage to anyone against his antecedent will and who is capable of carrying out its duties. Moreover, the conjugal act itself is also meritorious when virtuously motivated, e.g., to render the debt in justice, or to beget children out of religious motivation, to foster marital love, and when performed under due conditions the principle of which is that it be done in charity. The shamefulness of concupiscence often accompanying the marital act is not that of fault but of penalty coming from original sin. Even if the intensity of pleasure takes away the reason's use, it does not take away the order of reason, because the marital act is preordered by reason.[13] Even the natural contract is a sacred thing,[14] and thus its principal act is also sacred.

Matrimony, from the viewpoint of its coming into being (*matrimonium in fieri*), i.e., in relation to the transitory act (of internal and external consent) creating the relationship of man and wife, is defined as the lawful contract between a man and a woman by which is given and accepted the exclusive and perpetual right to those bodily functions apt to generate children, and by which they oblige themselves to share in a common life.[15] With respect to this relationship in its permanent state as already established by the mutual consent, i.e., the matrimonial bond or permanent and indissoluble

9. Cf. Summa Theol., Suppl., q. 41, a. 1; **III Cont. Gent.**, c. 122.
10. Cf. Denz.-Schön. 206; 461; 1012; Summa Theol., loc. cit., a. 3.
11. Cf. Summa Theol., II-II, q. 152, a. 2, ad 1; Suppl., q. 41, a. 2; **III Cont. Gent.**, c. 136.
12. I Cor. 7:9.
13. Summa Theol., Suppl., q. 41, a. 3. Cf. also **Gaudium et Spes**, n. 49.
14. Leo XIII, ency. **Arcanum Divinae Sapientiae** (10 feb. 1880), n. 19. (Some sections of this Encyclical are found in Denz.-Schön. 3142-3146.
15. c. 1013, 1. Cf. Pius XI, ency. **Casti Connubi** (31 dec. 1930). (Some sections of this Encyclical are found in Denz.-Schön. 3700-3724).

alliance of man and woman (*matrimonium in facto esse*), matrimony is defined as the lawful marital union of a man and a woman involving their living together in undivided partnership.[16]

Marriage as an office of nature is essentially a contract and a bond effected by the mutual exchange of consent; it is more properly the bond which is effected causally by the contractual consent. This conjugal bond is the complex of relations arising from the matrimonial contract and uniting the spouses in one society, the group of rights and obligations among which the exclusive and perpetual right and obligation of carnal intercourse is proper and exclusive to marriage as distinct from all other unions.[17] The sharing of bed, board, and cohabitation pertains to the integrity and perfection of the conjugal life and not to its essence, as is obvious in a marriage of conscience. The union of the two spirits through mutual love is not precisely the object but rather the condition of a happy married life.[18] Similarly, the union of material goods is a condition for bearing equitably the burdens of marriage; it can be and sometimes is determined by civil agreement. The principal purposes of marriage[19] are usually not to be achieved or well attained unless the integrity of the bond is also had.

The remote material of the contract of marriage is the persons of the contractants, embracing the mutual right to the body of each relative to procreation. The proximate material is the signs or words expressing this reciprocal exchange. The formula is the manner by which the acceptance of each other with mutual rights and obligations is exteriorly manifested.

16. P. Lombard, **IV Sent.**, d. 27, cap. **Sunt ergo.** Cf. also **Summa Theol.,** Suppl., q. 44.
17. The right (as distinguished from the use) to the acts of themselves apt to procreate is essential; if the right is not transferred (in the sense of being intended and not excluded) or if the party is not apt to generate, there can be no marital contract or union. Marriage bespeaks an order to carnal copulation, although the latter does not pertain to its essence but to its integriy.
18. **Gaudium et Spes,** n. 49.
19. **Ibid.,** n. 48: "By their natural character the institution of marriage and married love are ordained for the procreation and bringing up of children; they reach their peak or crown in these activities." **Cf.** also n. 50.

Marriage by its very nature is destined or ordained for the pro-creation and education of offspring. This purpose (and thus the right to its fulfilment) is intrinsic to marriage and must be intended, or at least not positively excluded, in contracting the union.[20] If it is lacking, no other purpose of itself suffices for true marital union, although it alone suffices without any other, but not very conven-iently. Other purposes intrinsic to the structure of marriage are: 1) *mutual help and comfort.* The spouses, endowed by God and na-ture with different and complementary inclinations and faculties, find mutual help and comfort in marriage, inasmuch as from it springs a happier life together, which is necessary for the education of off-spring, and a more tolerable forbearance of the burdens of a common life and of old age. It consists in mutual love and deepest friendship together with other helps and solaces of the spiritual and material orders, e.g., a sharing of goods.[21] 2) *the enjoyment of pleasure and*

---

20. **Ibid.** Paul VI, ency. **Humanae Vitae** (25 iul. 1968), n. 8: "Marriage .. is the wise institution of the Creator to realize in mankind his design of love. By means of the reciprocal personal gift of self, proper and exclusive to them, husband and wife tend towards the communion of their beings in view of mutual personal perfection, to collaborate with God in the generation and education of new lives."

21. **Gaudium et Spes**, nn. 48-49; 50: "But in fact marriage is not instituted merely for procreation. The indissoluble character of the personal pact and the good of the children themselves demand that mutual love should be properly shown between a married couple, that it should progress and mature. Even therefore if children, often so much de-sired, are lacking, marriage persists as a lifetime comradeship and keeps its value and indissolubility."
    There are certain goods or benefits or effects which follow from a validly and lawfully contracted marriage, substantial or essential goods which cannot be intentionally excluded and which safeguard the validity of marriage. Inasmuch as they accrue to the spouses they are called goods or benefits or blessings; inasmuch as they attract or move men to contract marriage they are called ends or goals. They compensate for the difficulties and trials of married life. They are: 1) the benefit or blessing of **offspring**, which founds the rights and obligations regarding the use of marriage and the rearing and formation of the offspring; 2) the good of **faith**, i.e., conjugal fidelity or mutual faithfulness of the spouses as regards bodily rights and what is conducive to leading a stable family life; 3) the **sacrament** or the hallowedness or sacredness of every marriage bond and the inseparableness of the spouses as a sing of the indivisible

the quieting of concupiscence. Although this is not essential, it is intrinsic to marriage in this state of fallen nature, as a remedy for weakness. It is an alleviation of concupiscence especially toward a third party and safeguards the achievement of unity of purpose in love. Fallen nature restrains concupiscence within reason only with difficulty; it is less excited to the forbidden if it is granted in marriage lawful things respecting the ordination of marriage. This quieting or healing of concupiscence is the acquisition of the virtue of conjugal chastity.[22]

B. *Sacramental Marriage*

Matrimony is also a sacrament of the New Law which confers grace for the sanctification of the lawful union of man and woman and for the religious and holy reception and education of offspring. It is a sign of the union of Christ with his Church, significative and productive of the grace derived from Christ, Head of the Church, whereby the marital union might be supernaturally fruitful of its proportionate likeness to the union of Christ and his Church. Christ while on earth certainly instituted it as a sacrament, elevating the natural bond to the higher state of a sign and cause of grace. He had consecrated and sanctified marriage by his presence in Cana of Galilee and had recalled marriage to its original perfection of unity and indissolubility. It is a teaching of faith that marriage is a sacrament and that a valid matrimonial contract between Christians is by that fact a sacrament.[23] The distinction between marriage as a natural contract and as a religious act of sacrament can relate only to the *effects* of Christian marriage and not to the marriage itself. Thus, strictly, the baptized cannot celebrate the matrimonial contract as the cause of civil effects and not also as the cause of supernatural effects or as a sacrament.

union of Christ with his Church—which is confirmed and strengthened in a marriage which is also a sacrament.

22. **Ibid.,** n. 50.
23. Eh 5:22-32; Trent, Denz.-Schön. 1797-1801; c. 1012; Cod. **Or.** De Matr., c. 1, 1; Pius XI, ency. **Casti Connubii;** Leo XIII, ency. **Arcanum Divinae Sapientiae.**

Elevation implies addition, and matrimony remains after its elevation what it was before, with the power of causing grace added. Thus, whatever properly belongs to a contract, belongs also to the sacrament, e.g., to contract through a proxy. Validly baptized non-Catholics, even if they do not admit or expressly deny that it is a sacrament, when they enter marriage with true consent, by that fact confect and receive a sacrament. Their intention, although erroneous, is sufficient; in the will to celebrate marriage or to contract a valid marriage is included the intention of doing that which in the Church is a sacrament. There is no sacrament and thus no marriage if their positive and prevailing will is not to receive a sacrament, as at least a virtual intention is required in the minister. The marriage of the non-baptized, when *both* spouses become subsequently baptized, automatically becomes a sacrament, even if they are not aware of the fact. The matrimonial contract and consent virtually perdure in the bond itself, which, with the advent of Baptism, becomes a sacred sign. The Church does not require a renewal of consent from such converts but rather exhorts them to receive the nuptial blessing.[24] If matrimonial consent has been withdrawn expressly, e.g., by a divorce, or if a new marriage is desired, the local Ordinary is to be consulted.

As in the natural contract the material of the sacrament is the outward manifestation of the *conferral* of marital rights; the formula is the external expression of the *acceptance* of these rights.

The ministers of the sacrament of Matrimony are the contracting parties themselves, as in the case of the natural contract.[25] The priest is only the qualified or official witness of the validity and lawfulness of the sacramental contract and thus may be called a minister of the juridical and religious solemnity only.

All the baptized who are free of any diriment impediment are capable of receiving the sacrament of Matrimony. The contracting

---

24. S. Off. 20 iun. 1860; 20 sept. 1848.
25. **Ibid.**, 11 aug. 1949: "In view of the peculiar nature of the sacrament of Matrimony, whose ministers are the contracting parties themselves and in which the priest acts as a witness **ex officio**, the priest can assist at the marriages of Communists." Cf. Pius XII, ency. **Mystici Corporis** (29 iun. 1943).

parties must be present to one another, either personally or by proxy, which holds also for baptized non-Catholics.[26] They must not have expressed a condition contrary to the essence of matrimony. They also receive the sacrament lawfully and fruitfully, if they are free from prohibitive impediments, in the state of grace, confirmed, possessed of parental consent if they are minors, and observant of all the ecclesiastical prescriptions for the celebration of marriage. The Church does not command but strongly advises the reception of Penance and the Eucharist before marriage.[27] This is the common practice, which is to be urged upon all nupturients, as well as the best man and the bridesmaid. Opportunity should be afforded them, usually at their last visit to the priest, for going to confession.

III. *Types of Marital Union*

A. *Valid.*

A valid or true marriage is a union which fulfills all the conditions requisite for validity, i.e., which is not vitiated by diriment impediment, by defective consent, or by the failure to observe the required form. The presence of a prohibitive or impedient impediment renders the marriage unlawful but valid. A valid marriage produces its juridical effects and makes the contractants to be spouses with all the rights and obligations thereof.

1. *sacramental only (ratum tantum)*. This is a marriage in which *both* parties are validly baptized and in which the union has not yet been consummated *(ratum et non consummatum)*. There must be valid Baptism present in both parties, since there cannot be a sacrament (and consequently its greater obligations) existing on the side of one party and not on the other; marriage does not limp. This is a union which is received or recognized *(ratum)* as a sacrament by the Church.[28] When a party or the parties who are unbaptized receive Baptism subsequent to having entered into a

---

26. c. 1088, 1; S. Off. 30 iun. 1949.
27. c. 1033.
28. Cf. c. 1015, 1; cf. also **Lumen Gentium**, n. 11; **Gaudium et Spes**, n. 48.

valid and legitimate marriage, the marital bond automatically becomes sacramental by reason of the Baptism now present in *both* parties.[29]

2. *sacramental and consummated* (*ratum et consummatum*). A sacramental union is consummated in which the spouses have performed the conjugal act, which consists in at least some penetration of and insemination in the female vagina by the male generative member. This act must be one placed *after* the celebration of the valid marriage. Once the parties cohabit after the marriage celebration, comsummation is presumed, until the contrary is proved.[30] A sacramental and consummated marriage is absolutely indissoluble by any power on earth.

3. *legitimate* (*legitimum*). This is a valid union (whether consummated or not) entered into according to the laws binding them between two unbaptized parties or between an unbaptized and a baptized party.[31] It is a *natural* bond only and not a sacramental union (which requires *two* baptized parties). Thus, even the marriage of a Catholic with an unbaptized according to the canonical form is only a natural bond. The marriage of two unbaptized parties is governed only by the natural law and by just civil laws. When one party alone is baptized (even though a non-Catholic) the marriage is by that fact ruled by ecclesiastical law (and the unbaptized party is indirectly bound), unless exempted in some respect, e.g., those baptized as non-Catholics are exempted from the Catholic canonical form of marriage.

B. *Invalid* (*nullum, irritum*)

An invalid or null and void marriage is a union lacking some

29. Consequently, between baptized parties a valid matrimonial contract cannot exist, unless it is by that fact a sacrament. Cf. c. 1012, 2; Pius IX, **Syllabus**, 8 dec. 1864, props. 66, 73 (Denz.-Schön. 2966, 2973). Cf. Paul VI, Address "Tout d'Abord," 4 maii 1970.
30. c. 1015, 2.
31. **Ibid.**, 3. "Legitimate" is also used only in the sense of "according to the law," however, in cc. 232, 2, 2º; 331, 1, 1º; 1075, without the specific meaning of **legitimum** of c. 1015, 3. Cf. Paul VI, Address "Tout d'Abord," n. 3: "As Holy Scripture teaches us: marriage is a great earthly reality before it is a sacrament."

condition for validity and in which an external manifestation or consent has no effect due to the presence of a lack of required form, or of defect in consent, or of a diriment impediment.

1. *in good faith.* A marriage celebrated in good faith by at least one of the parties is considered to be a putative (*putativum*) marriage, until such time as *both* parties become aware of the nullity of the matrimonial contract.[32] There remains the figure or appearance of a true marriage. However, to be considered *certainly* putative, the marriage must have been *celebrated before the Church*,[33] i.e., in the canonical form, either ordinary or extraordinary.[34] Only an outwardly correct contract will be recognized as putative, with consequent effects. Thus, any act in good faith which by external form of celebration has the appearance of a canonical marriage, although actually null due to some substantial defect, is certainly a putative marriage, e.g., if celebrated in good faith before a priest lacking necessary jurisdiction, or before a pastor and two witnesses outside his parish. An invalid marriage celebrated in any form which the Church regards as sufficient for those not bound to the canonical form is *probably* putative. In such a case, the local Ordinary is to be consulted.

2. *in bad faith.* A marriage is called *attempted* or an *attempt at marriage* or made in bad faith if one or both of the parties have knowledge of the nullity and yet have gone through the external form of marriage contract. A marriage contracted not *coram Ecclesia* by one who is bound to the canonical form, but contracted only civilly, is an attempted marriage; in the sight of the Church it has not even the appearance of a marriage and is rather concubinage,[35] which implies no form or appearance of marriage,[36] although the

---

32. **Ibid.,** 4. If one or both parties to the marriage begin to doubt its validity, it still remains putative until there is moral certainty of the nullity.
33. PCI 16 oct. 1949; cf. Codex Or., **de matrimonio, c. 4, 4.**
34. cc. 1094; 1098.
35. PCI 16 oct. 1949, n. 17.
36. Concubinage is distinguished from common law marriage, which is entered into without any kind of ceremony and in which a man and a woman live together as man and wife and present themselves as such to others. Some States recognize such a marriage as valid in civil law.

intent and will to be considered as spouses is expressed (thus differing from common concubinage).

C. *Public*

A marriage that is entered into according to the canonical form, either ordinary or extraordinary, by those bound to it, is called public (*publicum*) in law. It is recorded in the public parochial register. A marriage is called public in fact when notice of it has been divulged or when it is celebrated or takes place in such circumstances that it can be, and ought prudently to be judged to be, easily divulged.

D. *Secret*

A marriage can be called secret (*occultum*) when the banns are omitted and the marriage has been contracted secretly. In the strict canonical sense the only secret marriage is the *marriage of conscience* (*matrimonium conscientiae*).[37] It is not secret with respect to the Church but only to civil society. A marriage which is contracted secretly and without the legitimate form prescribed by the Church is called a *clandestine* marriage; it is always invalid for Catholics not dispensed from the form.

IV. *Properties of marriage*

The unbaptized, together with the baptized, are subject to the prescriptions of the natural and the divine law regarding the essential properties of the contract of marriage: unity and indissolubility. These properties are even more firmly attached to Christian marriage, since the sacramental union more perfectly reflects and signifies the perfect and lasting union of Christ with his Church.[38] Thus as the woman gives herself wholly and perpetually to the one man, so equally the man should give himself to the woman.

37. cc. 1104-1107.
38. c. 1013, 2; cf. S. Off. 20 iun. 1866; 17 aug. 1898.

A. *Unity*

The unity of matrimony, which is the union of one man with one woman to the exclusion of all other persons, is called monogamy. To this unity is opposed plurality or polygamy, whether simultaneous or successive.

1. *Simultaneous polygamy*. This is the union of one party with many spouses. It is divided into:

Simultaneous polyandry. This is the marital union of one woman with several husbands. It is historically of most rare occasion. It is opposed to the Scriptural command of two in one flesh[39] and to the purposes of marriage. The woman tends to become infertile, the uncertainty of the father renders the education of offspring impossible, the woman cannot remain faithful to multiple husbands, the natural subjection of woman to man is unrealizable, domestic concord cannot be achieved nor the remedy for concupiscence.[40] The union is intrinsically evil and can never be allowed.

Simultaneous polygamy or polygamy principally so-called. The marital union of one man with several wives is more commonly designated by the generic term of polygamy. Although it is not absolutely repugnant to the natural law, it is opposed to the secondary precepts and purposes of marriage,[41] rendering their fulfillment most difficult and hindersome. It existed among the Jews and Gentiles before the time of Christ and continues among some sects today. Christ recalled marriage to its pristine unity and made it unlawful and invalid for all men, baptized, Jew, unbaptized, to have more than one valid wife simultaneously.[42]

---

39. Gn 2:24; Trent, Denz-Schön. 1797-1798. **Gaudium et Spes**, n. 48: "As a mutual gift of two persons, this intimate union, as well as the good of the children, imposes total fidelity on the spouses and argues for an unbreakable oneness between them."
40. Leo XIII, **Arcanum Divinae Sapientiae**; Pius XI, **Casti Connubii**; **Summa Theol., Supp.**, q. 65, a. 1 ad 8-9.
41. **Summa Theol.**, loc cit., c.; **IV Cont. Gent.**, c. 124. This is why it is possible for the bill of divorce of the Old Testament (Dt 24: 1-4).
42. "If anyone says that it is lawful for Christians to have several wives at the same time and that this is not forbidden by any divine law, let him be anathema," Trent, Denz.-Schön. 1802; S. Off. 20 iun. 1866: "It is a most certain principle that a marriage celebrated by a man

2. *Successive polygamy.* This is bigamy in the canonical sense, or the second or repeated marriages validly entered into upon the lawful cessation of a previous bond by death or by lawful dissolution by the Apostolic power.[43]

B. *Indissolubility*

This is the property whereby marriage even as an institution of nature cannot be dissolved and it is called indissolubility or unbreakableness. Because of its intrinsic and inviolable firmness the conjugal *bond* should be lasting and stable and not be dissolved. Although this firmness certainly belongs to the natural bond, it is more strongly present in a sacramental marriage, in which the indissoluble union of Christ with his Church is more perfectly represented and signified, and thus it is called the good of the sacrament. This property is called firmness inasmuch as the intimate nature itself of marriage requires an indivisible bond; it is called indissolubility, since no human cause or agency can divide or break the *bond.* "What God has joined together, let *no man* put asunder."[44] Thus marriage is said to be indissoluble as diseases are said to be incurable, i.e., not excluding the power of God to interfere.[45]

1. *Intrinsic.* Matrimony cannot be dissolved by an intrinsic cause, such as the mutual consent of the parties themselves, and thus it is said to be intrinsically indissoluble. The primary precepts of the natural law would be violated; the principal ordination of marriage, the procreation and education of offspring, could not be realized

with a woman at a time when they are unbelievers is null and void by both natural and divine law, if there is living another woman to whom he had bound himself by a previous marriage."

43. cc. 1142-1143; Rm 7:3; 1 Cor 7:39.
44. Mt 19:6; Mk 10:9. Cf. **Gaudium et Spes**, n. 48.
45. There is a threefold indissolubility distinguishable: a) as to **bond,** inasmuch as the spouses cannot contract a new marriage while the preceding marriage perdures; b) as to **bed,** inasmuch as the spouses are bound to render each other the conjugal debt; c) as to **board** or dwelling, inasmuch as the spouses are bound to share the same table, dwelling, and other temporal goods necessary for the proper family living.

if at any time and at their own pleasure the parties themselves were able to sever the conjugal bond. The contractants in a marriage contract do not of themselves stipulate or determine the terms of the contract; these have already been instituted by nature and by divine law. Thus the terms of marriage are not proposed by the parties but to the parties, by God, the third and interested and authoritative party to every marriage. The parties are free to enter or not into the marital contract, but they assume the contract as stipulated, i.e., with the properties of unity and indissolubility. They are then bound by the marital bond contracted and are not free of themselves to change or sever it.[46]

2. *Extrinsic.* The marriage *bond* cannot be dissolved by any human authority outside the parties themselves, even by those holding the supreme natural·civil power or by those endowed with highest supernatural power simply as head of a supernatural society; it is thus said to be extrinsically indissoluble. To dissolve the bond by an extrinsic authority does not appear to be absolutely contrary to the purpose of the natural law but opposed to the secondary precepts.[47] However, the prohibition of the natural law has been reinforced by that of divine law. Although marriage could sometimes be dissolved by a bill of divorce (*libellus repudii*) under the Mosaic law (and the relaxation probably extended to the Gentiles), Christ in the New Law recalled marriage to its original indissolubility, so that no marriage by anyone can be dissolved henceforth by any human authority or power or for any cause but only in certain cases by the divine power itself.[48] God can dissolve any marriage

46. Cf. Paul VI, Address "Tout d'Abord"; **Summa Theol., Suppl.**, q. 67, a. 1; **III Cont. Gent.**, c. 123.
47. Cf. **Summa Theol.**, loc. cit., a. 2.
48. Mt 5:31-33; 19:3-12; Mk 10:2-12; Lk 16:18; I Cor. 7:10-11; Rm 7:2-3; cc. 1013, 2; 1129, 1; Trent. Denz.-Schön. 1805; 1807; Pius VII, Brief, 8 nov. 1803: "The decision of lay tribunals and of Catholic assemblies by which the nullity of marriages is chiefly declared, and the dissolution of their bond attempted, can have no strength and absolutely no force in the sight of the Church.... Those pastors who would approve these nuptials by their presence and confirm them with their blessing would commit a very grave fault and would betray their sacred ministry. For they should not be called nuptials but rather adulterous unions" (Denz.-Schön. 2705-2706); Pius IX, Syllabus, prop. 67: "By natural law the bond of matrimony is not indissoluble, and in

bond whatsoever (which exceptions are rare and special), either by direct action or by granting the power to dissolve the bond to men, either the spouses themselves (as in the case of the Pauline privilege), or to the Supreme Pontiff, dispensing in a divine and natural law not as head of the supernatural society with the general mandate to rule the faithful but by an extraordinary and vicarious power (the so-called Petrine power or privilege of the faith) as successor of St. Peter as the Vicar of Christ on earth.

The altogether adequate reason for the indissolubility of marriage as an office of nature and as a sacrament is very probably the positive will or precept of God. However, nature itself indicates the exigency. Every marriage, especially when consummated, is indissoluble by at least the secondary precepts of the natural law. Absolutely speaking, the primary purpose of marriage can in certain cases be achieved without perpetual indissolubility. However, notwithstanding this, marriage is of itself ordered to the primary purpose, which is protected and fostered by the properties of unity and indissolubility, even though the purpose cannot be actually realized, as in the cases of a sterile union or where the education of offspring is providable outside of the union; in the generality of cases the achievement of the primary purpose is impeded or made very difficult and far less perfect if the bond is held to be dissoluble. The secondary purposes cannot be enjoyed without this property. Dissolubility would cause the greatest inequality between man and woman, to the detriment of the woman. Mutual help in domestic partnership of itself ought to endure for life; love itself tends to perpetuity, since the total giving should be mutual and irrevocable. Nature intends the education and care of the offspring for his whole life;

various cases divorce properly so-called can be sanctioned by civil authority" (Denz.-Schön. 2967); Leo XIII, **Arcanum Divinae Sapientiae;** Pius XI, **Casti Connubii;** Pius XII, **Allocution to the Rota** (3 oct. 1941): "It is superfluous . . . yet it is not inappropriate to repeat that sacramental marriage which has been consummated is indissoluble by the law of God, so that it cannot be dissolved by any human power (c. 1118); whereas other marriages, though they are intrinsically indissoluble, have not absolute extrinsic indissolubility, but, granted certain necessary prerequisites (We are speaking, as you know, of cases which are relatively rare) can be dissolved, not only in virtue of the Pauline privilege, but also by the Roman Pontiff in virtue of his ministerial power."

the possibility of separation with a new marriage and the fragile union of peace endanger this. The concord of domestic and civil society is imperilled, and strife and the corruption of morals are given entrance.

V. *Contract of marriage*

The state or bond of matrimony is entered into or caused by way of contract. Every marriage is a contract, and for the baptized the contract in addition becomes sacramental or the sign and cause of sacramental grace. As a contract it thus pertains to the virtue of commutative justice since rights and obligations are assumed. These rights acquired by the matrimonial contract are inalienable; they can be diminished by no pact, nor transferred to others, e.g., by prescription,[49] nor directly limited by public authority.

Being essentially the legitimate consent of two parties to the same thing with the purpose of binding themselves, matrimony is a *true* contract. It is *consensual* and not real, i.e., it is perfected and takes its immediate effect by the very consent alone of the contractants and not by the actual exchange of any thing. Thus actual intercourse or use of marriage, or actual common life, do not constitute the contract. This matrimonial consent cannot be forced by any created power or supplied by any human power or be considered as supplied by any human authority.[50] In matrimony nature itself determines everything substantially pertaining to the contract and leaves nothing so to be determined or decided upon or varied by the contracting parties, whereas in other contracts they can by private decision determine many things as to the object, effects, obligations, firmness, perpetuity, etc., of the agreement. Thus the parties are so bound that by mutual consent or in any other way they can never rescind the matrimonial contract validly entered into or retain the right to pull out of the assumed obligation, either unilaterally or bilaterally.

49. Innocent XI, damnati S. Off. 4 mart. 1679 (Denz.-Schön 2150): "Intercourse with a married woman, with the consent of her husband, is not adultery, and so it is enough to say in confession that one has committed fornication."
50. c. 1081, 1.

The contract is perfectly *bilateral*, inducing in each rights and obligations or duties with respect to a perpetual life together as one, especially the mutual, exclusive, and perpetual right to each other's body for those functions of themselves apt for generation. As a relation it is a contract which can at no time limp or retain the force of a unilateral pact but must necessarily spring from both sides or be null and void. It cannot be stronger on one side than on the other; there cannot be a right or obligation on one side only, otherwise, e.g., one side would fornicate and the other side rightly use marriage.

Matrimony is a *natural* contract founded in nature and tending to the good of nature and of the whole race;[51] it is not a private contract but affects society. It preexisted any civil contract, e.g., with our first parents, and precedes any civil contract, e.g., with those unable civilly to enter marriage. It can be called civil only in that it depends secondarily on the civil power and with respect to accidental effects separable from the contract itself.

In addition to the above, the matrimonial contract is of a special type because it is of its very nature sacred and religious and not merely profane, even prescinding from its elevation to a sacrament.[52] It has God as its author and has the procreation and education of children of God as its purpose together with the mutual love and help of spouses in attaining their destiny in God. It is also a foreshadowing and representation both of the union of God with the souls of the just and of Christ with the Church through the Incarnation. Even among pagans matrimony can be called a sacrament in the wide sense of being a sign of a sacred thing. Among all peoples matrimony has been considered something holy and religious and surrounded with religious ceremonies.

VI. *Matrimonial consent*

Marriage is effected by the consent lawfully expressed of persons

51. Cf. Pius XI, **Casti Connubii**.
52. Ibid.; Leo XIII, ency. **Arcanum Divinae Sapientiae**: "Marriage has God for its author and was from the very beginning a kind of foreshadowing of the Incarnation of his Son; and therefore there abides in it something holy and religious, not extraneous but innate, not derived from men but implanted by nature."

who are capable according to law, and this consent no human power can supply. Matrimonial consent is an act of the will whereby each party gives and accepts a perpetual and exclusive right over the body for acts which are of themselves designed to generate offspring.[53] Consent is necessary and essential for the contract as its expression. It is the total cause of matrimony, as both material and formula of the contract and sacrament, formally constituting the contract and effectively the bond or state. Thus a proper understanding of this consent is important.

A. *Qualities*
The consent to the terms of marriage must be:

1. *internal.* The consent must be genuine, true and sincere, as internal act of the will and not falsified or merely theatrical or jocose. If in no way it is expressed explicitly or implicitly, the contract is null. Internal consent is always presumed to be in conformity with the words or signs used in the contracting of marriage.[54] A spouse who falsely gives consent sins seriously against truth, justice, and chastity, and is forbidden the use of marital rights. The innocent spouse may seek or render the debt, since the deception need not be believed until proven in the external forum.

2. *mutual.* There must be a reciprocal consent and not an unilateral donation and acceptance of rights and obligations; nor does it depend upon the approval of a third party, e.g., parents.

3. *free.* The expression of consent must be made by one capable of a perfectly human act, with the independence required by natural and ecclesiastical law, e.g., as in the case of child marriage in mission areas.

4. *deliberate and simultaneous.* Deliberate consent is required in undertaking such serious obligations, i.e., with full knowledge and will. By the natural law there must be at least a moral simultaneity of mutual consent, so that the consent of one perdures when the other consents, both being present.[55]

53. c. 1081; cf. **Summa Theol., Suppl.,** q. 45, aa. 1, 3; q. 48, a. 1.
54. c. 1086, 1.
55. Cf. cc. 1136; 1088, 1.

5. *of the present*. The contract must be consented to here and now. A promise of future contract is not marriage but espousals or betrothal (*sponsalia*).

6. *externally expressed*.

a. *requisites*. Matrimony as a human contract must be expressed by some human sensible sign; as a sacrament it requires that there be a sensible sign. The spouses are to express their matrimonial consent in words; and if they can speak, it is not lawful for them to employ equivalent signs.[56] Thus the baptized, even non-Catholics, if they can speak, are bound to express their consent in words for lawfulness; for validity it must be expressed in the juridical form by those so bound.[57] Also for validity it is necessary that the parties be present to each other in person or by proxy.[58] This binds baptized non-Catholics as well.[59] Thus consent given by letter, messenger, radio, telephone, telegraph, etc., is invalid for them. The unbaptized are not bound by any specific formalities in the expression or exchange of their consent. It suffices that they abide by what conforms to the natural law and by what is required for validity by the civil law or the estimation of the region.[60]

b. *interpreter*. Marriage may be contracted through an interpreter.[61] There must be a justifying reason, e.g., language barrier on the part of the pastor and witnesses, and the permission of the local Ordinary is needed for lawfulness.[62] The interpreter should be a Catholic adult who probably is under oath to satisfy the function faithfully and truthfully.

c. *proxy*. Without prejudice to diocesan statutes containing further regulations, for a marriage by proxy to be contracted validly there is required a special mandate for the contracting of marriage with a specific purpose, signed by the person giving the mandate and either by the pastor or the Ordinary of the place in which the mandate is given, or by a priest delegated by either of these, or at

56. c. 1088, 2.
57. Cf. c. 1099.
58. c. 1088, 1.
59. PCI 30 iun. 1949; Cod. Or. c. 79.
60. Cf. S. Off. 9 dec. 1947.
61. c. 1090.
62. c. 1091.

least by two witnesses. If the principal does not know how to write, this is to be noted in the mandate and another witness is to be added and the latter is also to sign the commission; otherwise the mandate is invalid. If before the proxy has made the contract in the name of the principal the latter shall have revoked the contract or become insane, the marriage is invalid, even in the case in which either the proxy or the other contracting party was unaware of the event. For the marriage to be valid the proxy must perform his function in person.[63]

For validity the proxy must be competent to execute his office personally. It is proper that the proxy be a Catholic adult of the same sex as the principal and in good standing. There must be for lawfulness a justifying reason for use of a proxy, e.g., impossibility of physical presence of one of the parties, and the permission of the local Ordinary.[64] Civil law acceptance of the use of a proxy must be considered; local and state laws and regulations should be known and observed. The principal or contracting spouse must personally designate the proxy and cannot entrust this designation to another.[65]

B. *Obstacles*

Being an act of the will, matrimonial consent is given in relation to the knowledge possessed beforehand. Thus there can be obstacles to valid consent both on the part of the intellect: want of reason, ignorance, error; and on the part of the will: force or fear, simulation, condition.

1. *want of use of reason.* By the natural law all those who are incapable of the use of reason cannot validly enter a matrimonial contract as long as they remain in that state, e.g., infants, the insane, those totally under the influence of intoxicants or drugs, those asleep, etc. The demented or partially insane, i.e., affecting certain matters, may contract marriage but not validly if the matters affected concern the substance of matrimony. Prudence often indicates that such weak-minded parties should be discouraged from marriage at all,

---

63. c. 1089. Cf. also Cod. Or. cc. 80, 82.
64. c. 1091.
65. PCI 31 maii 1948; cf. Cod. Or. cc. 80-82.

also deaf-mutes, unless it is prudently judged they can properly fulfill their marital obligations. In attacking a marriage bond the marriage must be considered valid until the want of reason is proved to
have existed at the time the contract was made. Civil law regarding
insanity antecedent and subsequent to marriage should be consulted.

2. *ignorance.* For matrimonial consent to be present it is
necessary that the contracting parties be not ignorant at least of
the fact that marriage is a permanent state between a man and a
woman for the purpose of procreating children. A lack of this knowledge is not presumed after the age of puberty.[66] A party invalidly
contracts marriage who does not know that marriage consists in the
mutual giving and accepting of the right over the body for the purpose of procreating. However, a general or vague or implicit knowledge of this necessary bodily cooperation suffices for valid consent.
It is more commonly held that, because of the very serious obligations
assumed, the matrimonial contract requires greater discretion of
judgment than that necessary to commit a serious sin.

Knowledge of the particular manner of procreation or the exact
technique of intercourse is not necessary for valid consent; it is
sufficient to intend to enter marriage as it is in itself and as practiced
by all men and women thus implicitly and deliberately willing all
that is connected with marriage. It is not any subsequent and more
exact knowledge—even that which, if known at the time of the marriage, would have deterred it—which invalidates, i.e., not the consent
which would not have been given but that which actually was given.
A false idea about the union of the bodies in marriage, e.g., that it
means only kisses, may be a substantial error invalidating the consent.

Knowledge that marriage is a permanent state does not mean a
knowledge that it is indissoluble, or an approval of its perpetuity and
indissolubility, but rather that it is not a transient or, as it were,
a momentary or experimental association (trial marriage), a mere
friendly arrangement or sex outlet. It suffices that the parties do not
positively exclude the essential properties of marriage, and, since
they are inseparable, they are implicitly consented to. Actual community of domestic life and mutual affection do not pertain to the

66. c. 1082.

essence of marriage and thus their absence does not affect the validity.

3. *error.* Error is a false judgment, which is substantial in marriage if it affects the very nature or object of the contract, and accidental if it does not. As with ignorance, error which is substantial invalidates marriage, but such an error is not presumed after the age of puberty. Since the will bears upon the object as known, error in the intellect always influences the will, but not every kind of error renders the consent null and invalid.

An error or mistake of *fact* will be about the person with whom the marriage contract is made or about a quality of that person. To be in error about the very identity of the person with whom one contracts marriage is substantial and invalidates the contract by the natural law itself, i.e., to judge that one is marrying the very party intended, whereas it is someone else.[67] To be mistaken or in error about some quality of the person with whom marriage is contracted is accidental, e.g., that the person is rich, or healthy, or a virgin, or has a different name, etc., and does not of itself invalidate marriage either by natural law or by positive law of the Church, even though the contract is based on it.[68] Notwithstanding error about the accidental qualities, the substance of the contract remains— consent to contract with the person of the other contracting party. However, error of quality will invalidate in two cases:

a) if the error as to quality amounts to an error of person.[69] This is most rare, unless in those areas where marriages are arranged with the parties never previously known to or seen by each other or in proxy marriages. Thus the quality must be one that identifies or is most proper and individual to a definite person, e.g., the *first-born* daughter. Similarly, if this accidental quality or characteristic is the necessary condition (*sine qua non*) of the marital consent or at least is implicitly demonstrable from the circumstances, the marriage is invalid, e.g., consent is given *only* on the supposition or condition of the presence of virginity.

b) if a free person contracts marriage with a person whom

---

67. c. 1083, 1.
68. Ibid., 2. However, it may be that, in an individual case, such an error is substantial.
69. Ibid., 1º.

he believes to be free but who is a slave in the strict sense of servile bondage.[70] This impediment is of ecclesiastical law only and thus does not bind the unbaptized marrying among themselves; civil law may prohibit such marriages.

An error or mistake of *law* concerns the nature or essential object and properties of the matrimonial contract, as in the case of ignorance. Thus, a *simple* error regarding the unity of the indissolubility or the sacramental dignity of marriage, even though the motivating reason for entering into the contract, does not invalidate the matrimonial consent.[71] A simple error is one which remains in the intellect without a positive act following in conformity with it. Thus, as the essence of matrimony has inseparably attached to it its essential properties, in consenting to marriage as it is in itself, consent is thereby also given to its properties of unity and indissolubility. To know a thing with all its properties and to will a thing differ; one can simply will a thing as it is in itself and not know very well its properties or be mistaken about them. Thus an error about the essential qualities of marriage does not necessarily invalidate it. The general intention to contract marriage as instituted by God prevails over the error. Although many today consider marriage to be dissoluble and not sacramental, e.g., Protestants, Jews, unbaptized, yet they normally will to contract marriage as it is. They probably would positively exclude these properties if they were later *questioned* about them, but they *did not* actually exclude them at the time the consent was given.

If either party or both parties by a *positive* act of the will should exclude marriage itself, or all right to the conjugal act, or any essential property of marriage, he contracts invalidly.[72] This is of the natural law. Thus the error is no longer simple, if it so influences the act of the will that this positive exclusion is made in the matrimonial consent. Such a positive exclusion may be *explicit*, e.g., an

70. Ibid., 2⁰.
71. c. 1084.
72. c. 1086, 2; S. Off. 11 mart. 1886: "Marriages are valid which are entered into when the contractants are solely in error that the bond of consummated marriage can be dissolved in the case of adultery or for other causes. However, if they are entered into under this expressed condition, they are to be considered as invalid."

agreement made to experiment with the marriage for a while and to break up by divorce if it turns out unhappily, or *implicit*, e.g., while intending to contract a true and proper marriage, one is at the same time deliberately disposed to terminate the contract by divorce in the future, should some special circumstance be verified, such as infidelity of the other party. Nevertheless, every marriage must be held to be valid in the external forum until the contrary can be proved.[73] No general rule of invalidity can be applied, but each individual case must be examined on its own merits, even in mission areas where polygamy and divorce are prevalent.[74] Civil law on fraudulent representation in a marriage contract should be consulted.

The knowledge or probable suspicion of the invalidity of a marriage does not necessarily exclude matrimonial consent.[75] This is with reference to consent as naturally valid, not as juridically efficacious. If the parties intend to contract marriage insofar as they can or as it depends on their will, the consent is valid, although inefficacious. Such consent is presumed to endure until it is proved that it was recalled.[76] This is important for cases involving radical sanation. Each case is to be judged by itself.

4. *force or fear*. Marriage is also invalid which is entered into under the influence of such force or of *grave* fear *unjustly* induced from *without* that to escape it one is compelled to choose marriage. No other fear, even though it provides the cause for the contract, entails the nullity of the marriage.[77] Force is coercion exercised by an extrinsic agent against the will of him who is subjected to it. Fear is a state of mental trepidation at the prospect of some imminent evil, so that the will shrinks from the evil and attempts to free itself from it by doing what fear induces it to do. Fear is absolutely grave, such as a brave man or one not easily intimidated

---

73. c. 1014.
74. Cf. S. Off. 9 dec. 1874.
75. c. 1085.
76. cc. 1093; 1139, 1; Cod. Or. c. 84.
77. c. 1087. Because of the uncertainty of the invalidity springing from ecclesiastical law alone or also from natural law, fear present in the contracting of marriage between two unbaptized doubtfully invalidates and must be submitted to the tribunal of the local Church.

might experience, e.g., death, exile, loss of all goods, etc.; relatively grave, inasmuch as it is grave for some people and not for others, e.g., because of age or temperament or health or intelligence or other circumstances. Reverential fear is the trepidation of the evil consequences impending as a result of offending a parent or superior. It is not of itself grave, but it may become so from contributing circumstances.

Where there is physical violence or duress forcing an external compliance with the will of the one exercising such pressure, the consent thus manifested is null by natural law as excluding a voluntary act, e.g., forcing a reluctant victim to nod his head or making his hand inscribe his signature. Also by the natural law a fear which is so intense that it removes the control of reason invalidates matrimonial consent. Whether in other cases the impediment of force or fear arises from the natural law, no authoritative declaration has been given, but in practice the Church does not dispense in what is even probably of divine law. It binds certainly a baptized non-Catholic and probably also the unbaptized marrying among themselves, certainly if the civil law declares marriage contracted in fear to be null.

The fear or pressure brought to bear from without may be unjust itself, e.g., threat of an unjust penalty such as to take life or unjustifiably ruin a good name, or unjustly brought to bear, e.g., a just penalty to be inflicted in an unjust manner such as to expel one's relative from one's home unless she marries a certain man. Moreover, one is said to be forced to enter marriage when there appears to be no other alternative to ridding oneself of the fear.[78] The unjust pressure must actually exist at the time of the celebration of the marriage.[79] The party forcing the marriage is bound to repair the unjust damage, and if he is party to the forced marriage and if there is no other means of reparation, he is bound to enter or to convalidate the marriage, if the innocent party or victim so desires.

---

78. Cod. Or. c. 78 requires that the unjust pressure be induced precisely to extort marital consent.
79. This must be distinguished from the reluctance or resistance which, in some mission areas, is shown by the bride as part of the ritual or ceremonial of marriage.

5. *pretense or simulation.* The internal consent of the mind is always presumed to be in conformity with the words or signs used in the contracting of marriage.[80] Simulated or feigned consent is present in marriage when, although exteriorly the words expressing matrimonial consent are duly and seriously pronounced, one or both parties withhold internal consent. The intention of the pretender may be not to contract marriage, or to contract it but not to assume its obligation, or not to fulfill its obligation. An intention not to contract marriage excludes consent and nullifies the contract. Likewise, the intention not to assume the obligations of marriage, since without it there cannot be true matrimonial consent.[81] The intention not to fulfill the matrimonial obligations does not invalidate consent, as this does not pertain to the essence of the contract. The intention to *violate* an obligation can exist with the intention to assume the obligation itself.

To feign consent is certainly a serious sin; it is a violation of truth, justice, chastity (if intercourse is intended) and perhaps religion by simulation in the case of the sacrament (although this is not agreed upon). The guilty party is bound to repair the injustice done, even by giving true consent, if this is the only way and it can be done without serious inconvenience. Lack of internal consent is clearly difficult to prove. Civil law in the U.S.A. does not generally admit it as a grounds for nullity.

6. *condition.* A condition is a circumstance in marriage upon which one makes his consent depend, so that the consent (if not revoked) takes its effect as the circumstance is verified or not. Thus the contract is consented to *only if* or *when* the condition placed is fulfilled (a *sine qua non*). A condition must thus be distinguished from a mode (*modus*) or prenuptial agreement or stipulation to do or to omit something *after* marriage is validly contracted and realized,

---

80. c. 1086, 1.
81. **Ibid.**, 2. The intention to contract marriage but not to receive the sacrament does not invalidate the contract, as the sacrament is inseparable with the Christian contract by the institution of Christ and does not depend on the contractant's intention, unless he positively excludes the contract itself if it is the only way to exclude the sacrament. To enter marriage as a joke is equivalent to feigning consent (S.C. Conc. 14 dec. 1889).

e.g., to move to another State, which neither affects the validity of the marriage nor rests the consent on it. Of itself a condition need not be expressed, but a merely internal condition is seldom easy to prove to have existed; it may relate to the past, the present, or the future. The use of a marital right is prohibited until the condition is clearly verified and the marriage is in possession.

If a condition placed refers to the present or past, the marriage will be valid or invalid as that on which the condition is based exists or not.[82] It does not suspend the validity.

If it refers to the future and its object is lawful, it suspends the validity or the marriage,[83] e.g., if your father recovers his health.

If it refers to the future and its object is something necessary, or impossible, or base, but not opposed to the substance of marriage, it is to be held as not having been made; if it refers to the future and is opposed to the substance of marriage, it renders the marriage invalid.[84]

a) A condition regarding a future necessary event or one impossible of fulfillment or a base object, i.e., contrary to right moral conduct, is considered in the internal and external fora as not seriously meant and thus nonexistent. This supposition will cede to contrary proof. Thus, if the object of the condition is necessary, e.g., consent to marry, if the sun rises on the morrow, the condition has no effect; if it is seriously meant, the marriage is valid when the circumstance is realized. If the object is impossible, e.g., if you grasp a star with your hand, the condition is void; but if it is seriously meant, the marriage will never be valid. If the condition is base but not contrary to the substance of marriage, e.g., if you kill your father or if you steal a certain sum of money, neither party is bound to observe the condition and it must be withdrawn; if it is not, the matrimonial contract is effective when the condition is fulfilled.

b) If the condition is base and against the substance or properties of marriage, i.e., an intention *not to assume* the obligations, it is destructive of true marital consent and nullifies the con-

82. c. 1092, 4º. Cf. prohibition of Cod. Or. 83.
83. Ibid., 3º.
84. Ibid., 1º, 2º.

tract, since a right to an essential element is not given but rather excluded. Whether the right itself or only the fulfillment of a right is withheld in certain conditions is difficult to ascertain. In the internal forum it depends upon the actual intention of the one placing the condition, in the external forum upon the proof that can be reached with moral certainty from indications and circumstances. Each case must be examined to ascertain whether an excluding condition or merely a stipulation (mode) or agreement was made; the latter is generally presumed until the former is proved and thus the marriage is considered to exist.

c) Matrimonial consent is valid only when the intention predominates to transfer (and not positively to exclude) the perpetual and exclusive and continual right to natural intercourse. A condition designed to exclude this transference perpetually or for a certain time or after a certain time (e.g., periodic continence or the non-use except on infertile days or the right only to onanistic relations) is contrary to the substance of marriage, vitiates the consent, and invalidates the contract (*contra bonum prolis*).[85] If this right is tranferred and the condition implies only the intention to abuse this transferred right, the contract is valid, as the sinful condition is not contrary to the substance of marriage.

d) If a restriction made on marital intercourse is absolute, without any limit of time, i.e., the marital right and obligation would be perpetually abused, the *presumption* (in the external forum) is that the right itself, i.e., the order to the object of the

85. There is a question here not of a desire or purpose of maintaining temporary or perpetual continence but of a condition whereby (especially when there is a mutual pact) the parties to the marriage intend to bind themselves in justice not to seek or to render the natural marital debt. Pius XII, **Allocution to Italian Midwives** (26 nov. 1951): "If at the time of the marriage at least one of the couples intended to restrict the marriage right, not merely its use, to the sterile periods, in such a way that at other times the second party would not even have the right to demand the act, this would imply an essential defect in the consent to marriage, which would carry with it invalidity of the marriage itself, because the right deriving from the contract of marriage is a permanent, uninterrupted, and not intermittent right of each of the parties, one to another. On the other hand, if the act be limited to the sterile periods insofar as the mere use and not the right is concerned, there is no question about the validity of the marriage."

contract, is excluded and thus no true marital consent and valid contract exists. This is especially true if a pact has been made acceding to this condition. If the condition is not absolute but limited to a certain time when this marital abuse is intended, the *presumption* is that true (although sinful) consent has been given and the marriage is presumed valid. This latter presumption considers that the right to the use was given but the fulfillment restricted. If the restriction is one of perpetual non-use (and not abuse), this is also against the substance of marriage if it implies that the conjugal right is not exchanged. However, such a condition of non-use is less clearly a vitiation of marital consent as is the condition of abuse. It is, moreover, not authoritatively determined nor generally agreed upon whether a condition of perpetual non-use or abstinence is in itself opposed to the substance of marriage. The condition may not be permitted, but a marriage so contracted must be *presumed* in practice to be valid.

e) A condition against the requisite fidelity or unity of marriage (*contra bonum fidei*) e.g., if you will commit adultery, invalidates the contract, if the intention is to exclude it and not merely not to observe it. A restriction of essential indissolubility (*contra bonum sacramenti*) e.g., only until I find someone more suitable, even though an implicit and hypothetical exclusion, always invalidates, as there can be no distinction between the intention to assume and to fulfill the property of indissolubility.

f) It is the more common view that a condition which is contrary to the Catholic upbringing of offspring is not one that is opposed to the substance of marriage, although it is sinful and unlawful. Moreover, although in a non-Catholic marriage ceremony or formula a condition contrary to essential indissolubility may be present and thus invalidate it, the marriage itself must not be presumed invalid until an investigation of the individual case proves that the consent itself was vitiated.[86]

Conditions affecting matrimonial consent which are not forbidden may be lawfully placed for a serious cause and with the permission of the local Ordinary.[87] However, such conditions are discouraged

86. Cf. S. Off. 6 apr. 1843; 24 ian. 1877.
87. The pastor must consult the local Ordinary before allowing even a

and when allowed should be made before witnesses and recorded in the matrimonial register (as well as the fulfillment).[88] The civil law of the U.S.A. does not recognize the effect of these conditions.

VII. *Ordinary juridical form of marriage*

The natural law requires for validity of the contract no special conditions of the form of entering into the contract or formalities but only that the ministers—the contracting parties themselves—externally manifest deliberate and mutual consent in some way. Divine law likewise has laid down no particular solemnities. Positive civil law is competent to make determinations or validating requirements concerning contracts for the sake of public good and order. This power can be exercised also regarding the matrimonial contract between two unbaptized parties. But, since the marriage of two baptized parties (a sacrament), and where even only one party is baptized, is subject exclusively to the competence of the Church, the positive ecclesiastical law can and does lay down certain conditions, formalities or solemnities, which must be observed by those wishing to enter a marital union. This is the canonical or juridical form (or formality) of marriage, rendering the contract juridically public or celebrated in the sight of the Church. Solemnities are substantial when required for validity, accidental when prescribed for lawfulness (to which the liturgical form of marriage pertains).

The first decree *"Tametsi"* establishing a juridical form of marriage was issued by the Council of Trent in 1563, prescribing the presence of the pastor of the parties and witnesses.[89] The form was again regulated by the universal decree of Pius X *"Ne temere"* promulgated in 1908 requiring the presence of the pastor of the place where the marriage was celebrated and witnesses.[90] With minor changes this became also the form prescribed by the present Code, effective as of May 19, 1918.

lawful condition (S.C. Sac. 29 iun. 1941). Baptized Orientals are forbidden to contract marriage lawfully with any condition whatever (Cod. Or. c. 83).

88. Cf. S.C. Sac., Instruction (14 iun. 1941), 9.
89. Trent, Denz.-Schön. 1816.
90. S. C. Conc., Decree (2 aug. 1907), Denz.-Schön. 3469.

A. *Valid form*

Only those marriages are valid which are contracted in the presence of the pastor, or the local Ordinary, or a priest (or deacon) delegated by either, and at least two witnesses, as regulated by the canons.[91]

1. *Pastor*

a. *designation*

The pastor is the qualified or authorized witness of the matrimonial contract in the name of the Church; as the specially selected or approved representative he actively receives the matrimonial consent, certifies the contract, and secures the due and fitting celebration of the sacrament in the name of the Church. Thus, since he is an assisting priest and not the minister of the sacrament but rather of the liturgical rite, he does *not* confect or administer a sacrament (thus, assisting in the state of serious sin, he does not commit a sacrilege). The power of assisting at marriage in his territory, which belongs to the pastor and to the local Ordinary and which is not jurisdiction in the strict sense although governed by the same principles and norms, is ordinary power attached by law to the office. The pastor and the local Ordinary enjoy this power cumulatively, so that the latter personally or through another can validly assist at any marriage in his diocese independently of the pastor.

The pastor for valid assistance at marriage is the one strictly so-called as well as those who are the equivalent.[92] Included therefore are: quasi-pastor,[93] vicar of a moral person,[94] administrator or priest in charge,[95] substitute vicar approved by the local Ordinary[96]

91. c. 1094, Cod. Or. c. 85: "Those marriages alone are valid which are contracted with a sacred rite, before the pastor, or the Hierarch of the place, or by a priest to whom the faculty of assisting at the marriage has been given by either and at least two witnesses, according to the cc. 89, 90." Cf. also note 109 below.
92. c. 451, 1, 2; cf. also The Celebration of Baptism, note 74.
93. c. 451, 2, 1º.
94. c. 471.
95. c. 472, 1º, 2º.

auxiliary vicar if he supplies for the pastor in everything.[97] Personal
pastors without territory validly assist at the marriages of their
subjects only. Pastors of national and language parishes in the U.S.A.
usually have a territory, and thus they enjoy cumulative power for
the *valid* assistance at all marriages in their territory. Chaplains of
the U.S. Military Ordinariate validly and lawfully assist at marriages
of their (personal) subjects anywhere, which power they share cumulatively with the pastor and local Ordinary of the place of celebration.[98]

A curate or assisting priest does not enjoy *ordinary* power to
assist validly at a marriage.[99] A chaplain or rector of a pious place
exempted from the local pastor lacks power to assist, unless he is
endowed with full parochial power;[100] likewise with other chaplains
and the rector of a seminary.[101] A priest assigned as full-time chaplain for the imprisoned and the prison officials is not a proper pastor
or assistant pastor unless so constituted by the local Ordinary; a
part-time chaplain should be delegated for each definite marriage
by the Ordinary or pastor of the place.[102] Cardinals, representatives
of the Holy See, bishops who are not local Ordinaries, a diocesan
officialis, do not enjoy power of assistance.

b. *conditions or qualifications*

For the valid exercise of his ordinary power of assistance at
marriage the pastor must have canonically assumed the office and

96. c. 465, 4; PCI 14 iul. 1922; and the same substitute vicar or a supply
priest in the pastor's absence due to sudden cause, as long as the Ordinary to whom his name has been given makes no other provision
(c. 465, 5; PCI **ibid.**); a substitute for a religious vicar can do likewise
after the approval by the local Ordinary and before approval by his
religious superior (PCI **ibid.**).
97. c. 475. None of the above substitutes can validly assist if the pastor
or local Ordinary has excepted this power (c. 474).
98. Unless the personal pastor enjoys the privilege of exclusiveness, the
pastor of the territory enjoys cumulative power with him. For the
Military Ordinariate cf. S.C. Consist. 23 apr. 1951.
99. cc. 476; 1096, 1; PCI 13 sept. 1933; 31 ian. 1942.
100. S.C. Conc. 25 ian. 1908.
101. c. 1368.
102. S.C. Conc. 3 feb. 1926.

be free from declared or imposed canonical penalties.[103] To disqualify him a suspension must be from office and not simply from jurisdiction.

A pastor validly assists at marriage *only* and *exclusively* in his own territory and not only of his own subjects but also of others (except in certain cases involving those of Oriental rites).[104] He may not validly witness the marriage of his own subjects outside his own territory without delegation of the pastor of that place. Places exempted from the jurisdiction of the pastor, e.g., a seminary or religious house, do not belong to his territory but are considered as in his territory for valid assistance at marriage.[105]

For validity the pastor must ask and receive the consent of the contracting parties without being coerced to do so by force or grave fear,[106] either by the contractants or by a third party even without their knowledge. Although fraud may be the cause of the assistance, the latter remains valid since free and not invalidated in law. The pastor must be physically present and aware of the necessary actions, which active assistance is required also in mixed marriages.[107]

c. *common error*

In the case of common error or of positive and probably doubt of law or of fact as to legitimate assistance, the Church supplies the power of assistance for the internal and external fora,[108] e.g., if the one to be married requests a particular priest to assist at his marriage, since he judges—as most of the parish would—that he has (since he has had) the faculty to do so; or if an assisting priest

---

103. c. 1095, 1, 1º; cf. Cod. Or. c. 86, 1, 1º; also PCI Cod. Or. 8 iul. 1952 on c. 86, 1, 2º.
104. c. 1095, 1, 2º.
105. S.C. Sac. 13 mart. 1910. He may also validly witness in an oratory under his jurisdiction but not in his territory.
106. c. 1095, 3º. The formula in the Rite of Marriage is not necessary for validity.
107. c. 1102, 1. Thus marriage before a completely intoxicated priest would be invalid due to lack of form (Rota 31 ian. 1929).
108. c. 209. PCI 26 mart. 1952: "Whether the prescription of c. 209 is to be applied in the case of a priest who, lacking delegation, assists at a marriage. Affirmative." Cf. The Celebration of Penance, III, B, 7.

thinks he is in his proper territory or that he has been properly
delegated or that as parochial vicar he is empowered to supply in
all things, etc. From the circumstances it will be judged whether
the error was common or private, whether the cause of the common
error is certain in that the public fact founding it is disposed to
result with a certain constraint in the error. Common error in the
form of marriage is not easily proved. More common teaching
maintains that in the case of such an error or doubt regarding a
priest who habitually assists at marriages, e.g., as a curate, or frequently helps out in this capacity, receives the suppliance of the
Church in these circumstances; not, however, in the case of a priest
who habitually is not engaged in marriage assistance, for a single
marriage. The practice of the Rota is and has been to declare as
null a marriage where the delegation—not otherwise habitually enjoyed by the priest—is absent in the particular case.

2. Delegated priest or deacon

a. delegation

The pastor (and the equivalent) and the local Ordinary who can
validly assist at marriage can also grant permission or delegation
to another priest or to a deacon to assist at marriage within the limits
of their territory.[109]

b. conditions or qualifications

It is the common opinion, to be followed in practice, that the one
delegated must be aware of his delegation and at least tacitly accept
it; thus one should not assist at a marriage unless he has a morally
certain presumption that delegation has been granted him. A delegation that has been extorted by grave and unjust fear or fraud is
nevertheless valid.[110]

The permission or delegation to assist at marriage must be ex-

---

109. c. 1095, 2. For a deacon see The Celebration of Holy Orders, notes
     60-61.
110. c. 103, 2.

pressly given to a definite priest or deacon for a definite marriage, and no general delegations are allowed except in the case of assistant pastor or deacons for the parish to which they are assigned; otherwise it is invalid.[111] No general delegation can be given. It should be noted that civil delegation is distinct from canonical delegation; thus in every case of assistance at marriage the priest or deacon must be careful to conform to the requirements of civil law in the place as to his competence to act in a marriage ceremony, e.g., to register for the performance of marriage.

Tacit or presumed permission does not suffice for valid marriage delegation. It must be expressed, either explicitly or implicitly, directly or indirectly conceded, made orally or in writing or by unambiguous sign. It is explicit when it is given clearly in so many words; implicit when contained in another act, e.g., in the appointment as administrator of a parish. The delegation need not be made personally but may be transmitted to the delegated priest through a third party. It is more desirable that the delegation be given in writing[112] but it may be given orally and even by telephone, telegraph, radiogram.

Delegation must be granted to a specific priest or deacon who is designated by name or by office, e.g., the present chaplain of such-and-such convent. The permission thus must be so granted that it clearly designates who the individual priest or deacon is; otherwise it is invalid. Delegation may not be given to the priest or deacon who will later be designated by the nupturients or by a religious superior.[113] Several may be delegated for the same marriage, as long as it is clear that definite individuals are designated, e.g., in a case where it is not certain that a certain priest or priests will be free to perform the marriage on the date set. The one delegated need not be known by the delegator, but a substantial error by the latter as to the identity of the one delegated renders the permission invalid.

A specific marriage must be the object of the delegation. The marriage to be performed must be designated by the names of the

---

111. c. 1096, 1. An episcopal delegate "ad universitatem negotiorum" does not have delegation to assist at marriage (PCI 25 ian. 1943).
112. A diocesan requirement that delegation be committed to writing is not for validity but only for the proof of the grant.
113. PCI 20 maii 1923.

parties or their office or in some way to individualize or identify the couple to be married for which delegation is given. Delegation can be given for the marriages on an itemized list but not merely for the time and place of a marriage without further identification.[114] Delegation cannot validly be given, therefore, for marriages generally, e.g., a pastor to delegate a priest or deacon to perform any marriages that might come up during his absence. It should be kept in mind that a temporary supply priest, (e.g., weekend, few weeks, summer), needs specific delegation for specific marriages, since he usually enjoys not even the status of a parochial vicar. A substantial error in the designation of the parties to be married invalidates the delegation. The restrictions and disqualifications noted for the pastor apply also to the delegated priest or deacon, as does the application of canon 209.

c. *subdelegation*

One who is delegated to assist at a marriage can further subdelegate another for this marriage *only* if this faculty of subdelegation is granted expressly with the delegation he receives, or if the delegate himself enjoys general delegation for all marriages, as in the case of a curate (*vicarius cooperator*). The designation is made by the subdelegator of the one subdelegated.

3. *Other witnesses*

These are the ordinary or common witnesses prescribed in addition to the priest or deacon who acts as qualified or authorized witness of the contract.[115] They must be at least two in number, more being permissible. For *validity* alone they may be of either sex, of any age, even separated Christians or the unbaptized, as long as they enjoy the use of reason and are capable of witnessing.[116] Thus those who are asleep, drunk, etc., deaf and blind (but not if only

114. Cf. Rota 23 dec. 1931.
115. c. 1094.
116. S.C. Sac. 12 mart. 1940. Cf. Sec. ad unit. Christ. fov. **Directorium,** 14 maii 1967, nos. 49, 58.

deaf or only blind) may not validly act as witnesses. They may use an interpreter in order to make aware when consent is requested and given. They must be physically present and attentive to the exchange of consent, even if their presence is induced by constraint or fraud or is accidental. It suffices that they are present and can testify to the contract; they need not expressly intend to be witnesses but merely know from what transpires that marriage is being contracted.[117] It is commonly maintained that for validity they need not have been designated beforehand by the contractants or the assisting priest.

B. *Those bound by the form for validity*

All baptized Catholics, both Latin and Oriental, including converts from heresy or schism, even though either the former or the latter should have later fallen from the faith, whether reared in the Catholic faith or not, when they marry among themselves or marry non-Catholics, whether baptized or not, even after obtaining a dispensation from the impediments of mixed religion or disparity of worship, are bound to the form.[118]

Baptism is not received in the Catholic Church necessarily by the fact that it is administered by a Catholic priest. It is by the expressed or tacit intention of being aggravated externally to the Church as manifested by himself in the case of an adult or in the case of an infant by his parents, legitimate guardians or in default of all these by the minister himself. One can be baptized in the Catholic Church even if the parents (or the minister) are non-Catholic.[119] Infants who are validly baptized in heresy or schism, if subsequently reared in the Catholic Church by their parents who have become converts, are considered as converts to the Catholic faith. Converts from unbelief or Judaism become immediately subject to the law of the canonical form by the reception of Catholic baptism.

117. S. Off. 6 maii 1742.
118. c. 1099, 1. A blessing is also required for validity in the form for Orientals (Cod. Or. cc. 85, 90).
119. **The Celebration of Baptism,** IV, A, 2-4; cf. cc. 1014; 1070, 2.

C. *Those not bound by the form for validity*

All non-Catholics, whether baptized or not, when they contract marriage among themselves.[120]

Before Jan. 1, 1949[121] persons born of non-Catholic parents, even though baptized in the Catholic Church, who have grown up from infancy in heresy or schism or unbelief or without any religion, when they contracted with a non-Catholic party; or with a Catholic Oriental who was not bound to any form. The parents may be two non-Catholics or only one non-Catholic, even if the promises were made, or two apostates,[122] and probably even one apostate. The exemption does not apply to the children of non-practicing Catholic parents.[123] It is often not easy to determine in the individual case the absence or presence of a Catholic upbringing. The practice of the diocese for sufficient certification should be consulted and observed.

Before May 2, 1949[124] Oriental Catholics when married among themselves, or with the baptized or the unbaptized who were not bound to a form, unless by the law of their own Rite they were bound by a canonical form.

Whenever Catholics, either Oriental or Latin, contract marriages

120. c. 1099, 2; Cod. Or. c. 90, 2; even if they belong to an atheistic sect (PCI 30 iul. 1934). Also exempted are those baptized in a non-Catholic or dissident Oriental sect (S.C. Conc. 28 mart. 1908). Although exempted from the canonical form, the parties are not exempted from the obligation to be physically present in person or by a proxy designated by the principal (cc. 1088, 1; 1089, 1; PCI 31 maii 1948; S. Off. 30 iun. 1949).

121. The effective date of the motu proprio "Decretum Ne Temere" of Pius XII (1 aug. 1948) abrogating the second comma of c. 1099, 2. It should be noted that these same persons were still bound by the impediment of disparity of worship when they married an unbaptized party (PCI 29 apr. 1940).

122. PCI 20 iul. 1929; 25 iul. 1931; 17 feb. 1930.

123. S. Off. 7 ian. 1947.

124. The effective date of the motu proprio "Crebrae allatae" of Pius XII (22 feb. 1949) establishing the Oriental Code on marriage. It had already been declared that a Latin rite woman who in virtue of c. 98, 4 declared she wished to transfer in matrimonio ineundo to the Oriental rite of the man, was still bound to the form for the celebration of marriage (PCI 29 apr. 1940; c. 1099, 1, 3°); thus the observance of the form preceded the change of rite.

with faithful who are non-Catholic Orientals, the canonical form of celebration for these marriages is of obligation only *for lawfulness; for validity* the presence of a sacred minister is sufficient, observing all the other requirements of law.[125]

In certain circumstances a Catholic may not be bound by the ordinary juridical form of marriage but by the extraordinary form, which is located below in section VIII.

D. *Dispensation from the Ordinary valid form of marriage*

Only the Holy See can dispense from the form prescribed by law for the valid contracting of marriage.[126]

125. S.C.E.O. Decretum **Crescens Matrimoniorum**, 22 feb. 1967. It should be noted that Vat. II Decree **Orientalium Ecclesiarum** stated that, when Eastern Catholics marry baptized Eastern non-Catholics, the canonical form obliged only **for lawfulness**; for **validity** the presence of a sacred minister sufficed, observing the other prescriptions of law. (This decree became effective in the USA on 21 Jan. 1965). The sacred minister referred to is taken to mean any sacred minister, including a deacon, accepted as validly ordained by the Eastern Orthodox and used by them to bless marriages. The other require-ments of the law to be observed (for lawfulness) are: dispensation from the canonical form for lawfulness, prenuptial investigation, promises, dispensation from mixed religion, etc. The local Ordinary who grants the dispensation from the impediment of mixed religion is the one who may dispense from the canonical form for lawfulness (Decree **Crescens Matrimoniorum**); he may be either the Ordinary of the Catholic party or the Ordinary of the place of the marriage. If the former, as is customary, the latter should be informed before-hand. Marriages of Latins which took place before an Orthodox minister before March 25, 1967 (the effective date of **Crescens Matri-moniorum**) would require a renewal of consent before a sacred minister (Catholic or Orthodox) or a radical sanation if the Orthodox party refuses.

126. Motu proprio, **De Episcoporum Muneribus**, 15 iun. 1966, IX, 7: Oriental Patriarchs may, for a very grave reason, dispense the faithful of their own rite from the canonical form in mixed marriages (**Crebrae Allatae**, c. 32, 2. The temporary faculty is granted to Metropolitans and other local Hierarchs (except Vicars General) outside the patri-archate and who have no superior below the Apostolic See to dis-pense from the canonical form in mixed marriages (and to sanate marriages because of defect of form) if the non-Catholic party cannot be persuaded to appear before the competent pastor and it is to be feared he will cause the Catholic party to adhere to a non-Catholic sect if the prescription of observing the form is urged in the case.

If serious difficulties stand in the way of observing the canonical form, local Ordinaries have the right to dispense from this form in any *mixed marriage.*[127] The celebration of marriage before a Catholic priest or deacon and a non-Catholic minister, performing their respective rites together, is forbidden; nor is it permitted to have another religious marriage ceremony before or after the Catholic ceremony, for the purpose of giving or renewing matrimonial consent.[128] Moreover, although the local Ordinary may permit a Catholic priest to officiate at a mixed marriage in a Protestant church but according to the canonical form, a non-Catholic minister may not officiate at a mixed marriage in a Catholic church even with a dispensation from the canonical form; this must be in a non-Catholic temple.[129]

E. *Those bound by a rite*

A rite is composed of a group of faithful who are ruled by laws and customs, rooted in ancient tradition, which pertain to the areas of liturgy and canonical order, and which group is recognized by the Apostolic See as autonomous and distinct from others.

Marriages of Catholics of *different* rites are to be celebrated in the rite of the *groom* and before his pastor.[130] This applies to the case of a Latin rite Catholic marrying an Eastern rite Catholic as well as to two Catholics of different Oriental rites. When both parties belong to the *same* Oriental rite, the pastor of the *groom* is to assist, unless a lawful custom or a just reason provides to the contrary.[131]

But they cannot grant the dispensation unless at least the Catholic party duly gives the guarantees and it is morally certain that all the children will be educated as Catholic. (S. Off. & S.C.E.O. 16 maii 1957).

127. Motu proprio **Matrimonia Mixta,** 31 mart. 1970, n. 9.
128. **Ibid.,** n. 13.
129. S.C.D.F., resp. 3 sept. 1968; cf. also NCCB, **Implementation of the Apostolic Letter on Mixed Marriages,** 16 nov. 1970.
130. c. 1097, 2; Cod. Or. c. 86, 3; PCI Cod. Or. (3 maii 1953) declared that the "nisi aliud particulari iure cautum sit" of the Latin Code is abrogated.
131. Cod. Or. c. 88, 3; CIC, c. 1097, 2.

The priest who assists at the marriage of the faithful of another rite always follows his own rite in the marriage ceremony.[132] An Eastern rite pastor does not *validly* assist in his territory at the marriage of two Latins, nor a Latin rite pastor validly assist in his territory at the marriage of two Orientals.[133]

The Oriental canonical form of marriage is now the same as that for the Latins with the exception that for the former the blessing of the assisting priest is also required for validity.[134] A single blessing suffices and no certain liturgical rite is required;[135] it suffices to follow the approved Eastern rite books and customs and laws.

Because of the very many faithful in the U.S.A. who belong to the various Eastern Catholic rites, it is necessary to be aware of what rites were not obliged to a canonical form prior to the present matrimonial law binding the entire Eastern Church. In the U.S.A. Greek Ruthenians have been bound by the form since August 17, 1914.[136] Maronites and Melchites in the U.S.A. were not bound;[137] Catholic Armenians in the U.S.A. were bound.[138] With regard to those whose origin was lower Italy or Sicily, it must be determined whether they pertain to the Latin or Italo-Albanian (Italo-Greek) rite. If the latter, they were not bound to the canonical form if they married in the U.S.A., but marriages contracted in Italy may have been subject to the form because so prescribed in the diocese of origin or celebration.

The pastor (and local Hierarch) can validly and lawfully assist at the marriages of the faithful of his rite within the boundaries of his territory also in places which are *exclusively* of another rite, provided the express consent of the Ordinary or the pastor or the rector of such places has been given.[139] As already noted, he cannot validly

---

132. PCI Cod. Or. 8 ian. 1953.
133. **Ibid.**, 3 maii 1953.
134. Cod. Or. c. 85.
135. PCI Cod. Or. 3 maii 1953.
136. S.C.P.F. (N.R.O.) decree "**cum episcopo**"; S.C.E.O., **motu proprio** "**Cum data fuerit**" (1 mart. 1929).
137. S.C.E.O. 12 apr. 1945.
138. Cf. S. Off. 14 iul. 1950 (private case).
139. Cod. Or. c. 86, 1, 2º; PCI Cod. Or. 8 iul. 1952. A Latin pastor is similarly restricted.

assist at the marriage of two faithful of the Latin rite nor can a Latin pastor validly assist at a marriage of two faithful of an Oriental rite.[140] If a priest of the Oriental rite of a Catholic party is available, either residing or ready to come to assist at the marriage in the local church of the Latin rite, the Latin pastor there has no right to assist at the marriage and he would be acting invalidly without proper delegation.

The pastor for assistance at marriage for an Oriental Catholic in the U.S.A.[141] is: 1) a pastor of his own rite who is subject either to an Ordinary of the same rite (true in the U.S.A. *only* of Ruthenians and Ukranians, Melchites, Maronites) or to the local Latin Ordinary; 2) a pastor of another Oriental rite or of the Latin rite expressly appointed to care for such Oriental Catholics or who becomes their pastor in virtue of the law itself. When a dispensation is required in the case of a mixed marriage the petition will be forwarded to the Latin Ordinary whenever the Catholic party belongs to an Oriental rite, except in the case of an Oriental having an Ordinary of his own rite when the dispensation is to be sought from the proper Ordinary.

F. *Dispensation to marry in another rite*

The local Ordinary may dispense and allow the marriage of two Catholics of different rites to be celebrated in the rite of the bride.[142]

The Apostolic See reserves the right to dispense: two Latin Catholics and allow them to marry in the Oriental rite, two Oriental Catholics and allow them to marry in the Latin rite; a Latin Catholic in order to marry a non-Catholic in the Oriental rite; an Oriental Catholic in order to marry a non-Catholic in the Latin rite. The Apostolic Delegate has the faculty to grant these dispensations.[143]

G. *Lawful assistance at the celebration of marriage*

1. *Pastor*

The pastor (or local Ordinary) lawfully as well as validly assists

140. cf. n. 133 above.
141. Cod. Or. cc. 86; 87.
142. S.C.D.F. 1 feb. 1957.
143. S.C.E.O., 1955, n. 36.

in his own territory at the marriage of spouses, either of which, it is legally ascertained, has a domicile or quasi-domicile or a month's residence in the place of celebration.[144] Regularly it is the lawfully constituted pastor of the bride who assists, unless a just reason excuses.[145] In marriages of mixed rite the ceremony takes place before the pastor of the groom, unless legal custom provides otherwise or a just cause excuses.[146] If the parties are wanderers (*vagi*) who are actually travelling and have no place of sojourn anywhere, the pastor of the place of celebration lawfully assists.[147]

Domicile and quasi-domicile are established according to the norms of law.[148] A month's residence is the morally continuous presence within the limits of the parish where the marriage is to take place, reckoning from moment to moment immediately prior to the celebration according to the calendar. It is not the intention but the factual residence for a month which is required, no matter what the reason for the residence may be, e.g., to avoid one's own pastor, to benefit by less expense, etc. One or two days absence is not considered to break the continuity of the month's residence.

One who is not, for at least one of the parties, the lawful pastor of marriage, must request permission of the latter, usually the pastor

144. c. 1097, 1, 2o; Cod. Or. c. 88, 1, 2o. All these lawfully constituted pastors have equal right of assistance.
145. c. 1097, 2. A light reason excuses.
146. Cod. Or. c. 88, 2. Cf. VII E above. (Ruthenians in the U.S.A. customarily celebrate marriage before the pastor of the bride; likewise, in everything they are subject to the Latin pastor of the place where they have no pastor of their own and no priest of another rite is designated to provide for Eastern rite Catholics. S.C.E.O. 30 maii 1955). If one of the parties pertains to the rite of the assisting priest, although the marriage is valid, for lawfulness the permission of the Apostolic Delegate or the Holy See is required, if the assisting priest is not of the groom's rite. If neither of the parties pertains to the rite of the assisting priest and there is no formally erected parish of the Oriental rite in the place or if there is merely a priest of another rite delegated to provide for the Eastern rite Catholics of the place, although any priest may validly assist in virtue of his own jurisdiction for marriage, for lawfulness the permission of the Apostolic Delegate or the Holy See is required (S.C.E.O. 10 dec. 1956).
147. c. 1097, 1, 3o; Cod. Or. c. 88, 1, 3o.
148. c. 92.

of the bride; grave necessity will excuse from seeking this permission,[149] e.g., to prevent a civil marriage, because of serious inconvenience to the pastor or the contractants, etc. This permission may be written or oral, expressed or tacit, or even reasonably presumed. The marriage between a Catholic and a non-Catholic is customarily celebrated in the parish of the Catholic party. A Latin pastor lawfully assists under the usual conditions at the marriage of Orientals who have no pastor of their own rite or when their own is not available.[150]

In every case the pastor does not lawfully assist unless he has legally ascertained the free status of the parties to marry in accordance with the law.[151] Moreover, a pastor who assists at a marriage without the permission required by law is not entitled to the stole fees and must remit them to the proper pastor of the parties,[152] usually of the bride. This is an obligation in justice, which regards the stole fees as such and not Mass stipends, donations given out of friendship, gratitude, etc.

2. *Delegated priest*

One lawfully delegated by the proper pastor must observe the norms for the use of the power of assistance as oblige the pastor. The stole fee by right belongs to the proper pastor.

3. *Other witnesses*

The ordinary witnesses should normally be Catholics who are in good standing. Excluded are adolescents, at least before the age of puberty and outside of necessity. Militant Communists, (i.e., adherents and defenders of the Communist system) cannot be lawful witnesses, but simply ascribed Communists can be tolerated outside the case of grave scandal, since they are not excluded from the celebration of marriage.[153]

149. c. 1097, 1, 3º; Cod. Or. c. 88, 1, 3º.
150. Cod. Or. c. 86, 3.
151. c. 1097, 1, 1º; Cod. Or., c. 88, 1, 1º.
152. c. 1097, 3.
153. S. Off. 11 aug. 1949.

Brethren of other churches may act as bridesmaid or best man at a wedding in a Catholic church. A Catholic too can be best man or bridesmaid at a marriage properly celebrated among separated brethren.[154]

VIII. *Extraordinary juridical form of marriage*

A. *Danger of death*

1. *Norm*

When it is impossible without serious inconvenience to have or to approach a pastor or Ordinary or delegated priest who can assist according to cc. 1095-1096, in danger of death marriage is valid and lawful when celebrated before witnesses alone.[155]

2. *Validity*

The danger of death may be from any internal or external source, as long as there is true danger of death prudently estimated. It must be at least a probable danger in the normal judgment of prudent people who consider that in the serious danger delay would prohibit the contract from taking place until an authorized priest could be reached or become available. The motive for entering the marriage may be varied, e.g., legitimation of offspring, to convalidate an invalid union, repair scandal, etc.

The impossibility or morally serious inconvenience of securing qualified assistance may be absolute, e.g., there is no time remaining, or relative, e.g., the inability to bear the expenses. The serious difficulty or danger may affect both spouses or either of them or a third person such as the pastor, even if it is due to a prohibition of the civil law.[156] The serious inconvenience must be real and proportionate to the non-observance of the ordinary juridical form and the real danger of serious scandal. The consent of the contracting parties

154. Sec. ad unit: Christ. fovendam, **Directorium,** 14 maii 1967, nos. 49, 58.
155. c. 1098.
156. PCI 25 iul. 1931; 3 maii 1945; S.C. Sac. 24 apr. 1935.

must be expressed in the presence of at least two competent witnesses.

3. *Lawfulness*

If any priest can be easily had, he must be called to assist together with the witnesses, but not under penalty of nullity of the marriage if this is not done for any reason.[157] It is required only for lawfulness. Probably excepted is a priest who is *vitandus* or under sentence of censure. The assisting priest would enjoy the faculties of dispensation of cc. 1044-1045. He should ask and receive the consent of the contracting parties.

B. *Outside the danger of death*

1. *Norm*

In the exact same impossibility of the assistance of an authorized priest (or deacon) but outside a case of danger of death, *and* when it is prudently foreseen that this condition of affairs will last for a month, marriage may be celebrated before witnesses alone.[158] This is at times applicable in mission fields or in areas of persecution of the Church.

2. *Validity*

There must be a continual and complete month which need not have already expired but is prudently foreseen will expire before the opportunity of contracting a qualified priest arises. The validity is not affected if the authorized priest appears suddenly and unforeseen after the contract has been made, or even if the parties waited until it would be impossible for the priest to be present. The serious inconvenience or impossibility is the same as noted above.

A normal prudent presumption and not a scrupulous inquiry of the pastor's absence suffices,[159] although a mistaken conviction made

---

157. c. 1098.
158. **Ibid.**
159. Rota 7 dec. 1926.

in good faith that an authorized priest was absent whereas in reality he was available will not make the marriage valid.[160] However, the mere fact of the pastor's absence is not sufficient but moral certainty is also necessary, based either on common knowledge or on inquiry, that for one month the pastor will neither be available nor accessible without serious inconvenience.[161] The pastor must be physically absent or, although materially present in the place, is unable because of serious inconvenience to assist at the marriage asking and receiving the consent of the contracting parties.[162]

3. Lawfulness

Even an unauthorized priest should be called in, if this can be easily done, as in the previous case. He enjoys the faculties of c. 1045. There are no formalities prescribed in this and the previous extraordinary case, except that the priest who assists ought to follow the ritual for marriage realizing that the asking and receiving of consent of the parties does not pertain to validity.[163] There is no serious obligation to supply later the ceremonies and solemnities of marriage. However, the spouses, witnesses, and the priest are bound *in solidum* to see that the marriage is recorded as soon as possible in the matrimonial and baptismal registers of the parish or diocese of the place of celebration.[164]

C. Marriage of conscience

This is not an extraordinary form of marriage but an extraordinary canonical circumstance in which the ordinary juridical form is observed.

160. Ibid., 30 ian. 1925.
161. PCI 10 nov. 1925.
162. Ibid., 10 mart. 1928; 25 iul. 1931.
163. An Instruction of S.C.P.F. (23 iun. 1830) indicated a way in which a marriage before two witnesses only may be performed: to make in the church (or if impossible, the home) before a group of people acts of faith, hope, charity, and contrition; exchange marital consent before the witnesses; offer up prayers of thanksgiving.
164. c. 1103, 3.

Only for the gravest and most urgent reasons, and by the local Ordinary in person, not by the vicar general without special mandate, can it be allowed that a marriage of conscience be contracted; that is, that a marriage be celebrated without the banns and in secret, according to the following norms.[165]

The permission to celebrate a marriage of conscience carries with it the promise and serious obligation of keeping secrecy on the part of the priest who assists at the marriage, the witnesses, the Ordinary and his successors, and even the other contracting party as long as the first does not consent to the divulgation of the marriage.[166]

The obligation of this promise on the part of the Ordinary does not extend to a case in which any scandal or serious harm to sanctity of marriage is imminent as a result of the observance of secrecy, or in which the parents fail to see to the Baptism of the children born of such a marriage, or have them baptized under false names, unless in the meantime within thirty days they give notice to the Ordinary of the birth and Baptism of the child, with the true indication of the parents, nor to a case in which they neglect the Christian education of the children.[167]

A marriage of conscience is not to be recorded in the usual matrimonial and baptismal registers but in the special book mentioned in c. 379, which is to be kept in the secret archives of the curia.[168]

IX. *Liturgical form of marriage*

Outside of necessity marriage is to be celebrated according to the rites of the approved liturgical books of the Church and of praiseworthy and sanctioned customs,[169] with proper regard respecting the obligation of rite.[170] The ceremonies concerning consent

165. c. 1104.
166. c. 1105.
167. c. 1106.
168. c. 1107.
169. c. 1100; Cod. Or. c. 91. This prescription does not affect validity. Cf. n. 171 below.
170. Cf. VII, E, F above.

placed by the qualified witness are essential and for validity.[171] The complete omission of the liturgical ceremonies outside of necessity is a serious sin, but their suppliance when omitted in necessity is not certainly of obligation, at least seriously.

Whenever marriage is celebrated within the Mass, the Mass for spouses is said and white vestments used, except on Sundays and solemnities when the Mass of the day is used with the nuptial blessing and, where appropriate, the special final blessing. On the Sundays of the Christmas season and throughout the year, in Masses which are not parish Masses, the wedding Mass (*pro sponsis*) may be used without change. When a marriage is celebrated during Advent or Lent or other days of penance, the parish priest should advise the couple to take into consideration the special nature of these times.[172]

It is not strictly necessary to apply the Mass for the spouses, unless they have contracted for the same, i.e., given a stipend.[173] A pastor or his delegate may assist at a marriage and another priest designated by either may celebrate the Mass and impart the solemn blessing. Confession and Communion are not obligatory but are to be strongly urged upon the spouses by the pastor.

In the celebration of a mixed marriage the liturgical form, if taken from the Roman Ritual, is from the *Rite of Celebration of Marriage*, whether it is a question of a marriage between a Catholic and a baptized non-Catholic or of a marriage between a Catholic and an unbaptized person. If, however, the circumstances justify it, a marriage between a Catholic and a baptized non-Catholic can be celebrated, subject to the local Ordinary's consent, according to the rites for the celebration of marriage within Mass, while respecting the prescription of general law with regard to Eucharistic Communion, which is to be considered when plans are being made to have the mixed marriage at Mass or not.[174]

171. c. 1095, 1, 3o Even the assisting priest of c. 1098 should employ the essential ceremonies.
172. S.C. Rit., 19 mart. 1969, **Ordo Celebrandi Matrimonium**, n. 11 (U.S.C.C., **Rite of Marriage**). Cf. nn. 12-18 for adaptations within the competence of episcopal conferences.
173. S. Off. 1 sept. 1841; S.C. Rit. 30 iun. 1896.
174. Motu proprio **Matrimonia Mixta**, 31 mart. 1970, n. 11; **Rite of the Celebration of Marriage**, nos. 39-54, 55-66, 1938; Sec. ad unit. Christ.

The celebration of marriage before a Catholic priest or deacon and a non-Catholic minister, performing their respective rites together, is forbidden; nor is it permitted to have another religious marriage ceremony before or after the Catholic ceremony, for the purpose of giving or renewing consent.[175]

With the permission of the local Ordinary and the consent of the appropriate authority of the other church or community, a non-Catholic minister may be invited to participate in the Catholic marriage service by giving additional prayers, blessings, or words of greeting or exhortation. If the marriage is not part of the Eucharistic celebration, the minister may be also invited to read a lesson and/or to preach.

In the case where there has been a dispensation from the Catholic canonical form and the priest has been invited to participate in the non-Catholic marriage service, with the permission of the local Ordinary and the consent of the appropriate authority of the other church or communion, he may do so by giving additional prayers, blessings, or words of greeting and exhortation. If the marriage service is not part of the Lord's Supper or the principle liturgical service of the Word, the priest, if invited, may also read a lesson and/or preach.[176]

X. *Time and place of celebration*

Marriage may be celebrated at any time of the year[177] and at any time of the day, unless local regulations limit it.

When a marriage is celebrated during Advent or Lent or other days of penance, the parish priest should advise the couple to take into consideration the special nature of these times.[178]

Marriages between Catholics are to be celebrated in the parish church; the pastor or local Ordinary may permit marriage in an-

fovendam **Directorium,** n. 39; NCCB, **Implementation of the Apostolic Letter on Mixed Marriages,** 16 nov. 1970, n. 17.

175. Motu proprio, **Matrimonia Mixta,** n. 13.
176. NCCB, **Implementation,** nos. 16-17. Cf. **Directorium,** n. 56.
177. c. 1108, 1; cf. Cod. Or. cc. 97; 98.
178. **Rite of Marriage,** no. 11.

other church or public or semipublic oratory (no special cause is needed). Special permission is required from the local Ordinary for marriage to be celebrated in a private house, a chapel of a seminary or of a house of religious women.[179]

The ordinary place of marriage, therefore, is in the parish church or other sacred place. For serious reasons the local Ordinary may permit the celebration of mixed marriage, when there has been no dispensation from the canonical form and the Catholic marriage service is to be celebrated, outside a Catholic church or chapel, provided there is no scandal involved and proper delegation is granted (e.g., when there is no Catholic church in the area, etc.). If there has been a dispensation from the canonical form, ordinarily the marriage service is celebrated in the non-Catholic church.[180]

XI. *Registration of marriage*

A. *Marriage register*

Record of the celebration of a marriage must be inscribed in the marriage register as soon as possible by the pastor or by his substitute, with the names of the spouses and of the witnesses, the place and date of celebration, as well as other items prescribed in the ritual books, or by the local Ordinary, even though some other priest has been delegated to assist at the marriage.[181] Likewise any convalidation or dissolution of marriage is to be inscribed in this register. There is a serious obligation to record a marriage promptly (*quamprimum*), which regularly means within at least three days. It is not a serious fault if the record is kept over a longer period on a sheet distinct from the marriage register, unless delay in the proper inscription raise the danger of failure to record properly in the register. The pastor is bound in conscience to supervise the proper recording of marriages. If a marriage has been contracted according to the extraordinary form, the priest, if one assisted, and

179. c. 1109, 1, 2.
180. NCCB, Implementation, nos. 19-20.
181. c. 1103, 1; S.C. Sac., Instruction "Sacrosanctum" (29 iun. 1941), n. 11, b.

otherwise the witnesses and the spouses are all bound, jointly and severally (*in solidum*), to make sure that the marriage is inscribed in the required registers as soon as possible,[182] and by the pastor of the place of celebration.

Priests responsible should make sure that non-Catholic ministers also assist in recording in their own books the fact of a marriage with a Catholic.[183]

In a mixed marriage for which there has been granted a dispensation from the canonical form, an ecclesiastical record of the marriage shall be kept in the chancery of the diocese which granted the dispensation from the impediment, and in the marriage records of the parish from which the application for the dispensation was made. It is the responsibility of the priest who submits the request for the dispensation to see that, after the public form of marriage ceremony is performed, notices of the marriage are sent in the usual form to (a) the parish and chancery as noted above and (b) the place of Baptism of the Catholic party. The recording of other mixed marriages is not changed.[184]

B. *Baptismal register*

Celebration of marriage must be recorded also in the baptismal register of the parties in the place where each has been baptized in the Catholic Church. If the place of Baptism is not that of the celebration of marriage, the pastor of the place of celebration is to send all the requisite details, either directly or through the episcopal curia, to the pastor of the place of Baptism of each spouse for inscription in the baptismal register; written assurance that this has been done should be received and placed in the dossier of the marriage.[185]

C. *Civil register*

The assisting priest, besides qualifying by civil law to witness

---

182. c. 1103, 3. For registration of a marriage of conscience, cf. VIII, C above.
183. Matrimonia Mixta, no. 10.
184. NCCB, Implementation, nos 12-13; cf. S.C.E.O. Decretum **Crescens Matrimoniorum**, 22 feb. 1967.
185. c. 1103, 2; S.C. Sac. c(f. n. 181 above), n. 11, b, c, d, e.

a marriage in a particular place, should also be careful to fulfill the requirements of the civil law respecting the proper civil registration of a marriage contracted. Most often it is required that the witnessing priest sign the civil marriage license and return it to the civil authorities within a specified time.

XII. *Banns of marriage*

A. *Obligation*

The banns of canonical proclamations are the public publication or notification whereby a future or intended marriage is made known to the whole populace so that any canonical impediment that is known might be disclosed. Before a marriage is celebrated it is to be ascertained that no obstacle exists to its valid and lawful celebration. Thus the pastor must publicly proclaim the parties who are to contract marriage.[186] This is a serious obligation (affecting only the lawfulness of the marriage) incumbent upon the pastor, even though he is otherwise morally certain of a lack of impediment in the case. It is commonly held that outside of necessity the omission of one bann—and probably of even two—is slightly sinful, if the pastor is morally certain of the absence of an impediment; it is certainly a serious sin to omit three publications.

B. *Form*

No special formality of publication is prescribed; the practice of the diocese is followed. The contractants should be clearly named and identified as to parish, the publication that is being made (1st, 2nd, 3rd), which publication has been dispensed, and the obligation of the faithful to reveal any impediments of which they are aware.

C. *Time*

The banns are published on three successive Sundays or feasts

---

186. cc. 1019, 1; 1022; cf. Cod. Or., cc. 13-21.

of precept in that place.[187] The successive days are not required for validity; the interval of one day without publication is not more than a slight sin, unless the days are so close that there would not be sufficient time to reveal impediments or if some other sound reasons justify the interval. The banns are usually published at the more important Mass or at the one which is more fully attended.

D. *Place*

The publications must be made in the proper parish where each party has a domicile or quasi-domicile. The request of the other pastors to publish the banns usually comes from the pastor of the bride, who is to assist at the marriage. They should be published also in each place where the parties have had the residence for six months after attaining puberty (14 years for a boy, 12 years for a girl), but in such cases the local Ordinary should be consulted, who may direct instead that other proofs be collected.[188] If the pastor has a positive suspicion that an impediment exists, he should also consult the local Ordinary respecting briefer periods of residence.[189]

Although the practice is to publish the banns in the parish church, they may also be published in any church or public oratory during Mass or other sacred functions attended by a large number of the faithful, as long as they are published by the authority of the pastor.[190] With the permission of the local Ordinary the banns of those with no fixed abode (*vagi*) may be published in the place where they are actually residing or intend to contact marriage.

E. *Omission*

Publication of the banns is omitted in marriages with non-Catholics, whether baptized or not.[191] It is also omitted in marriages of conscience,[192] of rulers of states, in danger of death, and in a

187. c. 1024. For the exceptional method cf. c. 1025.
188. PCI 3 iun. 1918.
189. c. 1023.
190. c. 1024.
191. c. 1026—unless the local Ordinary judges it advisable that it should be made.
192. c. 1104.

case of necessity when the marriage cannot be deferred without serious inconvenience and there is not time to apply for a dispensation, e.g., when there would be scandal or infamy in delay. Often there is need to procure a dispensation in the case of convalidation of a marriage. A modest tax according to their means may be paid by the parties to the diocesan chancery for the dispensation.

F. *Dispensation*

The local Ordinary of the parties can in his prudent discretion and for a just cause dispense from the banns, even in another diocese than his own. If there are several Ordinaries of the parties, that one in whose diocese the marriage is celebrated has the right to dispense; in case it is to be celebrated outside the proper diocese of the parties, then any proper Ordinary can dispense.[193] Diocesan faculties sometimes delegate pastors the power to dispense for a just cause from one or more publications. Reasons proportionate to the number of banns for which a dispensation is sought should be presented, e.g., the pregnancy of the woman, the danger of incontinence when a marriage has already been attempted civilly, prudent fear that the marriage will unjustifiably be interfered with.

G. *Interval*

The pastor should not assist at a marriage until he has at hand all the necessary documents for a valid and lawful contract of marriage. Moreover, unless there is a reasonable cause otherwise, he should wait until three days have elapsed since the last publication. If the marriage is not contracted within six months the banns must be republished, unless the local Ordinary judges otherwise.[194] If another pastor has conducted an investigation or has completed the publications, he should immediately by an authentic document notify the pastor who is to assist at the marriage of the result of his effort.[195]

193. c. 1028. This includes also the Military Ordinary of the Military Ordinariate.
194. c. 1030.
195. c. 1029.

H. *Existence of impediments*

1. *Obligation of disclosure*

All the faithful are bound, if they are aware of any impediment, to make known the same to the pastor or local Ordinary before the celebration of marriage.[196] This obliges also by the natural and divine law (even the unbaptized) in order to prevent sin or harm to the parties to the marriage or to the common good, as well as irreverence to the sacrament. All are bound at the earliest moral possibility to disclose an impediment of which they have certain or at least seriously probable knowledge.

Sacramental knowledge of an impediment absolutely forbids its revelation. A mere natural secret or one confided under a promise of secrecy does not excuse, since the harm resulting from the disclosure usually is not proportionate to the seriousness of the law and the evil effects of silence. Knowledge gained through a professional secret more probably excuses, e.g., a physician or lawyer professionally consulted, a priest consulted outside of confession, etc. There is no obligation of disclosure when greater harm which is done to the parties to the marriage by the disclosure, however, is usually outweighed by the advantages accruing to them.

2. *Continuance of the banns*

If a pastor is in doubt about the existence of an impediment, he must pursue his investigation further by questioning witnesses (if this would not disgrace the contractants), and even the parties themselves if necessary, under oath. He is to make or to finish the publications if the doubt has arisen before they have begun or have finished. If he prudently judges that the doubt still exists, he must not assist at the marriage without consulting the local Ordinary.[197]

A pastor who discovers with certainty that an impediment exists which is occult, he is to make or to finish the publications and to report on the matter, without mentioning names, to the local Ordi-

196. c. 1027.
197. c. 1031, 1.

nary or to the Sacred Penitentiary. If the impediment is public and is detected before the banns are published, he should not proceed further until the impediment has been removed, even if he knows that a dispensation has been obtained for the forum of conscience only. If the impediment is discovered after the first or second publication he is to complete the publications and refer the matter to the local Ordinary. Finally, if no doubtful or certain impediment is discovered, when the banns have been finally published, the pastor is to admit the parties to the celebration of their marriage.[198]

XIII. *Pre-marital Investigation*

A. *General Norms*

The Church has established certain carefully framed laws in order to insure that marriage might be lawfully, and especially validly, entered into and be productive of the abundant graces coming from this sacrament, and which cannot be disregarded without grave injury to the sacrament and serious sin for the recipient of the sacrament. Ministers of the Church who by allowing the faithful to celebrate marriages that are forbidden are gravely deficient in the duty committed to them of previously making a careful investigation lest marriages be contracted in defiance of the sacred canons. The causes of invalid or unlawful marriages can be reduced to three points: a) a marriage impediment in the strict sense, b) a defect of consent, c) a defect of canonical form.[199]

Before a marriage is celebrated it should be made certain that no obstacle exists to its valid and lawful celebration. In danger of death, if other proofs are not available and if adverse indications are absent, sufficient proof is obtained in the sworn statement of the contractants that they are baptized and are not disqualified by any impediment,[200] which statement would be insufficient if their veracity

198. Ibid., 2, 3.
199. S.C. Sac., Instruction "Sacrosanctum" (29 iun. 1941), concerning the norms to be observed by a pastor in making the investigation before admitting parties to marriage, nn. 2, 3.
200. c. 1019; Cod. Or. c. 9. When it is impossible to obtain the normal attestations of freedom to marry, it is left to the local Ordinary to accept other proofs, not excluding supplementary affidavits (PCI 3 iun. 1918). Thus, when records are unobtainable, the priest should

were open to suspicion or if they contradicted each other. The manner of arriving at the requisite knowledge of the freedom of the parties to marry has been established and current diocesan forms and questionaires usually cover the required information.[201]

B. *Pastor of investigation*

The pastor who enjoys the right of assisting at a marriage must carefully inquire beforehand and in good time whether any obstacle to the marriage contract exists. The prospective spouses should notify their pastors of their intention to marry in sufficient time to permit the proper investigation to be made before the proclamation of the banns. In ordinary cases the investigation should be made in practice one month before the proposed date of the marriage; when the parties are from different parishes and especially different dioceses, a proportionately longer period should be allowed. The regular place for holding the investigation is the parlor or office of the rectory.

The pastor who conducts the investigation will be the proper pastor of the bride, unless there is a just reason to the contrary. The pastor (or Military Chaplain) of the groom, either on his own initiative or at the man's request or that of the bride's pastor, should also confirm by examination the latter's freedom to marry, the result to be sent in writing as soon as possible to the bride's pastor, together with other necessary documents which may be in his parish archives. The pastor who grants delegation or permission to another to assist at a marriage is to conduct the investigation himself even if he is morally certain of the freedom of the parties, although he may delegate this duty to another for a just and not necessarily serious cause. The pastor also is to secure the *nihil obstat,* as noted below.

At the time of the investigation the parties intending marriage must reveal any hidden impediments, as otherwise they expose themselves to the proximate danger of serious sin in the case of a diriment impediment. When an impediment is occult but of a defamatory nature, e.g., crime, and will not be divulged, it need not be revealed

refer the matter to the local Ordinary rather than decide on his own. Diocesan forms often include a form of supplementary or suppletory oath.

201. Cf. no. 199 above.

to the pastor but to a confessor who, using a fictitious name, can recur to the Sacred Penitentiary for a dispensation in the internal forum. The pastor is to take the bride and bridegroom separately and question discreetly whether they are disqualified by any impediment, whether their consent—especially that of the woman—is free, and whether they are sufficiently instructed in Christian doctrine, (unless it is clear from their qualifications that this last inquiry would be pointless), especially relative to a correct idea of the sanctity and indissolubility of Christian marriage and the obligations undertaken as understood in the Church. The least that should be known also are the Commandments of God and of the Church, the obligation of receiving the sacraments, the Our Father, Hail Mary, Creed, Acts of Faith, Hope, Charity and Contrition. Defect of knowledge and even a refusal to take instructions is not of itself cause for refusal to assist at a Catholic marriage.

The pastor, in seeking to establish and to verify the free status of the parties through appropriate documents and the testimony of reliable witnesses whenever necessary, especially gains this information by his direct questioning of the parties. It is important that on their first visit the prospective spouses be received kindly, affably, and sympathetically; usually they feel strange and uncomfortable in the circumstance and in the place, and thus they need to be put at their ease immediately. The pastor or interrogating priest must conduct himself in a way so as to inspire confidence and respect and to arouse an appreciation of the sacredness and seriousness of the sacrament. He should speak distinctly and with all due prudence, modesty, circumspection, particularly with regard to impediments and other circumstances which could suggest shame or loss of reputation. His questions should be framed in ways to accommodate the understanding of each party, phrased to safeguard the rightful sensibilities of the parties; at times he will have to be plainspoken and firm in order not to diminish respect for and observance of the truth and the law.

C. Questionary

1. Oath and identification

A preliminary oath is required (but not preceptive) of each party attesting to the truth of their replies, once the sacredness and sanction of oaths has been explained to them. If either a Catholic or a non-Catholic party refuses to be questioned under oath, the pastor should not insist upon it but merely note the refusal and the reason for it in the questionary. Moreover, if the party questioned is unknown to the pastor personally, he should require other identification which has a photograph.

2. *Residence*

Interrogation to establish the residence of each party is necessary in order to determine the lawfulness of the pastor's assistance at the marriage in his territory, especially in the case of those with no fixed abode (*vagi*) or who are emigrants from a distant country or who belong to another Rite. The pastor must also discover in what dioceses the parties have lived (including the Military Ordinariate) for at least six months after attaining the age of puberty.

3. *Baptism*

The fact of Baptism must be established with certainty. The pastor, unless it was conferred in his own territory, is to require proof of the Baptism of both parties, or of the Catholic party in a disparity of cult case. Official proof of Baptism or transcript from the baptismal register would be not more than six months old so as to include also all other pertinent information. The seal of the parish and the pastor's signature should be affixed to make the document authentic. If a written certification is impossible, e.g., the records have been destroyed by fire or contact with a distant country is not possible, the sworn evidence of relatives or other reliable witnesses or of the party himself, if he was an adult when baptized, will suffice. Diocesan forms for such an affidavit are usually available.

A doubtfully established Baptism of a professed Catholic should be referred to the local Ordinary. A pastor who, after a diligent investigation to establish the facts, remains in doubt as to the Baptism or its validity in the case of a non-Catholic, should petition a dispensation not only from mixed religion but also *ad cautelam* from disparity of worship.

4. *Confirmation*

Proof of Confirmation is usually put on the baptismal certificate or on a separate Confirmation certificate, or in lieu of either on the sworn testimony of affidavit, as with Baptism. Catholics should be confirmed before entering marriage, if this can be done without grave inconvenience.[202] The pastor should try to arrange conveniently the reception of this sacrament before, but at least as soon as possible after, the marriage takes place.

5. *Confession and Communion*

The pastor should urge upon the parties as strongly as possible to confess their sins before entering into marriage and to receive Communion worthily.[203] An opportune time for confession should be indicated to the parties. It is usually recommended that the entire bridal party receive the Eucharist at the wedding ceremony, or at least on the day (unless non-Catholics are involved, which sometimes may indicate another arrangement). Opportunity for private confession may be afforded at the last visit of the parties with the priest or at the wedding rehearsal, although in time to handle any hidden impediment that may appear. Recommendation of a general confession is left to the prudence of the pastor or priest preparing the couple.

6. *Unworthy Catholics*

If a public sinner or one laboring under censure refuses to make a sacramental confession or to be reconciled with the Church before marriage, the pastor is not to assist at the marriage, unless a serious reason demands and, if possible, not without consultation with the local Ordinary.[204] The investigation may also reveal that one of the

202. c. 1021, 2.
203. c. 1033.
204. c. 1066. A serious reason would be danger of an attempted civil marriage, of scandalous concubinage, of serious harm to the innocent party, of complete defection from the faith, etc.

parties has notoriously abandoned the Catholic faith, without becoming affiliated with a non-Catholic sect, or has joined societies forbidden by the Church, in which cases the pastor is gravely forbidden to assist at the marriage without the previous permission of the local Ordinary who is to provide adequate guarantees and safeguards.[205] The Ordinary likewise should determine whether the banns should be published and if any of the sacred rites pertaining to a nuptial Mass and blessing should be eliminated. The sense of this prohibition usually excludes one who has given up the practice of his religion without being ascribed to any sect or notoriosly professing anti-religious tenets. It is forbidden to possess open or secret membership in societies explicitly condemned by the Church, whether by censure or not, or which exact an oath or pledge of blind obedience or of secrecy even from ecclesiastical authority.[206]

7. *Minors*

The pastor is directed to dissuade minors from contracting marriage without the knowledge of or contrary to the reasonable opposition of their parents; if they nevertheless insist on going ahead, the pastor may not *lawfully* assist without previous consultation with the local Ordinary.[207] In ecclesiastical law a person is a minor until his twenty-first birthday:[208] the age in civil law may vary from State to State beginning with age eighteen.

The reasons for the parental refusal must be weighed by the pastor against the reasons of the minor for wishing to enter the marriage. If the parental opposition is prudently judged reasonable

205. c. 1065. The norms of cc. 1065-1066 are applied to those who join or favor the Communist party and who publish, propagate or read books, periodicals, daily papers, or sheets which promote the doctrine or action of Communists, or who write in them; for those who profess the materialistic and anti-Christian doctrine of Communists, and especially those who defend or propagate it, [militant Communists] the norms governing the impediment of mixed marriage are applied (S. Off. 1 iul. 1949; 11 aug. 1949).
206. cc. 2335; 684; S. Off. 20 aug. 1894; III Baltimore, n. 247.
207. c. 1034. Cod. Or. c. 24. Some dioceses have a special prohibition against "teen-age" marriages.
208. c. 88, 1.

after questioning and investigation, e.g., because of the immoral or irreligious character of the other party, the pastor must dissuade them from the marriage and failing this to refer all facts to the local Ordinary. If parental consent is judged to be unreasonably withheld, he should try to win their consent; if they remain adamant, the pastor may go ahead with the marriage, even without consulting the Ordinary if the latter has expressed no special prohibition or reluctance. However, civil law must always be kept in mind regarding parental consent and requisite age for marriage. Usually a diocesan form is available with which to secure and record parental consent.[209] Where the parties have known each other only a short time, or know little about each other so that the pastor fears the lack of a sufficiently solid basis for so important a union, or there is a difference of religion or other factors of disruption, even if pre-marital pregnancy has occurred, the pastor is to be most prudent in favoring and permitting the marriage and to strive to defer it.

D. *Nihil obstat*

When the bride and groom belong to different parishes in the *same* diocese all the documents and testimony pertinent to the intended marriage *may* be sent to the diocesan chancery so that a *nihil obstat* may be granted by the episcopal curia, i.e., a written authorization to proceed with the marriage in the diocese since the evidence submitted appears to establish the free status of the parties to marry. This procedure is recommended but not prescribed by the Instruction *"Sacrosanctum"*; however, it may be prescribed by diocesan law.

When the pastors are of *different* dioceses and the pastor of the bride is to celebrate the marriage, all the documents pertinent to the marriage are to be transmitted to the bride's pastor through the diocesan chancery of the pastor of the groom and not directly from pastor to pastor.[210] It is for this chancery, then, to issue a

---

209. In lieu of parents, guardians, or adopting parents must give consent. If the parents disagree, the father's consent should ordinarily prevail, unless civil law requires the consent of both parents. Consent is required generally only for the first marriage of minors.

210. The request for information and necessary documentation is made

testimonial letter (*litterae testimoniales*) certifying the groom's freedom to marry. If the pastor of the groom is to celebrate the marriage, the documents concerning the bride are to be sent to him through the diocesan chancery of the bride's pastor together with the testimonial of the latter chancery of her freedom to marry. Moreover, the pastor who is to assist at the marriage *must* obtain the *nihil obstat* of his own chancery before proceeding to the celebration of the marriage, i.e., he is to send to the chancery all the documents relating both to the groom and to the bride for certification of the free status of the parties to contract marriage within the diocese. When the pastor who assists at the marriage in his own territory is neither the proper pastor of the bride nor of the groom, each pastor should consult his own regulations, but the ultimate responsibility of securing certificates of freedom rests with the pastor of the place of celebration of the marriage.

In due time before the marriage the pastor whose duty it is to seek the *nihil obstat* should send the above-mentioned documentation to his chancery together with a transcript or list or summary of the available relevant documents (*status documentorum*), which transcript the chancery uses in issuing the *nihil obstat*. The authenticated transcript and the dossier or file of documents should be preserved in the files of the parish where the marriage is celebrated. A pastor who permits a marriage to be lawfully contracted outside his parish before a priest who is in other respects legally competent is to use this form or transcript in granting permission.

E. *Documentation*

The following summary of documentations will be more or less required of the priest seeking a *nihil obstat* according as the marriage case requires. Diocesan law or practice may demand further information. Explanation of them is found in connection with the matters to which they relate.

1) Transcript or summary of the dossier of documents.

2) Certificate of the priest of the freedom of each party to marry.

> directly by pastor to pastor; the transmission, however, of the same is made through the diocesan chancery.

3) Prenuptial questionary or inquiry form properly signed and annotated where necessary.

4) Formula of oaths or affidavits (supplementary or suppletory oaths) a) of witnesses to prove freedom to marry, b) of the party intending marriage regarding freedom from all impediments when direct proof is lacking, c) of parents or guardians of their lack of objection to the marriage of a minor.

5) Baptismal certificate including Confirmation and other notations duly issued within six months.

6) Certificate of publication of the banns or of the Ordinary's dispensation.

7) Death certificate of a previous spouse executed by competent authority according to diocesan regulations.

8) Authentic record of a papal dissolution, decree of nullity (whenever a marriage has been attempted), Pauline privilege or a privilege of the faith.

9) Civil divorce decree with date and place of issuance.

10) Ordinary's decision regarding any previous marriage.

11) Promises or guarantees (*cautiones*) required in mixed marriages and properly executed in the form prescribed.

12) Civil certificate of marriage in a case of revalidation with place and date of issuance.

13) Dispensations from impediments.

14) Parental consent for the marriage of minors.

15) Delegation for valid assistance at the marriage.

16) Permission for lawful assistance at the marriage.

17) Permission of the local Ordinary for
   a) persons of no fixed residence (*vagi*) or emigrants.
   b) apostates, public sinners or persons under censure.
   c) a lawful condition to be attached to the marital contract.
   d) minors to marry without parental consent.

18) Curial testimonial of the *nihil obstat*.

19) Assurance received of registration in the marriage and baptismal registers.

20) Civil license with date and place of issuance.

F. *Pre-marital instruction*

The pastor is not to fail to instruct the parties, according to their varying capacity, on the sanctity of the sacrament of marriage, the mutual obligations of the spouses, the obligations of parents toward their children, the impediments to marriage and the requirements for valid consent.[211] All parties to marriage today need some pre-marital instruction or vocational guidance, which may generally be secured in marriage courses in Catholic schools, closed retreats, etc. The pastor should usually recommend or even insist upon attendance at pre-Cana or Cana conferences (where it is not otherwise of diocesan regulation). However, if he knows that the parties have not the necessary knowledge, the pastor's obligation to impart sufficient instruction is serious. If the parties are known to be fully instructed, he may give a short talk on mutual love and forbearance, sympathy and patience, the Catholic education of offspring, and the graces which attend the married state and flow from the sacrament itself. Such is the personal instruction which is given over and above the required parochial instructions and the examination involved in the questionary.

In the case of a mixed marriage many dioceses require a series of instructions for the non-Catholic party; pre-Cana and Cana conferences are sometimes accepted or prescribed; the pastor himself should introduce the non-Catholic party to the Catholic attitude and practice regarding the nature and obligations of marriage, the role of the Church and the practices of Catholics, Catholic teaching on conjugal chastity and birth prevention, Catholic Baptism and education. The education and attitude of the non-Catholic will influence the approach of the priest in his instruction.

The practice of reserving instruction on conjugal chastity and its implications for the sacramental confessional is not in accord with the character of the judgment exercised in this tribunal nor with the desire of the Church. If either or both parties are found to be completely ignorant or in error regarding the conjugal act or the

211. cc. 1033; 1018; cf. Pius XI, Encyclical "**Casti Connubii**" on preparation for marriage.

physical cooperation necessary between husband and wife, he should refer them to morally sound and mature relatives or to a Catholic physician for adequate instruction in the nature of the marriage act, while indicating at the same time that all acts ordained to the proper accomplishment of the marriage debt are lawful and even sacred or meritorious. In these matters the instructor must speak with great discretion in order to avoid any degree of offence or scandal.

XIV. *Impediments to marriage*

A. *Authority over marriage*

It is of faith that the Church can establish diriment impediments to marriage, dissolve a *ratum* marriage, and that matrimonial causes or cases belong to ecclesiastical tribunals.[212] It is at least theologically certain that the government of Christian marriage, i.e., between two baptized persons, pertains exclusively to the Church and is not possessed cumulatively with the civil power. It is commonly held that a marriage between a baptized and an unbaptized person is governed by the law of the Church.

Civil authority, for the good of society, can and ought to make just laws (which bind in conscience) for the temporal effects of marriage,[213] the separable civil effects, e.g., inheritance, dowries, social status, titles, registration, union and administration of goods, as long as they are not evil in themselves nor expressly proscribed by the Church. Inseparable civil effects exclusively reserved to the Church in the case of the baptized are, e.g., legitimacy of children, the right of parties to mutual marital relations, questions affecting or depending on the validity of marriage.

The Church does not have authority directly over the marriages of unbelievers. However, all marriage is governed by the divine law. The Church as the one authentic interpreter of the natural and divine law may speak on all marriage by her Teaching Authority. She

---

212. Trent, Denz-Schön. 1804; cc. 1038: 1119; Pius XI, ency. **Casti Connubii**; Leo XIII, ency. **Arcanum**.
213. Cf. c. 1961; Leo XIII, loc. cit.; Pius XI, loc. cit.; Pius XII, **Allocution to the Rota** (6 Oct. 1946).

alone can give a judgment as to what natural marriage is valid before God. It is most common teaching that the marriage of unbelievers is governed not only by natural and divine law but also by civil law exclusively and properly. The practice of the Church confirms this. Thus the civil power probably may establish both diriment and prohibitive impediments for their unbeliever subjects, as long as they are not contrary to natural or divine positive law (although it is sometimes not clear which quality of impediment the lawgiver intended). However, there can be no perfect divorce or dissolution of the natural bond granted, as this is forbidden to all by positive divine law in the New Testament. Marriage between unbelievers is a juridic fact with consequent effects even for the faithful inasmuch as it constitutes an impediment of existing bond. The civil power may justly regulate espousals or betrothal, the valid form of celebration, civil effects, recognize and define causes of nullity, etc. In mission territories care and consideration must be given to the various kinds of marriage possible or current in the area, such as unions entered into according to tribal customs, according to the marriage statutes of the government, or in other ways, and the effects obtained by various acts placed.[214] The mission law of the territory must be consulted; nullity of a legitimate marriage contracted contrary to tribal or civil law is to be referred to the local Ordinary.

B. *Circumstances of impediment*

A matrimonial impediment is a circumstance present in the parties on account of which marriage, by disposition of law either natural or divine or ecclesiastical (or even civil), cannot be lawfully or even validly celebrated. It is a circumstance which disqualifies a person from contracting marriage, if they are not prohibited by law from doing so.[215] Even though an impediment exists on the part of only one party, it affects the right of both parties, disqualifies both.[216] An impediment directly affects a marriage

214. Cf. S. Off. 23 iun. 1938 on Chinese civil form of marriage.
215. c. 1035. Cod. Or. c. 25.
216. c. 1036, 3. Cod. Or. c. 26, 3.

inasmuch as it is a contract and only consequently as a sacrament. Not every cause rendering a marriage unlawful (e.g., serious sin, omission of banns) or null (e.g., fear, error, lack of jurisdiction) is a canonical impediment, but only those recognized as impediments by law are canonical impediments.

C. *Division of impediments*

Matrimonial impediments are divided on the basis of:

1. *origin*

Impediments are *natural, divine* or *human* as they are founded in the natural, divine or human law (ecclesiastical or civil).

2. *effect*

impedient. A prohibitive or impedient impediment gravely prevents the lawful contracting of marriage, saving its validity.[217]

diriment. A diriment impediment nullifies a marriage contract, so that a marriage cannot be even validly contracted.

3. *extension*

absolute. An absolute impediment prevents marriage from being contracted with any person whatsoever, e.g., sacred orders, absolute impotency.

relative. A relative impediment forbids marriage with a certain person, while permitting it with others, e.g., consanguinity, affinity, relative impotency.

4. *duration*

perpetual. An impediment is perpetual which always endures unless there is room for dispensation, e.g., consanguinity.

temporary. An impediment is temporary which ceases with the lapse of time, e.g., age.

5. *dispensation*

dispensable. An impediment from which the Church can and

217. c. 1036, 1-2. Cod. Or. c. 26, 1-2.

customarily does dispense is called dispensable, e.g., spiritual relationship.

indispensable. An impediment from which the Church either cannot or customarily does not dispense is called indispensable, e.g., absolute impotency, episcopacy.

6. *grade*

The grade or degree of impediment is based on the difficulty of obtaining a dispensation or the reluctance in granting the same.[218] An impediment is called:

minor: (it should be noted that these are nevertheless diriment impediments)

1° consanguinity in the third degree collateral.

2° affinity in the second degree collateral.

3° public propriety in the second degree.

4° spiritual relationship.

5° crime arising from adultery with a promise or an attempt at marriage, even civil marriage.[219]

major: all other impediments. If false reasons are alleged in seeking a dispensation from a minor impediment, the dispensation is still valid; it is invalid in the case of a dispensation from a major impediment.[220]

7. *knowledge.*

An impediment is *certain* or *doubtful* inasmuch as a prudent doubt is excluded or admitted; the doubt may be of law or of fact. Ignorance does not excuse from impediments.[221]

When there is a doubt of law regarding an impediment of ecclesiastical law, the impediment does not bind. If the doubt is

---

218. c. 1042. Cod. Or. c. 31, 1, which are more extensive.

219. The local Ordinary may dispense, for a just and reasonable cause, from all matrimonial impediments of minor grade, even in cases of mixed marriages, provided, in the latter case, the prescription of cc. 1061-1064 are observed. (Motu proprio **Pastorale Munus**, n. 19) Cf. also c. 1054 on falsity in petition.

220. It is probable that all other **diriment** impediments are major in view of Cod. Or., c. 31, 2: "All other diriment impediments are of major grade."

221. c. 16, 1; S. Off. 11 mart. 1868.

only of fact regarding an impediment of the divine law, the impediment binds and marriage is forbidden, e.g., in doubt whether a previous marriage has been dissolved. If the doubt of fact regards an impediment of ecclesiastical law, the Ordinary may dispense, if it is an impediment from which the Roman Pontiff customarily dispenses.[222]

8. proof.

An impediment is *public* which can be proved in the external forum, otherwise it is *occult*.

An occult *impediment* refers to the possibility of proof in the external forum; an occult *case* refers to the lack of notoriety of an impediment, whether it is known or not by others. Thus an impediment may be public by nature, i.e., which is customarily evident, e.g., age, sacred orders, consanguinity by legitimate birth; or by nature occult, i.e., which is customarily secret, e.g., crime, private vow, consanguinity by illegitimate birth. An occult impediment may become known in fact or remain a secret; a public impediment may not be known in fact and thus remain in certain circumstances classed as an occult case; it may be known by only a very few discreet people who will keep it a secret. It may be public in one place, e.g., where the impediment was contracted, but occult in another, e.g., where the marriage is celebrated; or public at one time and becoming later occult, e.g., after ten years. To determine how many people must be in the know in order to render a case no longer occult, the common rule of thumb is four or five people in a town and eight to ten in a city, which numbers may increase or lessen as these individuals are discreet, hostile, garrulous, etc. For an impediment to be by nature public, it is not necessary that it be known as an impediment but only that the fact be public, e.g., uxorcide.[223]

---

222. c. 15. Cf. c. 1069. However, marriage is not forbidden in a case of doubtful impotency (c. 1068, 2).
223. c. 1037. Cod. Or. c. 27: "An impediment is considered to be public which arises from a public fact or which can be proved in another way in the external forum; otherwise it is occult." Cf. PCI 25 iun. 1932.

D. *Impedient impediments*

1. *Simple vows*[224]

a. *notions.* A vow is a deliberate and free promise made to God of a possible and better good and which obliges from the virtue of religion. It is public if accepted by a legitimate ecclesiastical superior in the name of the Church; otherwise it is private. It is reserved when only the Holy See can dispense, absolute when its fulfillment is not made contingent upon a future event. Only an external vow is considered in canon law, but an internal vow of itself will by the natural law impede the lawful celebration of marriage. Violation of the vow is a serious sin against the virtue involved and against the virtue of religion. All private vows are simple vows, even though reserved to the Holy See. No simple vow nullifies or invalidates a marriage unless the Holy See so declares, as in the case of Jesuit simple vows regarding attempted marriage subsequent to profession. The following *simple* vows, whether public or private, reserved or not, absolute or condition, perpetual or temporary, prohibit the lawful contracting of marriage, because the observance of their obligations is incompatible with the married state and runs the proximate risk of violation.[225]

b. *vow of virginity.* The vow of virginity is a promise made to God to abstain perpetually from the first complete act of carnal pleasure, in or out of marriage, by which virginity is lost. If the voluntary violation is merely internal, virginity is restored after the sin has been forgiven, but any external consummation of a voluntary venereal act effects an irreparable loss, as the preservation of physical integrity cannot ever be restored. Usually this latter is lost by voluntary emission of seed in man and by intercourse or other actions by which the hymen is culpably broken in a woman. The vow imposes a serious obligation and yet the party who contracts a valid marriage may not ask for the marital debt the first

---

224. c. 1058. Cf. Cod. Or. c. 48 as it also varies somewhat from the Latin rite.
225. c. 1307; 1308; 1058, 2.

time but is bound to render the debt when requested. Since after the intercourse the object of the vow can no longer be realized, the debt may thenceforth be requested and received. A private vow of virginity can be dispensed by the local Ordinary, the Superior of a clerical exempt institute, a confessor who is a Regular, and a confessor with delegated faculties.[226]

c. *vow of perfect chastity.* This is a promise made to God to abstain, whether perpetually or for a time, from every deliberate act of venereal pleasure (even though virginity has been lost) in or out of marriage. Within a valid marriage the party may not request the marital debt but may accede to the reasonable and lawful request of the other party. Upon the death of the spouse the vow revives its vigor and forbids a second marriage, if it is perpetual or has not elapsed or been dispensed. A private vow of perpetual and perfect chastity made absolutely after the completion of the eighteenth year of age is reserved to the Holy See.[227] The quinquennial faculties of the bishops permit dispensation of the reserved vow for just and reasonable cause for a marriage about to be contracted. The Apostolic Delegate can commute or dispense the reserved vow.

d. *vow of celibacy.* This is a promise made to God not to marry. If nevertheless marriage is contracted validly, the marital debt may be lawfully asked and received, since the object of the vow is limited to abstinence from the celebration of the marriage. If this vow is absolute and perpetual, it forbids a second marriage upon the dissolution of the first; otherwise it ceases as an impediment. This vow is dispensable as in the vow of virginity.

e. *vow to receive sacred orders.* A vow made to God to receive the diaconate or the priesthood indirectly forbids marriage, inasmuch as its fulfillment is practically impossible. It is a vow that is to be fulfilled unless the one assuming it is otherwise impeded, e.g., being refused admittance into sacred orders. If marriage does take place, the marriage debt may be lawfully sought and received. The obligation of the vow continues even after the dissolution of the marriage, unless circumstances, e.g., children, or

226. cc. 1313-1314.
227. c. 1309.

age have changed and render its fulfillment impossible. It is dispensable as in the case of the vow of virginity.

f. *vow to embrace the religious state.* This vow made to God to embrace the religious state, whether in a diocesan or pontifical institute, whether of perpetual or temporary, simple or solemn vows, indirectly forbids marriage, as in the previous case. If the marriage is contracted, the marital debt may be lawfully requested and received. After the marriage is dissolved, the vow renews its force, unless age or other circumstances make its realization impossible. It is dispensable as in the case of the vow of virginity, except in the case of a vow to enter a religious institute of solemn vows, which is reserved to the Holy See[228] and is dispensable as noted for the vow of perfect chastity.

2. *Legal relationship*

In those places where legal relationship arising from adoption renders a marriage unlawful in civil law, the marriage is also unlawful in canon law.[229] In the U.S. jurisdiction legal adoption is not a prohibitive impediment in civil law.

3. *Mixed religion*

a. *impediment.* Mixed religion is not as such an impediment of the divine or natural law, but in the nature of things there does exist the danger of perversion or of religious indifference. Thus the Church everywhere most severely forbids the contracting of marriage between two baptized parties of whom one is a Catholic and the other a validly baptized member of a non-Catholic community; and if there is danger of perversion for the Catholic party and the offspring, the marriage is also forbidden by the divine law itself.[230]

228. c. 1309.
229. c. 1059; Cod. Or. c. 49.
230. c. 1060. Cod. Or. cc. 50-54. Cf. Paul VI, motu proprio **Matrimonia Mixta**, 31 mart. 1970; motu proprio **Causae Matrimoniales**, 28 mart. 1971; Pius XI, ency. "**Casti Connubii.**" "The Church greatly desires that Catholics marry Catholics and generally discourages mixed marriages. Yet, recognizing that mixed marriages do occur, the Church, upholding the principles of divine law, makes special arrangements for them. And recognizing that these marriages do at times encounter special difficulties, the Church wishes to see that special help and

The Church in her experience is wisely reluctant to permit such a union, since it is often harmful to the intimacy of the union and the happiness of the spouses, dangerous to the faith and even the morals of the Catholic party and especially the children because conducive to indifferentism.

b. *subject*. Both contracting parties must be validly baptized. Catholics include all who have been baptized in the Catholic Church or converted to it and have not become members of a false religion, an heretical or schismatical or atheistic sect.[231] Non-Catholics include those who have been baptized as non-Catholics and who have remained in their non-Catholic community or who have given up their affiliation with a non-Catholic or an atheistic sect.

c. *dispensation*. The local Ordinary of the Catholic party for a just cause, even in the case of the use of the Pauline Privilege, and taking into account the nature and circumstances of times, places, and persons, may dispense from the impediment of mixed religion

support are extended to the couples concerned. This is the abiding responsibility of all." (NCCB, **Implementation of the Apostolic Letter on Mixed Marriages**, 16 nov. 1970).

231. S. Off. 28 dec. 1949: "Whether, in adjudicating matrimonial cases, Baptism conferred in the sects of the Disciples of Christ, the Presbyterians, the Congregationalists, the Baptists, the Methodists, when the necessary matter and form were used, is to be presumed invalid because of the lack of the requisite intention on the part of the minister to do what the Church does or what Christ instituted, or whether such Baptism is to be considered valid, unless the contrary is proved in the particular case. In the negative to the first part; in the affirmative to the second part."

PCI 30 iul. 1934. Formal Communists, i.e., Communists in the full sense of the term who profess the materialistic and anti-Christian doctrine of the Communists and especially those who defend or propagate it, are Communist-apostates and the guarantees or promises (**cautiones**) must be required of them before marriage; whether they also must be dispensed from the impediment of mixed religion is controverted depending on whether the Communists are considered a religious or atheistic sect or not. Material Communists, i.e., mere affiliates of the Communists without subscribing to their doctrine, are Communists-aggregates and the guarantees may be required of them in the prudent judgment of the local Ordinary. Cf. S. Off. 1 iul. 1949; 11 aug. 1949.

and also from the impediment of disparity of worship *ad cautelam* if there is a prudent doubt about the validity of the Baptism of the non-Catholic party),[232] when it has been found impossible before marriage either to bring the non-Catholic party to the true faith or to deter the Catholic party from the marriage.

To obtain the dispensation from the local Ordinary the Catholic party shall declare that he is ready to remove dangers of falling away from the faith. He is also gravely bound to make a sincere promise to do all in his power to have all the children baptized and brought up in the Catholic Church. At an opportune time the non-Catholic party must be informed of these promises which the Catholic party has to make, so that it is clear that he is cognizant of the promise and obligation on the part of the Catholic. Both parties are to be clearly instructed on the ends and essential properties of marriage, not to be excluded by either party.[233]

The declaration and promise by the Catholic, necessary for dispensation from the impediment of mixed religion (or disparity of worship) is made in the following words or their substantial equivalent: "I reaffirm my faith in Jesus Christ and, with God's help, intend to continue living that faith in the Catholic Church. I promise to do all in my power to share the faith I have received with our children by having them baptized and reared as Catholics." The declaration and promise are made in the presence of a priest or deacon either orally or in writing as the Catholic prefers.[234]

At an opportune time before marriage, and preferably as part of the usual pre-marital instructions, the non-Catholic must be informed of the promises and of the responsibility of the Catholic. No precise manner or occasion of informing the non-Catholic is prescribed.

232. Motu proprio. **Matrimonia Mixta**, n. 3; **Pastorale Munus**, n. 20.
233. **Matrimonia Mixta**, nos. 4-6.
234. NCCB, **Implementation of the Apostolic Letter on Mixed Marriages**, nos. 5-6. The form of the declaration and promises is not altered in the case of the marriage of the Catholic to the communion of spiritual benefits in such a Christian marriage. The promise and declaration should be made in the light of the certain, though imperfect, communion of the non-Catholic with the Catholic Church because of his belief in Christ and Baptism (**ibid.**, no. 7).

(In every case local diocesan norms are to be followed). It may be done by the priest, deacon or the Catholic party. No formal statement of the non-Catholic is required. But the mutual understanding of this question beforehand should prevent possible disharmony that might otherwise arise during married life.[235]

The priest who submits the request for the dispensation must certify that the declaration and promise have been made by the Catholic and that the non-Catholic has been informed of this requirement. This is done in the following or similar words: "The required promise and declaration have been made in my presence. The non-Catholic has been informed of this requirement so that it is certain that he (she) is aware of the promise and obligation on the part of the Catholic." The promise of the Catholic must be sincerely made and is to be presumed to be sincerely made. If, however, the priest has reason to doubt the sincerity of the promise made by the Catholic, he may not recommend the request for the dispensation and should submit the matter to the local Ordinary.[236]

Penalties formerly in effect for transgressors have been abrogated with retroactive effect.[237]

E. Diriment impediments

1. Want of age

a. *impediment.* A valid marriage cannot be contracted by a man before he has completed his sixteenth year, by a woman before she has completed her fourteenth. Although a marriage contracted after the completion of the stated ages is valid, nevertheless pastors of souls are to make every effort to prevent the marriage of youths before that age at which, according to the accepted usage of the

---

235. Ibid., no. 8.
236. Ibid., nos. 9-10. Cf. also IX Liturgical Form of Marriage above.
237. "The penalties decreed by Canon 2319 of the Code of Canon Law are all abrogated. For those who have already received them the effects of those penalties cease, without prejudice to the obligations mentioned in number 4 of these norms." (Matrimonia Mixta, no. 15).

country, marriage is customarily contracted. The age is computed according to the norm of law.[238]

b. *subject.* Assurance for the primary purpose of marriage, the health of the spouses, and offspring and the maturity needed for family life and the rearing of children are protected by this law of the Church. On the other hand, too great a disparity of age in couples to be married is not recommendable but is no impediment. The natural law itself forbids marriage to all who have not the necessary use of reason validly to contract marriage by giving true matrimonial consent. The attainment of natural or physiological puberty is not necessary for the validity of marriage. Ecclesiastical law specifies only the definite age for valid marriage.[239] It binds only the baptized, including non-Catholics; in practice it includes the marriage of a baptized with an unbaptized party (the civil impediment binds marriages among the unbaptized). A civil birth certificate is acceptable proof of age; a baptismal certificate will indicate only the maturity of the party. The impediment of nonage in civil law, as well as the age requiring parental consent in civil law, must be considered also.

c. *cessation.* The impediment of nonage normally ceases with the attainment of the required legal age; it is rarely dispensed. In doubt of the fact of the age, the local Ordinary is to be consulted, especially in the missions, who may dispense by c. 15, if and when expedient. The Apostolic Delegate may dispense from this impediment of ecclesiastical law for a serious reason. A marriage invalid due to nonage requires for validation a renewed act of consent according to the prescribed form of marriage.[240]

238. c. 1067. Cod. Or. c. 57; cf. legislation on this impediment previous to the Oriental Code. Cf. c. 34, 3, 3⁰.
239. Sufficient discretion to effect true matrimonial consent is presumed after puberty (c. 1082, 2).
240. cc. 1133, 1135. By quinquennial faculties the bishops may grant a sanation "for marriages invalidly contracted because of some impediment of ecclesiastical law ... in case there is great inconvenience in requiring a renewal of consent from the party who is ignorant of the nullity of the marriage; provided, however, that the former consent continues to exist and that there be no danger of divorce. The party who knows of the impediment is to be informed of the effect of the

2. *Impotency*

For a proper understanding of this impediment and of other matters of marital concern regarding reproduction, it is necessary first to describe briefly the anatomy or structure of the reproductive organs and their physiology or functions.

a. *male reproductive organism.* The external organs of reproduction are the testicles (testes) and the male member or penis. The testicles are oval-shaped glands which produce the microscopic bodies or fertilizing germ cells, called spermatozoa, which by way of intercourse unite and fuse with the female germ cells. Each normal spermatozoon (in appearance like a tadpole and one five-hundredth of an inch in length) keeps up a whipping motion with its long tail-like portion enabling it to travel in the seminal fluid about eight inches an hour. Lodging in the female uterus after intercourse the sperm cells retain this mobility and capacity to unite with the female cells for about two days, after which they slowly perish. In an ordinary ejaculation at the time of intercourse, hordes of these spermatozoa are emitted. The testicles, encased in a protective sack, called the scrotum, delicate and sensitive to pain, are indispensable for procreation. They contain a mass of tubules (total length of a thousand feet) which subsequently run into larger ducts or tubes at the upper end of the testicles, called the epididymes. The testicular glands also produce an essential secretion, from the Leydic cells, called hormones, which are greatly responsible for the peculiarly male characteristics which mainly appear at puberty.

The penis is the immediate organ of sexual union or coitus. It is a soft spongy organ (about four inches long and an inch in width) attached at its root to the pelvis and hanging limply above the scrotum. Due stimulation or excitement of desire causes the blood to surge into its spongy tissues whereby it swells, elongates (about six inches), spontaneously lifts itself, becoming very firm and stiff; this process is called erection. The tip of the penis is a bulbous gland

sanation, and the usual entry is to be made in the baptismal and marriage records." The local Ordinary may not dispense from the impediment of nonage for contracting a valid marriage, if the want of age amounts to more than a year (motu proprio **de episcoporum muneribus,** IX, 11).

supplied with abundant sensitive nerves, an enlarged cone-shaped structure called the glans penis, which is covered with a movable or retractable membrane of skin known as the prepuce or foreskin. Frequently the minor operation of circumcision is performed on male infants or even on adults for medical or hygienic reasons, which removes all or part of the prepuce. When penetration of the female genitals occurs this foreskin is pushed back exposing the tip; the friction of the coitus gradually excites these nerve endings until the peak or climax of nerve excitation is reached, which is called orgasm, when emission occurs by the sperm fluid being strongly expelled into the female receptacle or vagina. Thereupon the penis returns to its quiescent or flaccid state.

The internal reproductive organs include the seminal vesicles with vasa deferentia, prostate gland, Cowper's glands. The seminal vesicles are two small pouch-like organs situated near the upper sides of the bladder where the ureters from the kidneys join it. They generally act as reservoirs for the sperm cells which are continually produced in the testicles. These cells are transmitted to the vesicles through the groin, i.e., from the scrotal sack into the pelvic cavity, by means of seminal ducts or tiny tubes, called vasa deferentia. The seminal vesicals themselves are attached to the outer side of each vas deferens in forming the ejaculatory duct and secrete a seminal fluid which mixes with the sperm cells before going into the prostate gland.

The prostate gland, chestnut-like in form, situated at the neck of the bladder, surrounds the urethra, i.e., the bladder outlet or central canal through which both urine and semen pass on their way outside the body. It secretes a fluid apt for carrying or giving mobility to the spermatozoa stored in the vesicles. The Cowper's glands are two small, rounded, lobulated bodies of the size of peas, situated at the urethra, which secrete a clear alkaline fluid that, after erection, cleanses the urethral tube of any acidity left by the passage of urine. This precoital fluid lubricates the canal and exudes in drops from the tip of the penis, acting also as a lubricant in coition. At the moment of orgasm both seminal vescicles and prostate expel their contents into the urethra in spurts. This seminal fluid or semen is a mixture of the consistency of the white of eggs.

b. *female reproductive organism.* The external organs or those which can be easily discerned are the vulva, labia, clitoris, hymen. The vulva or genitals is a mouth-like organ with thick and fleshly outer lips or folds, usually in apposition, called the labia maiora, about three inches in length. The vulva forms a triangle with the point or apex to the back and the base at the front of the body, which base is covered with hair rooted in a fatty cushion called mons veneris. The vulva is closed or slightly open, soft and flabby except during intercourse when the blood gathering in the spongy tissues gradually swells them and makes them firm. Beneath the labia maiora are the labia minora which are two thinner, hairless, and more sensitive lips or folds parallel to the former. While separated at the bottom they are joined at the top in a V-shape to form a kind of hood for the clitoris and enclose and protect the entrance to the vagina (also called introitus or vaginal orifice) and the urinary canal.

The clitoris is a small organ in the shape of a bean, frequently about one fifth of an inch across the tip. It is a kind of stub glans penis, since it bears a resemblance to the male penis and is constructed in a similar fashion though minus the urinary canal. Its role is highly important in producing the female orgasm. Beneath the labia are two openings into the body—the urinary orifice (meatus) or small upper one, and the vagina or large lower one which is often partially sealed by the hymen or maidenhead, a membrane perforated to allow passage of the menstrual flow. Although the hymen is usually ruptured in the first marital act, many other natural or accidental factors may cause this.

The vagina, where the penis deposits its seminal fluid, is a tube-like organ of four to six inches in length lying along an uphill line thirty degrees above the horizontal and extending to the opening or neck of the uterus. Normally the vaginal walls are in a collapsed condition touching each other but they are capable of great distension. Sexual stimulation causes the vulvo-vaginal glands underneath the labia maiora to exude their secretion into the groove between the edge of the hymen and the labia minora to serve as the needed lubricant for coition.

The uterus or womb is the organ of gestation of the living fetus.

Its tip or neck (cervix uteri) projects downward about one-half inch into the vagina at its far end, with a very small canal, about one eigth of an inch in diameter, in its center as the outlet for the uterus and the entrance for the sperm cells. Resembling a flattened pear in shape the body of the uterus lies upward from the vagina and normally tilts slightly forward toward the bladder (thus the uterus in a person in a standing position normally lies horizontal or level with the floor). In itself a very small organ (three inches long, two inches at its widest, one inch thick), it is capable of enormous growth during the period of pregnancy. Its mucous lining is destined to lodge and nourish the fertilized ovum until maturity and to account for the menstrual cycle. When the fetus is fully formed after normally nine months, it is forced down into the vagina and thence expelled.[241]

At the wide part of the uterus are the fallopian tubes, one at each side, which act as passageways into the uterus for the ova or egg cells which have matured in and been discharged by the ovaries. These tubes, four to five and one-half inches long, terminate in large fringe-like structures that pick of the ova floating in the pelvic cavity. An ovum is a tiny cell, about one tenth of an inch in size, built like an egg with white, yolk, nucleus, and thin shell; it takes three to four days to reach the uterus. In its journey it may be met and fertilized by some one (and only one) of the hordes of sperm cells in opposite transit. The ovaries, a few inches from the uterus, one on each side, and behind and below the fallopian tubes, are oval-shaped organs, which are attached to the uterus by rope-like appendages. They are packed with a large supply of ova or egg cells which begin to mature at puberty and rather regularly thereafter during adult life until the menopause or period of change of life.

Each ovary normally releases a mature ovum every other lunar month, about fifteen days before the commencement of the menstrual flow. If the ovum is not fertilized it will disintegrate and pass out with the next menstruation. The ovaries also act as glands for an

241. The new infant is covered at birth with the amnion or thick pellucid membrane containing the amniotic fluid in which the fetus floats suspended by the umbilical cord. This membrane must be broken and the infant released.

internal secretion which contains the female hormones that help to regulate the development of the peculiarly female characteristics.

c. *impotency and sterility.* The human action as such is the only action over which the human individual has control and thus responsibility, and consequently the only action which can be made the object of the marital contract. In the process which leads to generation of offspring in marriage the specifically human act is the conjugal act. True conjugal intercourse and thus consummation of the marriage consists in the penetration of the female vagina by the male penis with insemination in the vagina with true seed. It is required and suffices that "a man in some fashion, even though imperfectly, penetrates the vagina and immediately effects, in a natural manner, a semination, at least partial, within the vagina, with this reservation that the entire male organ need not enter the vagina."[242] Thus, those things which pertain to copulation alone are within the control of the individual and not subsequent acts which are solely of nature itself. For this reason the parties in marriage mutually transfer the rights to those acts which *of themselves* are *apt* for generation; the action of nature itself in the process of generation or procreation is neither included nor excluded. The impediment of impotency is therefore the inability to copulate (*impotentia copulandi*).

Anything which is extraneous or accidental to copulation itself and which frustrates the passage of the seed of generation is a lack of fertility or sterility (*impotentia generandi*). It is a failure in some phase of the natural process of the physiological functions that operate independently of the human will and control, e.g., the movement of the semen within the female organism, the descent of the ovary, the fecundation of the same, the fertility of the male sperm itself. Thus the inability of nature itself to accomplish its purpose where copulation is not impeded is the defect of sterility and not of impotency.

d. *types of impotency*

as to time: impotency may be antecedent, if it existed prior to or at the time of the marriage contract; *subsequent*, if it arose after a valid and indissoluble contract was entered into.

242. S. Off. 12 feb. 1941.

as to extent: it may be *absolute*, i.e., extending to marriage with any person; *relative*, i.e., limited only to marriage between particular individuals and not others.

as to origin: impotency is *natural*, if it is from nature or has existed from birth; *artificial* or *accidental* if it has been acquired from an accidental cause, such as surgery, disease, accident.

as to certainty: it is *certain*, if its existence or presence can be certified or proven with at least moral certainty; otherwise it is *doubtful*.

as to duration: impotency is *temporary*, if it will cease in time or can be overcome by human effort, e.g., surgery; *perpetual*, if in the prudent judgment of experts it will never cease or if it cannot be cured without danger to life or be removed by lawful means. Perpetuity is usually unlikely in cases of functional impotence.

as to cause: impotency is *organic*, mechanical or anatomical, if it arises from an anatomical defect in the genital organs themselves, when either the organs are lacking or are inept for perfect copulation; it is *functional*, when due to some lack of stimulation preventing normal functioning, or due to some organic defect or abnormality in another part of the body or to some disease of the nervous system, or due to some psychical cause arising from the purely mental or psychological makeup of the person, e.g., homosexuality, ejaculatio praecox, vaginism.

e. *canonical impediment of impotency*. By the natural law itself a marriage is rendered invalid by *antecedent* and *perpetual* impotency on the part of either the man or the woman, whether known to the other party or not, whether it is absolute or not. If the impediment of impotency is doubtful because of either a doubt of law or a doubt of fact, the marriage is not to be hindered. Sterility neither invalidates marriage nor renders it unlawful.[243]

There must be real and true impotency which is both antecedent and perpetual and which must be proved with moral certainty. The

243. c. 1068. The Holy See has condemned as contrary to the natural law direct sterilization, e.g., Pius XI, ency. "Casti Connubii"; S. Off. 21 mart. 1931; and artificial insemination, e.g., S. Off. 26 mart. 1897; 24 iul. 1929; Pius XII, Allocutions 29 sept. 1949; 29 oct. 1951; Paul VI ency. **Humanae Vitae**, n. 14 (25 iul. 1968); Vat. II, Const. **Gaudium et Spes**, n. 51.

presumption is in favor of the power to copulate until the contrary is proved. It is difficult to prove antecedent and perpetual impotency, especially if arising from a psychic cause. It is not necessary that it actually existed or was evident before marriage but that the proximate causes of the impediment existed then and thus it was virtually antecedent.

Impotency is judged to be present in a man in the following instances: absence or ineptness of the male organ or penis, its inability to erect at least sufficiently to allow proper penetration of the vagina (sexual anasthesia), lack of both testicles, excessive venereal excitement resulting in an uncontrollable loss of seed before penetration can take place (sexual aphrodisia or eiaculatio praecox), absence of true seed which has been elaborated in at least one existent and vital testicle (mere apposition of both genital organs with semination at the orifice of the vagina is not apt of itself for generation). All agree that the presence of spermatozoa in the ejaculate is not necessary for true semen. However, it is controverted whether it is necessary that the seed be elaborated in the testicles (at least one). The majority view affirms this requirement and thus the man who has undergone double or bilateral vasectomy is impotent. Others, denying the requirement of a testicular component in the ejaculate, hold that the doubly vasectomized man is not certainly impotent and thus not impeded from contracting marriage. Double vasectomy signifies the excision or ligation of the vasa deferentia, thus precluding the transit of fluid from the testicles. The condition is perpetual if at the same time irremediable.[244] Therefore, recognizing that in such a case doubtful impotency may be indicated, in practice the priest will always consult the local Ordinary before petitioning a declaration of nullity or at least a dissolution of an unconsummated marriage, when prudent judgment indicates a valid doubt about the application of the impediment.

In the following cases impotency is considered to exist in a woman: absence of a vagina, impenetrability of the vagina due to narrowness or to vaginism—which is the spastic contractions of the

---

244. The (then) Holy Office (28 sept. 1957) has stated that in a case of double vasectomy, marriage according to c. 1068, 2, is not to be impeded.

muscles surrounding the opening of the vagina and rendering penetration impossible; this functional impediment has a psychic origin and is usually not permanent. On the other hand, the occlusion or retroversion of the uterus or its absence (hysterectomy) which leaves the vagina perfectly intact,[245] the severance or ligation of the both fallopian tubes (fallectomy) or their radiation (oopherectomy), the removal of both ovaries (ovariotomy) cause sterility but not impotency, since it is accepted in practice that they do not pertain to the act of copulation. Controversy prevails in the case of a woman with an artificially constructed vagina, especially if it is open at the inner end to the uterus, as to the existence of the impediment of impotency. In this case, as above with double vasectomy, the pastor will consult the local Ordinary before making any petition, and also before approving of any such vaginal surgery before marriage.

f. *obligations.* The pastor or confessor does not usually inquire about impotency. If he becomes aware of it and the parties are in good faith, he should not immediately warn them, since it is usually very difficult to separate and material sins may become formal ones. A dispensation from at least an unconsummated marriage will be petitioned (if there is a doubt of the fact of the impotency being antecedent or perpetual and irreparable). Only in a rare and exceptional case will an arrangement to live as brother and sister be admitted. When certain and antecedent impotency is discovered after marriage the parties lose all right to the marital act; they may exercise their right until the impediment becomes certain or nullity declared. A woman is bound to submit to surgery to remedy an impediment, if the operation is relatively easy and ordinary, but not if it is truly dangerous. Separation is not urged as long as there is reasonable hope of substantial fulfilment of the marital act; if there is no hope, acts are permissible which do not expose either party to the proximate danger of pollution. A sterile party is bound to reveal this defect to the other partner, whether the

---

245. An occlusion severing the connection between the vagina and the uterus, and which is intrinsic to the vagina, e.g., by a traverse membrane, constitutes impotency, but often it is remediable and thus temporary. Cf. Rota (Appellate Tribunal of Bologna) 5 aug. 1954.

defect is discovered before or after marriage is celebrated; also in the case of subsequent impotency.

Medical science and civil law are not always in accord with canon law regarding the definition of impotency and the consideration of cases. In almost all the American States impotency is grounds for annulment or divorce (but not double vasectomy). Concealment of sterility is often treated as impotency, but knowledge by the innocent party of the other's defect often precludes judicial action.

3. *Marriage bond*

a. *impediment.* One who is bound by the bond of a previous marriage, even though it was not consummated, attempts marriage invalidly, without prejudice, however, to the privilege of the faith. Even though the former marriage is invalid or dissolved for any reason, it is not therefore allowable to contract another marriage before the nullity or dissolution of the previous one has been established in accordance with the law and with certainty.[246] This impediment of *ligamen* is a diriment impediment of the natural and divine law, and thus binds all without exception. The exception of the privilege of the faith refers to the Pauline privilege whereby the previous valid bond is dissolved at the moment the second is contracted and not before.

b. *conditions.* The freedom of a party from a previously existing bond of marriage, even though it is certainly known to be invalid, must be canonically certified.[247] This applies also to revali-

---

246. c. 1069. S.C. Sac., Instruction "**Sacrosanctum**" (29 iun. 1941): "6. The impediment of the bond of an existing marriage calls for some special remarks because of its importance. Pastors must take great care lest any persons break the law, knowingly or unknowingly, by entering upon a fresh marriage with the bond of the previous marriage still binding them, even though the invalidity of the first marriage is not only very doubtful but certain. They must know that by canon 1069, 2, the nullity of any marriage can be established only by a canonical proof."

247. A petitioner may wish to convalidate a subsequent union and thus be declared free of the bond of the previous marriage because of the death of the previous partner or because of a defect or impediment

dation. Where the previous spouse is deceased, the death must be proved by authentic document.[248] The testimony of the surviving spouse is of no value. The authentic death certificate (normally from the pastor of the place of burial) should be compared with the certificate of the first marriage to insure that the same party is involved and that there is no prohibited degree of consanguinity. Mere lapse of time and the presumptions of civil law (or of military authorities or an insurance company, etc.) are canonically insufficient proofs, unless other evidence and indications, in the judgment of the local Ordinary, warrant a declaration of freedom.

Whenever it is discovered that a party has at any time possessed marital status, even only civilly, and the death of the previous spouse is not authentically certified, the case must be referred to the local Ordinary, who will proceed according to the norms of law. Petition for a declaration of freedom or decree of nullity should be made according to the forms or procedures required in the diocese, with the collection of baptismal certificates pertaining to the previous marriage, impediments dispensed, divorce decrees, record of convalidation or affidavit of non-convalidation, marriage certificates, affidavits of the three parties in the two marriages. Where the previous bond has been dissolved by papal dispensation (or solemn profession), the authentic document to this effect must be obtained, or the certification on the baptismal certificate. A second marriage or convalidation cannot be allowed until there is moral certainty of the absence or the removal of the impediment of ligamen, as well as assurance of the non-convalidation of the union. Investigation of the possible existence of the impediment of crime must always be made and dispensation secured *ad cautelam.*

The impediment of marriage bond may also be present in the

in the first marriage. On the other hand, the petitioner may have married a divorced person and now wishes to be freed on the basis of the latter's previous valid and extant bond, or the petitioner has married a second time—the first partner dying after this second marriage was entered into—and now desires freedom from the second marriage.

248. Or the sworn testimony, according to the norms of law, of two reliable witnesses (or one first-class witness) who knew the deceased, were congnizant of the fact of his death, and agree on circumstances of its occurrence (cf. S. Off. 13 maii 1868).

case of a common law marriage. From the viewpoint of the Church this type of informal marriage implies that two parties—neither of whom are bound to the canonical form of marriage—have exchanged true marital consent effective of a valid marriage according to the natural law, but without any religious or civil ceremony. Civil law in some States and U.S. jurisdictions recognize common law marriages as valid, but not in others. When both parties to the union are unbaptized, the validity or invalidity will be regulated by the law of the particular civil jurisdiction. If at least one party is validly baptized (as a non-Catholic), the local Ordinary must decide on the validity of the common law union, regardless of the attitudes of the civil law. A common law marriage of baptized non-Catholics enjoys the presumption of validity. In common law marriage in general the assumption of marital status as indicative of true marital consent is presumed, until proven otherwise, when the parties themselves live as man and wife, are publicly considered as married, perform public acts as a married couple, e.g., joint bank account or income tax return, registration for voting, housing, etc.

c. *obligations.* If it becomes morally certain during the second marriage that the first spouse is still alive, the second marriage is invalid, but the children are considered legitimate inasmuch as they are born of a putative marriage. A doubt about the death of the first spouses arising after the second marriage must be carefully investigated. Meanwhile the doubting party, being a possessor in bad faith, must refrain from requesting the debt but may render it. If both parties are in doubt, both must abstain. If the existence of the first spouses becomes certain, the parties must separate from bed and also from cohabitation, if the case is public. If the doubt persists after careful investigation, the present partners are considered to be possessors in good faith and thus may continue fully as spouses in a presumed valid marriage,[249] until the second marriage is declared null by an ecclesiastical tribunal because of a positive and insoluble doubt of the validity of the first marriage,[250] or until the existence of the first partner becomes certain.

d. *penalties.* Bigamists, i.e., those who attempt marriage

249. S. Off. 22 mart. 1865.
250. PCI 26 iun. 1947.

while bound by a previous bond become automatically infamous, public sinners, and irregular, subject to the impediment of crime and of the excommunication of the Third Council of Baltimore.[251]

4. *Disparity of worship*

a. *impediment.* A marriage contracted by a non-baptized party with a person who has been baptized in the Catholic Church or converted to it from heresy or schism, is null. If at the time the marriage was contracted the person was commonly considered to be baptized or if his Baptism was doubtful, the marriage is to be regarded as valid according to the norm of c. 1014, until it is certainly established that one of the parties was baptized and the other unbaptized.[252]

No baptized has an unrestricted right to marry an unbaptized party. The divine law itself prohibits (but does not invalidate) such a union when there is any danger of perversion to the spouse or offspring; from this law there is no dispensation. The impediment of ecclesiastical law is diriment, nullifying a marriage, whether the danger of perversion is present or not; lacking the danger, the impediment is dispensable.

b. *conditions.* One of the parties must be unbaptized. The other party must be baptized in the Catholic Church. Thus, the impediment is drawn in the present law in a restricted sense. It binds only those whose Baptism (or conversion) binds them or aggregates them to the external communion of the Catholic Church, as acknowledged members of the Catholic Church. This is determined in an adult Baptism by his own intention, in an infant Baptism by the intention of the parents or guardians or the minister in lieu of either (a Catholic baptizes an infant in danger of death in the Catholic Church, even against the wishes of the parents). Thus, the impediment does not bind validly baptized Protestants who remain unconverted to the Catholic Church when marrying the unbaptized. On the other hand, non-Catholic or separated (Orthodox) Orientals

251. cc. 2356; 984, 4°; 985, 3°; 1075, 1°; III Baltimore, n. 124; cf. also c. 1053 an automatic dispensation from crime.
252. c. 1070; Cod. Or. c. 60; Motu proprio **Matrimonia Mixta,** n 2.

are bound by this impediment.[253] Likewise bound were those who
were born of non-Catholic parents but baptized in the Catholic
Church and raised outside the Church, although they formerly were
not bound by the canonical form of marriage,[254] unless they were
baptized unlawfully.[255]

If there is doubt of the Baptism of the non-Catholic party in the
case of a marriage about to be contracted, a dispensation from the
impediment should be sought *ad cautelam*. (A doubtfully baptized
Catholic should be rebaptized conditionally). If in the case of a
marriage already contracted a doubt should arise over the Baptism
of one or of both parties, the marriage must be *presumed* to be
valid until the contrary can be proved and the certainty of non-
Baptism established. In judging marriage cases certain presumptions
of the validity of Baptism in non-Catholic sects prevail, until a
particular case established the contrary.[256]

The requirements of just and serious reasons for seeking a dispensation, the obtaining of sincere promises or guarantees, and the
prohibition of any other marriage ceremony must be strictly observed, as in the impediment of mixed religion.[257]

c. *dispensation.* The local Ordinary may dispense from the
impediment of disparity of worship under the conditions as noted
above for a dispensation from the impediment of mixed religion.[258]

5. *Sacred Orders*

a. *impediment.* Clerics in sacred orders attempt marriage

253. Cod. Or. c. 60, 1. The impediment existed also prior to the present
    Oriental Code of 2 maii 1949 (cf. S. Off. 18 maii 1949; 17 apr. 1950).
254. PCI 29 apr. 1940; c. 1099, 2.
255. An infant of non-Catholic parents, who is baptized by a Catholic
    priest or layman contrary to the law ((cc. 750-751) outside the danger
    of death and who is educated outside the Church, is probably not
    bound, but the local Ordinary should be consulted in practice.
256. Cf. n. 231 above. There must be certainty also that the marriage
    has not been validated or sanated.
257. c. 1071. Cf. text above, IX D 3.
258. A dispensation from this impediment does not imply a dispensation
    from any other. S. Off. 16 apr. 1931 (S.C.P.F. 20 maii 1931); 30 iun.
    1932.

invalidly.[259] Sacred orders in the Latin Church are diaconate and priesthood (with episcopacy).[260] The impediment is of ecclesiastical origin. The ordination must be valid and free; ignorance, force and fear would be difficult to prove juridically today because of the oath taken before diaconate.[261]

b. *dispensation.* In ordinary cases the Holy See alone dispenses from this perpetual impediment.[262] In danger of death or of urgency any priest may dispense from this impediment in the case of the diaconate.[263]

c. *penalties.* A cleric in sacred orders (and his accomplice) incurs an excommunication simply reserved to the Holy See for attempting marriage, even civilly; he is irregular *ex delicto* and is liable to further penalties after warning with failure to amend.[264] If he is a religious he is automatically dismissed from the institute, suspended, and deprived of clerical garb.[265]

6. *Solemn vows*

a. *impediment.* Marriage is invalidly attempted by religious who have taken solemn vows or simple vows to which by a special provision of the Holy See the effect of invalidating marriage has been added.[266] The solemn vows must be actually and validly taken. If one party is a cleric in sacred orders, the impediment is two-fold and multiple if both parties have solemn vows.

b. *dispensation.* The impediment is of ecclesiastical law and in ordinary cases is dispensed by the Holy See alone; in danger

259. cc. 1072; 132.
260. The present Oriental Code (c. 62) extends this same impediment also to the subdiaconate, although in the Oriental Church (with the exception of the Armenians) it is not a sacred or major order.
261. Motu proprio **Ad Pascendum**, 15 aug. 1972, V. Previously an oath was taken before subdiaconate.
262. Motu Proprio **De Episcoporum muneribus**, IX 12. S.C.D.F. **Normae,** 13 ian. 1971 and 26 iun. 1972. Local Ordinaries cannot dispense by c. 81 (PCI 26 ian. 1949).
263. cc. 1043-1045.
264. cc. 2388, 1; 985, 3º; 188, 5º.
265. c. 646, 1, 3º.
266. c. 1073. Cod. Or. c. 63. The simple vow of the Jesuit has this invalidating effect on marriage.

of death or of urgency any priest may dispense.[267] A religious automatically dismissed from the religious institute for attempting marriage, even civilly, is not freed from his vows, unless the particular
constitutions or the Holy See provide otherwise.[268] In this latter case,
since the vows have ceased to have their effect, the impediment does
not exist and no dispensation is required to contract marriage.

An indult of secularization permits perpetual residence outside
the cloister and separates the religious from his institute. He must
lay aside the habit and conduct himself as a secular in all that
concerns Mass, the divine office, and the use and administration of
the sacraments. He is freed from his vows but is bound by such
sacred orders as he may have received.[269] An indult of laicization,
a step beyond secularization, reduces the religious to the lay state.

c. *penalties.* A religious (of either sex) with a solemn vow
of chastity (and the accomplice) who attempts marriage, even
civilly, incures an automatic excommunication simply reserved to the
Holy See. He is irregular *ex delicto*, automatically dismissed from
the institute, and liable to further penalties.[270]

7. *Abduction*

a. *impediment.* Marriage is invalidly contracted between
an abducted woman and a man who has abducted her with a view
to marriage as long as she remains in his power. But if the abducted
woman, withdrawn from the power of the man who abducted her
and established in a place where she is secure and free, consents
to have him as a husband, the impediment ceases. With respect to
the invalidity of marriage, the violent detention of the woman is
considered equivalent to abduction (*raptus*), that is, her violent detention by the man for the purpose of marriage in a place where
she dwells or to which she has freely come.[271]

---

267. Motu proprio **De Episcoporum Muneribus,** IX, 12. Local Ordinaries
    cannot dispense by c. 81 from reserved vows (PCI 26 ian. 1949).
    Cf. cc 1043-1045.
268. Cf. cc. 646, 1, 3o; 669, 1.
269. c. 640.
270. cc. 2388, 1; 985, 3o; 646, 1, 3o.
271. c. 1074. Cod. Or. c. 64.

b. *conditions.* For the impediment to be present it must be a woman who is abducted or kidnapped; the man purposing to marry her must abduct her himself or through an agent acting under his orders; the abduction must be precisely for the purpose of marriage; the abductor must remove the woman from one place to another which is morally distinct, even though close by; the abductor must use violence, either physical force or threats or fraud and deceit; the woman must not have consented to the abduction or at least to its purpose of marriage; the woman must be under the power of the abductor in the place where she is taken. For the impediment to be present in the case of violent retention (*sequestratio*) of the woman all the above conditions must be verified, with the exception of removal to another place. The impediment binds only the baptized, and it suffices that one party is baptized.

The above conditions establish the matrimonial *impediment* of abduction. This latter is of wider scope, including the kidnapping of a woman for lustful purposes and the elopment with or seduction of a girl who is still a minor and who consents to her removal unknown to or against the will of her parents or guardians.[272] Abduction or kidnapping is also a crime in civil law but not an impediment to marriage.

c. *dispensation.* Abduction is an impediment of ecclesiastical law. Dispensation is not granted as long as the woman is in the power of the abductor. Where there has been an incidence of abduction, the pastor should not assist at the marriage even if the woman now actually free and safe from duress consents to marry her abductor (in which case the impediment ceases). The local Ordinary is competent to dispense.[273]

d. *penalties.* The crime of abduction automatically excludes the delinquent from legitimate ecclesiastical acts and makes him liable to further penalties.[274]

8. *Crime.* Marriage between persons who by complicity have perpetrated certain nefarious crimes is forbidden by ecclesiastical law under pain of invalidity. The parties become incapable and dis-

---

272. Cf. c. 2353. Cf. Rota 8 ian. 1948.
273. Cf. Motu proprio, **De Episcoporum Muneribus,** IX, 11-16.
274. cc. 2353; 2354, 1.

qualified. The crime may be one of a threefold species (or fourfold, as the first species has two formalities).

a. *impediment. Adultery with promise of marriage (neutro patrante homicidio)*. Persons who, during the existence of the same lawful marriage, have consummated adultery together and have mutually promised each other to marry incur this impediment.[275] The adultery must be true in that at least one of the parties is validly married, consummated by natural carnal intercourse, formally recognized by both parties as adultery inasmuch as they know that at least one party is validly married. The promise itself must be true and not merely a proposal or desire, serious, free from duress or deceit, absolute and not conditional, with the object of entering into marriage *after* the death of the other spouse[276] with the existence of the valid marriage known to be the impediment to the fulfilment of the promise, reciprocally made and accepted, externally manifested and not revoked before committing the adultery if it precedes the latter. The adultery and promise must be before the valid marriage which they violate ceases to exist. This crime is an impediment even if only one of the parties to it is baptized.

Adultery with attempt of marriage (neutro patrante homicidio). Those who, during the existence of the same lawful marriage, have consummated adultery together and have attempted marriage, even civilly.[277] The adultery must be characterized as above. The attempt at marriage (even civil marriage) may take place before or after the adultery, but during the existence of the valid marriage; it produces the same effects as a promise of marriage. Marital consent (even though ineffectual and providing the attempt was not withdrawn before the adultery) must be present and mutually expressed, together with mutual knowledge of the existing bond (which knowledge may come to one party later and yet the adulterous union is continued). A person validly married who subsequently divorces and remarries while still bound by the first marriage, consummating the

---

275. c. 1075, 1º. Cod. Or. c. 65, 1º.
276. It is most probable that the promised marriage must be a valid contract, i.e., according to the canonical form, and not a promise of merely a civil marriage (cf. Rota 30 apr. 1957).
277. c. 1075, 1º. Cod. Or. c. 65, 1º.

second union, incurs this impediment, as well as the second partner who is aware of the situation. Although some hold that a belief in good faith by one party that the first marriage bond is severed by divorce and thus that adultery is not formally present removes the grounds for the impediment,[278] in practice dispensation from the impediment is sought *ad cautelam*. The other elements noted in the first species pertain also here.

Adultery and conjugicide without conspiracy (uno patrante homicidio). Those who, likewise during the existence of the same lawful marriage, have consummated adultery together, and one of whom has killed the lawful spouse.[279] The adultery requires the same conditions as above. The conjugicide is committed by only one of the adulterers, even against the will of the other; it must be consummated in that the death of the lawful spouse actually follows the placing of the cause of death, and follows also the commission of the adultery, the murder of the lawful spouse (of either adulterous partner) being committed with the intention of marriage with the adulterous partner. In this species of crime only the baptized party who has committed adultery and conjugicide incurs the impediment; if the adulterous murderer is the unbaptized party, neither party incurs the impediment.

Conjugicide with conspiracy (utroque patrante homicidio). Those who, even without committing adultery, have by mutual cooperation, physical or moral, brought about the death of the lawful spouse.[280] Thus adultery is not required. There must be true cooperation[281] of both parties in the killing of the lawful spouse of either, which efficaciously results from their conspiratorial action, with the added intention (at least on the part of one conspirator) of marrying each other subsequently.

  b. *multiplicity.* The impediment of crime may be multiplied when several species are verified in one and the same marriage or when more than one marriage is injured by the crime. Probably adultery with a promise and an attempt at marriage also is only

278. S. Off. (24 iun. 1959) answered a private query supporting this position.
279. c. 1075, 2º. Cod. Or. c. 65, 2º.
280. **Ibid.**, 3º.
281. **Cf.** c. 2209, 1-3.

one impediment in the one case, as is also the repetition of the promise or of the adultery or of the attempt. Thus multiple crime exists when both parties are mutually known to be married in the case of adultery, of conjugicide, and when both lawful spouses are murdered. It suffices to explain the circumstances of the case in seeking a dispensation rather than enumerate the number of species —which may not be so obvious.

      c. *dispensation.* This impediment does not cease with the lapse of time. Crime in the absence of conjugicide is a minor impediment and it alone is dispensable by the local Ordinary.[282] When murder is public, the Church does not dispense. All species of the impediment are dispensable in danger of death and of urgency.[283]

      Permission for a new marriage granted with a dispensation from the impediment of *ligamen* or bond in the presumed death of a spouse includes a dispensation from the minor impediment of crime, as also when the Holy See dissolves an unconsummated sacramental marriage.[284] It is necessary that pastors and confessors be vigilant in discerning the presence of crime, either public or occult, in their investigations or considerations of marriage cases. Conjugicide has been a diriment impediment of civil law only in Puerto Rico.

9. *Consanguinity*

      a. *notion of blood relationship.* Consanguinity (*cumsanguine—unitas*) or blood relationship is a natural moral bond or relation between persons which is based on carnal generation (legitimate or illegitimate, full-blood or half-blood) and which unites them in blood. Consanguinity exists in the *direct* line if one of the persons is the direct ancestor or progenitor of the other, in the *collateral* or

---

282. Motu proprio **Pastorale Munus**, n. 19. Cf. Motu proprio **De Episcoporum Muneribus**, IX, 13. The Bishop may also, by his quinquennial faculties, dispense from this impediment when it is occult, without any plotting of death for a marriage already contracted or to be contracted. The Apostolic Delegate may dispense from the crime of c. 1075, 2 and 3 if the delict is certainly occult.

283. cc. 1043-1045. The penalties of cc. 2354; 985, 4⁰; 2356; 2357, 2, are applicable to delinquents in crime.

284. c. 1053; PCI 26 mart. 1952.

indirect and oblique line if neither person is the direct ancestor of the other but both are descended from a common ancestor or progenitor. Consanguinity is multiplied as often as the proximate common ancestor is multiplied. More remote ancestors multiply consanguinity only when that are reached by the parties by distinct lines.

An *ancestor* in blood relationship is the person—male or female —from whom as from a common stock (*stipes*) or root (*stirps*) two or more persons descend through carnal generation. A *line* (*linea*) is the series of persons who spring from the same ancestor, either directly or collaterally. The *direct* line is *ascending* if the order of blood relatives is counted back to the common ancestor, e.g., son to father to grandfather, etc.; it is *descending* if the reverse order of compilation is used, e.g., father to son to grandson, etc. The *collateral* line is *equal* when the blood relatives are equidistant from the common stock, otherwise it is *unequal*. When both parents in the common stock are the same progenitors there is only one line; when only one parent is common—in half-blood relationship—each parent must be considered separately in computing lines of relationship, when the respective descendants wish to intermarry.

A *degree* (*gradus*) is the measure of distance between blood relatives and their common ancestor. These degrees are computed in the *direct* line according to the number of persons in the line without counting the common ancestor. In the *collateral* line they are computed according to the number of generations in one branch (*or* according to the number of persons in the line without counting the common ancestor) if the branches are *equal*, but in the longer branch if the two are *unequal*. The unequal collateral line is expressed by "second degree touching first," "second degree mixed with first," or as the degree of relationship requires. Thus, the collateral branch more distant from the common ancestor determines the degree of relationship, the longer line as it were drawing over to it the shorter line. The presence or absence of the canonical impediment in this case is determined by the more remote or longer line.

It should be noted that the terms denoting blood relationships in common language usage do not always correspond with the canonical terminology respecting the same degrees of relationship.

b. *impediment.* In the *direct* line of consanguinity marriage is invalid between all ancestors and descendants, legitimate or not. In the *collateral* line it is invalid up to the *third* degree inclusively, but the impediment is *multiplied* only as often as the common ancestor is multiplied. Marriage is never to be permitted as long as there remains any doubt that the parties may be related by blood in any degree of the direct line or in the first degree collateral.[285] If one line goes beyond the third degree collateral, the impediment ceases, e.g., fourth degree touching third—a man may marry his second cousin-once-removed or his third cousin. Baptized non-Catholics are bound by this impediment. The purpose of the prohibition is to preserve the reverence which blood relatives owe each other, the good of society, moral good, and the physical good of the offspring.

Because of the differences in the laws establishing the impediment of consanguinity in the Latin and Oriental Codes, it is necessary in *interritual* marriages to know also the impediment as it binds the Oriental party.[286] In the direct line marriage is invalid between all ancestors and descendants, legitimate or not. In the collateral line it is invalid up to the sixth degree inclusively, but the impediment is multiplied as the common ancestor is multiplied. Marriage is never to be permitted while there exists any doubt of blood relationship in any degree of the direct line or in the second degree of the collateral line. In the direct line the degrees are computed according to the number of persons in the line without counting the common ancestor. In the collateral line there are as many degrees as there are persons in *both* branches without counting the common ancestor. By this computation the sixth degree collateral, when the branches are equal, is the same as the third degree collateral of the Latin impediment (second cousins). When the collateral branches are unequal, the "fourth degree collateral touching on second" as expressed according to the Oriental computation is an impediment

---

285. c. 1076. Marriage must not be allowed if, before the birth of the woman who is to be married illicit and secret intercourse occurred which may give rise to a doubt that she may be the daughter or sister of the intended groom (PCI 3 iun. 1918).
286. Cod. Or. c. 66.

to marriage, whereas the same expression according to Latin computation is not.

    c. *dispensation.* Consanguinity is an impediment of divine and natural law in the direct line certainly to the first degree and probably to the other degrees, in the collateral line probably to the first degree. It is certainly of ecclesiastical law in the other collateral degrees. The unbaptized are bound only by the divine and natural law, and by just civil law; upon conversion of a married party the marriage stands as valid, unless the impediment is certain.[287]

    Dispensation in the direct line in any degree is never granted; likewise in the first degree collateral. The local Ordinary for a just and reasonable cause may dispense from the second degree collateral equal and from the third degree collateral even when the third degree touches first.[288] The Apostolic Delegate is competent to dispense from the second degree collateral touching first. In danger of death and in a case of urgency the degrees which are certainly of ecclesiastical law may be dispensed.[289] It should be noted that the civil law regarding consanguinity as an impediment in each State should be kept in mind.

    A genealogical tree should accompany every petition for dispensation from consanguinity.[290] A clear statement of the existing relationship which is an impediment to marriage should be made, in the complete manner as exemplified in the figures below. When a dispensation from the impediment of consanguinity or of affinity is granted in any degree of the respective impediment, it is valid in spite of an error regarding the degree made in the petition or in the rescript granting the dispensation, provided that the actual degree is less close than the one specified, and in spite of the failure to mention another impediment of the same kind in the same or a less close degree.[291] Thus, a mistake whereby a dispensation is requested

---

287. Cf. c. 1014.
288. Motu proprio **Pastorale Munus**, n. 19; motu proprio **De Episcoporum Muneribus**, IX, 14.
289. cc. 1043-1045.
290. Cf. S. C. Sac., Instruction "Sacrosanctum" (29 iun. 1941), 5.
291. c. 1052. PCI (8 iul. 1948) stated that the dispensation is valid also for another impediment of the same species in an equal or lower degree, which in good or bad faith was omitted from the petition.

or granted for a second degree collateral whereas the actual degree is third does not invalidate the dispensation, even if another third or second degree equal or unequal is actually present.

    d. *penalties.* Those who attempt and consummate marriage within the forbidden degrees of blood relationship without a dispensation are guilty of the crime of incest. They are automatically infamous, excluded from legitimate ecclesiastical acts and liable to further penalties. Clerics are punished with more severe penalties.[292]

10. *Affinity*

    a. *Notion of in-law-ship.* Affinity or in-law-ship is a relationship arising from a *valid* marriage between two persons whereby each party is related to the blood relatives of the other.[293] It is natural *fact* and thus is contracted by the valid marriage of the unbaptized, although it becomes an *impediment* only for the baptized. Affinity arises from a valid marriage, whether ratified only or ratified and consummated, which must now be understood to refer not only to a sacramental union but also to any valid marriage, whether consummated or not; this natural relationship only becomes also an impediment where at least one party is baptized or becomes baptized.[294] Thus the natural foundation or fact of affinity may be placed before or after the reception of Baptism, but the new marriage to which it is an impediment must take place after the Baptism of at least one of the parties.

    Affinity is computed in such wise that the blood (even half-blood) relatives of the husband are related by affinity to the wife in the same line and degree as they are related by consanguinity to him, and vice versa.[295] By this reckoning a man is related in the direct line to his mother-in-law, grandmother-in-law, etc., and to his step-daughter, step-grand-daughter (i.e., any children of his wife by a previous marriage), and to his daughter-in-law and grand-daughter-in-law, step-parent or step-grand-parent. In the collateral line he is

292. cc. 2357-2359.
293. Cf. c. 97, 2.
294. **Ibid.**, 1; S. Off. 31 ian. 1937.
295. c. 97, 3.

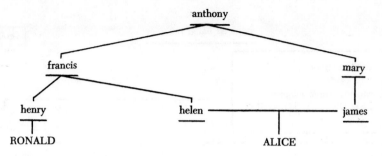

RONALD and ALICE are related in the second degree collateral equal (first cousins) through one common ancestor *Francis*, and in the third degree collateral equal (second cousins) through the other common ancestor *Anthony*.

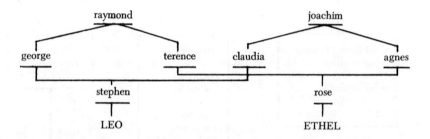

Two brothers have married two sisters. LEO and ETHEL are related doubly in the third degree collateral equal (twice second cousins) through the common ancestors *Raymond* and *Joachim*.

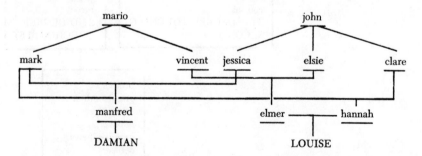

DAMIAN and LOUISE are related twice in the third degree collateral equal (second cousins) through the common ancestors *Mario* and *John*, and once in the second degree collateral equal (first cousins) through the common ancestor *Mark*.

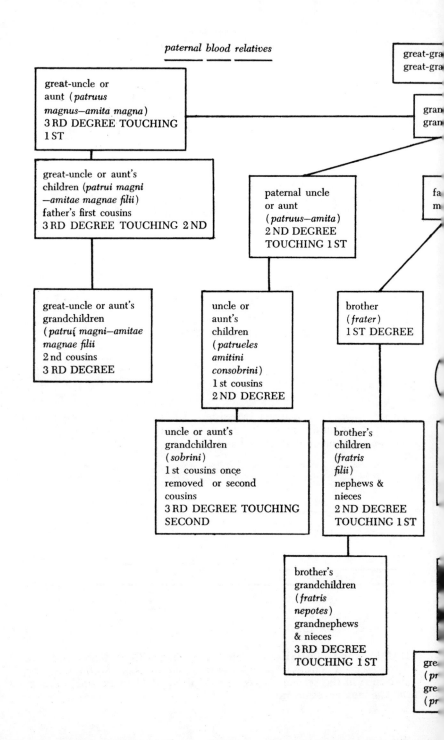

paternal blood relatives

great-uncle or
aunt (*patruus
magnus—amita magna*)
3 RD DEGREE TOUCHING
1 ST

great-gra
great-gra

gran
gran

great-uncle or aunt's
children (*patrui magni
—amitae magnae filii*)
father's first cousins
3 RD DEGREE TOUCHING 2 ND

paternal uncle
or aunt
(*patruus—amita*)
2 ND DEGREE
TOUCHING 1 ST

fa
m

great-uncle or aunt's
grandchildren
(*patrui magni—amitae
magnae filii*
2 nd cousins
3 RD DEGREE

uncle or
aunt's
children
(*patrueles
amitini
consobrini*)
1 st cousins
2 ND DEGREE

brother
(*frater*)
1 ST DEGREE

uncle or aunt's
grandchildren
(*sobrini*)
1 st cousins once
removed or second
cousins
3 RD DEGREE TOUCHING
SECOND

brother's
children
(*fratris
filii*)
nephews &
nieces
2 ND DEGREE
TOUCHING 1 ST

brother's
grandchildren
(*fratris
nepotes*)
grandnephews
& nieces
3 RD DEGREE
TOUCHING 1 ST

gre
(*pr
gre
(*pr

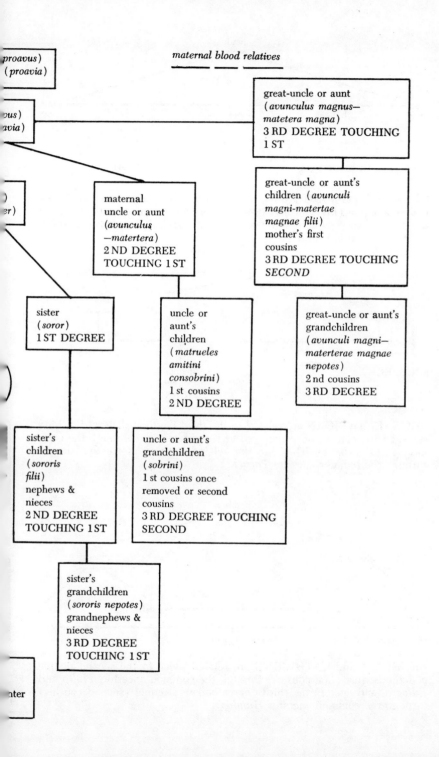

maternal blood relatives

(*proavus*)
(*proavia*)

vus)
avia)

great-uncle or aunt
(*avunculus magnus—
matetera magna*)
3 RD DEGREE TOUCHING
1 ST

)
er)

maternal
uncle or aunt
(*avunculus
—matertera*)
2 ND DEGREE
TOUCHING 1 ST

great-uncle or aunt's
children (*avunculi
magni-matertae
magnae filii*)
mother's first
cousins
3 RD DEGREE TOUCHING
SECOND

sister
(*soror*)
1 ST DEGREE

uncle or
aunt's
children
(*matrueles
amitini
consobrini*)
1 st cousins
2 ND DEGREE

great-uncle or aunt's
grandchildren
(*avunculi magni—
materterae magnae
nepotes*)
2 nd cousins
3 RD DEGREE

)

sister's
children
(*sororis
filii*)
nephews &
nieces
2 ND DEGREE
TOUCHING 1 ST

uncle or aunt's
grandchildren
(*sobrini*)
1 st cousins once
removed or second
cousins
3 RD DEGREE TOUCHING
SECOND

sister's
grandchildren
(*sororis nepotes*)
grandnephews &
nieces
3 RD DEGREE
TOUCHING 1 ST

nter

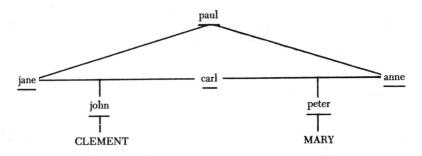

CLEMENT and MARY are related (by half blood) in the second degree collateral equal (first cousins) through one common ancestor *Carl*, and in the third degree collateral equal (second cousins) through the other common ancestor *Paul*.

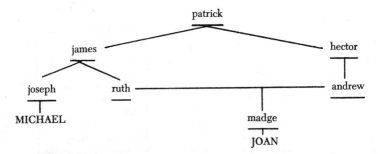

MICHAEL and JOAN are related in the third degree collateral touching second (first cousins once removed or second cousins) through the common ancestor *James*. They are not related within a forbidden degree through the remoter ancestor *Patrick*.

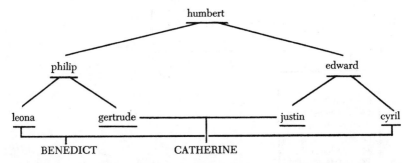

BENEDICT and CATHERINE are related twice in the second degree collateral equal (first cousins) through the common ancestors *Philip* and *Edward*, and once in the third degree collateral equal (second cousins) through the common ancestor *Humbert*.

related to the wives of his brothers, uncles, grand-uncles or great-uncles, nephews and grand-nephews, cousins, and to similar collateral relatives of his own wife.

b. *impediment*. Affinity in the direct line in any degree invalidates marriage; in the collateral line, to the second degree inclusively. The impediment of affinity is multiplied: 1) as often as the impediment on which it is based is multiplied; 2) through a subsequent marriage with a blood relative of one's deceased spouse.[296] Persons who are related by affinity to a third person are not, however, related thereby by affinity to each other, e.g., a man's brother's wife is not related by affinity to the same man's sister's husband. The purpose of the impediment is to lessen a danger to chastity, to foster mutual reverence among in-laws, and to embrace others in a wider range of charity and friendship through marriage.

For Orientals the common law of affinity places an impediment arising from a valid marriage, whether consummated or not, in all degrees of the direct line and to the fourth degree inclusively of the collateral line.[297] Since the Oriental computation is followed, this impediment (and its multiplication) parallels that of the Latin Code. The Oriental Code also sanctions two particular laws regarding affinity where they are operative, namely, an impediment of affinity existing between the blood relatives of one spouse and the blood relatives of the other spouse to the fourth degree inclusively (computed by totaling together the degrees of consanguinity on each side); likewise, when two persons successively are married to the same third person and when two persons are successively married to two persons who were blood relatives, to the first degree (unmultiplied).

c. *dispensation*. Affinity as an impediment is of ecclesiastical law; it is a permanent impediment and ceases only by dispensation. Affinity in the direct line may be dispensed only by the Apostolic See and, especially when the marrige has been consummated, it is most rarely dispensed. The local Ordinary may dispense from the degrees of the collateral line.[298] The emergency faculties

296. c. 1077.
297. Cf. Cod. Or. cc. 67-68.
298. Cf. Motu proprio **De Episcoporum Muneribus**, IX, 15.

of dispensation from matrimonial impediments in cases of danger of death or of urgency exclude dispensation from affinity in the direct line when the marriage has been consummated.[299]

d. *penalties.* Those who attempt marriage while bound by the impediment of affinity are liable to the penalties for incest.[300] Civil laws vary in the degree in which affinity is established as an impediment to marriage, with consequent penalties for incest

11. *Public propriety*

a. *impediment.* The impediment of public propriety or decency (*honestas publica*) arises from an *invalid* marriage, whether consummated or not, and from public or notorious concubinage; it invalidates marriage in the first and second degrees of the direct line between the husband and the blood relatives of his wife, and vice versa.[301]

One foundation for the imperiment is an invalid marriage, due to lack of true consent, to defect of form, or to the presence of a diriment impediment. It makes no difference whether consummation took place or whether the union was entered into in good or bad faith (thus a putative marriage incurs the impediment), as long as there is at least an appearance of marriage, an apparent contract. When at least one party is bound by the canonical form of marriage, an attempt at a purely civil marriage, when there is no cohabitation, has not even the appearance of marriage, and consequently does not incur the impediment.[302] Usually public or notorious concubinage accompanies this civil act (or a marriage attempted before a non-Catholic minister), and thus the impediment is incurred.

Concubinage is a *modus vivendi* or relationship between a man and a woman which has a certain semblance of marital life. The parties cohabit as man and wife in sexual intercourse, without necessarily dwelling in the same abode or without necessarily involving financial arrangements, and even though the woman is already

299. cc. 1043-1045.
300. Cf. c. 2357.
301. c. 1078. Cod. Or. c. 69.
302. PCI 12 mart. 1929.

married. There must be a certain unity and continuance or perma-
nence in the carnal relations of the man and the same woman, so
that a condition of acceptance of the state of relationship exists or
an understanding perdures between them to live in an apparently
marital fashion. This stability or understanding is thus lacking in
the approach to a prostitute or in the frequency of fornication, even
with the same woman. The concubinage must also be public or notorious in the sense of canon 2197.

The degree of relationship is computed in the same way as for
consanguinity, but only in the direct line and to the second degree.
It is more commonly held that this impediment is multiplied, e.g.,
by entering into an invalid marriage or concubinage with the daughter
of a woman with whom one has already incurred this impediment.

b. *dispensation.* Being of ecclesiastical law only, this impediment does not bind the unbaptized marrying among themselves.
Becoming baptized and remaining in the conditions of the impediment, it begins to bind. The impediment is permanent and thus can
be removed only by dispensation. The local Ordinary may grant a
dispensation from either degree[303] (provided, of course, that it is
certain that one of the parties is not the offspring of the other).
The impediment may also be dispensed in danger of death or of
urgency.[304] Public propriety may be incurred in some cases of common law marriage. In rectifying an invalid marriage or in witnessing
a marriage after concubinage, dispensation from this impediment
may be indicated.

12. *Spiritual relationship*

a. *impediment.* Because of the spiritual relationship which
exists, marriage cannot be validly contracted between the one who
baptizes and the one baptized or between a baptismal sponsor and
the one baptized.[305] The Baptism conferred must be valid and abso-

303. Cf. Motu proprio **De Episcoporum Muneribus,** IX, 11-16.
304. cc. 1043-1045.
305. c. 1079. Cod. Or. c. 70 states that spiritual relationship as an impedi-
    ment exists between the one baptized and the sponsor, and between
    the sponsor and the parents of the one baptized, but not between
    the baptized and the minister. A spiritual relationship may have

lute, whether solemn or private. The impediment is not incurred if only the ceremonies are supplied or if the Baptism was conditionally conferred, unless the sponsor was the same person in both Baptisms. The minister must have been validly baptized himself at the time of the conferral of the sacrament, and the sponsors must have validly exercised their function.

b. *dispensation.* This impediment is of its nature permanent and is removed only by dispensation. It may be multiplied if the minister of the Baptism is also, by proxy, the sponsor of the one baptized. The local Ordinary may dispense; dispensation is applicable in a case of danger of death or of urgency.[306]

13. *Legal relationship or adoption*

Those who are disqualified in civil law from contracting a valid marriage because of the legal relationship arising from adoption are also impeded by canon law from contracting a valid marriage in the same circumstances.[307] This impediment has been applicable in the U.S.A. jurisdiction only to Puerto Rico. It is dispensable as in the case of public propriety.[308]

XV. *Matrimonial dispensations*

A. *Notions*

A matrimonial dispensation is a form of relaxation in a particular case of some impediment in order to contract or to convalidate a marriage and which is granted by one who has the authority. In the *external forum* it is a dispensation sought in the sight of the Church and in the expressed names of the contracting parties, not only that a marriage may be validly and lawfully contracted but also that the same may be proved, even before an ecclesiastical

existed in a marriage entered into by two baptized non-Catholics and thus the basis of contesting such a marriage in a subsequent case may exist.

306. Cf. Motu proprio **De Episcoporum Muneribus,** IX, 11-16; cc. 1043-1045.
307. c. 1080.
308. Cf. no. 306 above.

judge. In the *internal forum* it is a dispensation sought in the sight of God and in the area of conscience either sacramental or extrasacramental, with fictitious names used for the parties involved, to the effect that marriage may be validly and lawfully contracted or convalidated in good conscience without it being proved in the external forum. Unless stated otherwise, a dispensation from an occult impediment granted for the internal, extrasacramental forum is to be accurately recorded in the register kept in the diocesan secret archives (and thus the real names are then supplied), and, should the impediment later become public, no further dispensation for the external forum is necessary; but such further dispensation is necessary, if a dispensation is granted only for the internal sacramental forum.[309]

When a dispensation is granted immediately and directly to the petitioner it is said to be given *in forma gratiosa;* when, however, its execution is committed to a Bishop, confessor, or other priest, it is said to be granted *in forma commissoria.* Rescripts in the external and internal fora issued by the Holy See are usually in the latter category; Ordinaries may use either type of grant.

B. *Competent authority to dispense.* The Apostolic See, i.e., the Roman Pontiff acting through the Sacred Congregations in the external forum and through the Sacred Penitentiary in the internal forum, may dispense from all matrimonial impediments of purely ecclesiastical law (although refraining in practice regarding certain ones), but not from those of divine or natural law. The faculties enjoyed by the Apostolic Delegate and by the local Ordinary have been noted in their respective places, as well as the faculties granted in the common law to certain persons in danger of death or of urgent necessity.

C. *Taxes and expenses*

The Sacred Penitentary grants dispensations absolutely gratis. Those granted by the Holy See in the external forum are subject to varying moderate payments on the score of taxes, alms, expenses, etc., except in the case of the poor. Local Ordinaries may demand nothing on the occasion of granting a dispensation unless it is but a moderate tax to defray expenses of the chancery,

309. c. 1047.

except in the case of the poor. Delegation received by indult from the Holy See to dispense should be expressly mentioned in the dispensation.[310]

D. *Causes or reasons*

There must be reasons or causes which justify the granting of a dispensation. The priest who submits a petition is bound in conscience in each case to verify the real existence and the objective gravity of the cause or reason cited. The reason should be proportionate to the nature of the impediment from which the dispensation is sought. A primary, final or motivating reason (*causa motiva*) is one that of itself suffices for the granting of the dispensation; a secondary, persuasive or subordinate reason (*causa impulsiva*) does not of itself suffice but together with others may suffice. Canonical reasons are those who are ordinarily accepted by the Roman Curia or by the diocesan curia; otherwise they are non-canonical and may be accepted in an extraordinary case. The following are the more common canonical and non-canonical causes or reasons.

Canonical Causes

Primary

a) *spes fundata conversionis partis acatholicae.* There is evidence for prudent hope of conversion such as the fact that the non-Catholic has begun instructions to become a Catholic, not merely his good will or friendliness toward the Church or his signing of the guarantees and taking the pre-marital instructions.

b) *promissio amplectendi religionem catholicam.* The non-Catholic has promised in writing or before two witnesses to enter the Church after marriage, with sufficient reason being manifested for the delay.

c) *spes fundata conversionis familiae.* The hope that a non-Catholic family will be brought into the Church by the marriage is well-based on clear and definite circumstances.

d) *periculum apostasiae ex negata dispensatione.* The

310. c. 1057.

danger of perversion or fear of defection to a sect if the marriage is not allowed must not arise from the ill will of the parties or from a threat; the circumstances giving substance to the validity and degree of the fear should be indicated.

e) *bonum prolis natae ex partium fornicatione.* A child has been born to the parties in illicit intercourse.

f) *bonum prolis natae ex anteriore matrimonio.* In this and the previous situation a dispensation may be indicated, all things being equal, since, it can be proved, marriage alone will insure the Catholic Baptism and upbringing of the offspring.

g) *copula publica seu notoria.* The relationship must be already notorious or in the circumstances will most probably become so.

h) *scandalum aut infamia mulieris.* The scandal or loss of reputation due to pregnancy or to conduct short of intercourse can be prevented only by marriage.

i) *praegnantia ideoque legitimatio prolis.* Marriage provides for the welfare of the child and also of the mother lest she remain unwed.

j) *periculum publici concubinatus.* The couple will likely live in public concubinage.

k) *cessatio publici concubinatus.* This and the previous reason are usually reduced to the danger of marriage outside the Church or to a convalidation of an attempted marriage.

l) *grave periculum incontinentiae.* Marriage, all other things considered, will prevent scandal and danger to salvation.

m) *periculum matrimonii mere civilis vel coram ministello.* The same remarks apply as in d) above. Direct interrogation of the Catholic party on probable intentions if the dispensation is not forthcoming should not be made but by discreet indirect method information is to be gleaned by the priest indicating the presence and degree of danger of an attempted marriage and even of defection, as in the case of a weak or lax Catholic of unfortunate background, etc.

n) *convalidatio matrimonii attentati coram magistratu vel ministello.* These are cases of marriages invalid in bad faith before a minister or a justice of the peace.

o) *revalidatio matrimonii catholici*. An apparently valid marriage according to the canonical form and contracted in good faith but in which an invalidating element has been discovered.

p) *remotio gravium scandalorum*. Marriage is indicated to remove hatreds, enmities, etc., as well as concubinage.

secondary

q) *aetas superadulta*. The age must be at least the woman's twenty-fourth year completed. The exact age must be noted, and it must be well founded that the woman will have no other opportunity to marry. This cause does not pertain to a widow, unless special circumstances are present.

r) *paupertas viduae catholicae*. The age of the widow and the number of children, if any, should be noted. Marriage may furnish the opportunity for support for the widow and her children, and prevent danger of incontinence if the woman is young.

s) *angustia loci*. Applicable only where neighborhoods are small and separated and the Catholics few in number, thus reducing marital possibilities.

t) *copula occulta iam habita*. This reason indicates the danger of incontinence, the grounds for possible future scandal, and the like. Because of the secrecy involved, the cause may not be presented without permission of the parties.

u) *nimia, suspecta, periculosa familiaritas, necnon cohabitatio sub eodem tecto, quae facile impediri nequit; copulae suspicio*. The purpose is to prevent scandal in that the situation of familiarity or cohabitation is such as naturally to give rise to suspicions of illicit relations.

v) *periculum incestuosi concubinatus*. This danger is more impelling than otherwise, since it is between parties related by blood or marriage.

w) *bonum pacis*. The public peace and the extinction of quarrels, etc., between families or individuals would be served.

Non-canonical Causes

a) *on behalf of the man. Orator infirmitate detentus*. The

man has an infirmity. *Orator viduus prole oneratus.* The man is a widower with children.

     b) *on behalf of the woman. Oratrix orbata.* The woman has lost one or both parents. *Oratrix ex natalibus illegitimis.* The woman was born out of wedlock. *Oratrix infirmitate, deformitate vel alio defectu detenta.* The woman has an infirmity, deformity or some other defect. *Oratrix iam ab alio deflorata.* The woman has lost her virginity.

     c) *on behalf of both parties. Utriusque oratoris boni mores.* The good character of the parties. *Munificentia oratorum erga bonum publicum.* The generosity of the parties toward the common weal. *Viri aut mulieris adiutorio indigentia.* One party, e.g., with a family to rear, needs the help of the other. *Mutuum auxilium in provecta aetate.* Mutual aid in advanced age.

     d) *on behalf of the marriage itself. Omnia iam parata sunt ad nuptias.* Everything is prepared for the wedding. *Propositum matrimonii contrahendi iam divulgatum.* The intention of the parties to marry is well known. *Pertinacia propositi matrimonii.* The fixity of purpose to wed. *Convenientia matrimonii.* The great benefits resulting from the marriage. *Bonum parentum indigentium ex adiutorio alterius vel utriusque.* Provision is made for the welfare of a needy parent or parents.

E. *Procedure*

     The formularies for various matrimonial dispensations to be petitioned from the Holy See or from the local Ordinary are found exemplified in the approved authors or in the regulations and forms laid down by the particular diocese. A petition is usually addressed to the local Ordinary, who either himself dispenses or forwards the petition to Rome. A petition to the Sacred Penitentiary may be sent directly, especially when there is any danger to the seal, or through the Ordinary with fictitious names used. One or more of the reasons for the dispensation should be supplied and a covering letter stating in detail the circumstances of the case should also be forwarded to the Ordinary. Besides the reasons for the dispensation there should also be included the number and lowest species of the impedi-

ment in question, the name and exact address of the person to whom
the rescript is to be returned, whether or not the marriage has already been contracted and with the prescribed form, whether contracted in good faith or with a view to a more easily obtainable dispensation after the banns had been published. In the external forum
the names, parish, and diocese of the parties are to be mentioned,
with the customary statement of the financial condition of the petitioner. The priest or confessor should execute the rescript exactly as
laid down and make the proper registration.

F. Case of danger of death

1. Law

When the danger of death urges, local Ordinaries, in order to
provide for peace of conscience, and, if the case warrants, the
legitimation of offspring, can dispense both from the form to be
observed in the celebration of marriage and from each and every
impediment of ecclesiastical law, whether public or occult, even multiple, except the impediments arising from the sacred priesthood and
affinity in the direct line after a marriage has been consummated;
they may do this for their own subjects wherever they may dwell
and for all those actually dwelling in their territory, provided that
scandal is avoided and that the usual declaration and promise of
the Catholic party are given if a dispensation is granted from disparity of worship or mixed religion.[311] In these very same circumstances, but only in cases in which not even the local Ordinary can
be reached, the same faculty of dispensing is enjoyed by a pastor,
a priest who assists at marriage in conformity with c. 1098, 2°,
and a confessor, but this last enjoys it only for the internal forum
in the course of a sacramental confession.[312]

2. Pastor

a. *valid exercise.* The pastor enjoys the same faculty of

311. c. 1043. Cod. Or. c. 33.
312. c. 1044. Cod. Or. c. 34.

dispensation in the very same circumstances as it is enjoyed by the local Ordinary, but this may be exercised validly only when the local Ordinary cannot be reached. Thus there must be a physical or moral impossibility of contacting the Ordinary in time to receive back the necessary delegated faculty to dispense in the needs of the case. The use of the telephone or telegraph is not obligatory, as they are considered in law to be extraordinary means[313] over and above the ordinary means of contact, such as by recourse to the Ordinary personally or in writing, but this recourse may even be normal and recommendable especially if a case is complex.

There must be a prudent judgment or at least a serious probability of death ensuing, whether from intrinsic or extrinsic causes, but not necessarily an imminent danger (*articulus mortis*) or a certainty of death.[314] For validity also the purpose of the faculty must be present, namely, peace of conscience and/or the legitimation of offspring. The disturbance of conscience to be quieted or peace of mind to be effected may refer to the party other than the one in danger of death or than the one laboring under the impediment. It need not be restricted to a need for sacramental absolution but may include some other serious cause or obstacle that is disturbing; thus the prevention of more sin, the settlement of dissension or of an injustice would suffice. The alternative motive of legitimation of offspring is usually but not always also a matter for peace of conscience. Legitimation is effected by this faculty of offspring already conceived or born and of adulterine or sacrilegious offspring born after the parents validly marry.[315] It is disputed whether this faculty includes also adulterine or sacrilegious offspring already born; the affirmative opinion is at least probable and may be safely followed.

The pastor may dispense in the circumstances from the canonical form required for the validity of marriage. Thus he may dispense from his own presence and/or that of one or both qualified witnesses. He may not dispense from the obligation of giving or renewing consent. His faculty extends to both internal and external

313. PCI 12 nov. 1922. If there is no danger in delay, it is not an extraordinary means to have recourse through the Apostolic Delegate (PCI 27 iul. 1942). Cf. also Cod. Or. c. 34, 2.
314. The circumstance is the same as for the confessor's faculty of c. 882.
315. Cf. c. 1051; also cc. 1114; 1116.

fora, to all his subjects anywhere and to those persons present in his parish, even though they are not his subjects. Since this power given to the pastor for the circumstances is ordinary power, it may be delegated (even habitually) and subdelegated,[316] e.g., to the curate (*vicarius cooperator*).

When there is question of a dispensation from mixed religion or from disparity of religion the declaration and promise of the Catholic party must be given even in danger of death, which in an extreme case may be given at least implicitly.

b. *lawful exercise.* The pastor may not lawfully exercise this faculty in the circumstances if scandal cannot be avoided. Thus he must act in the circumstances in a way that safeguards his actions against scandal, such as revealing publicly that a dispensation has been granted and the marriage "fixed up," when the invalidity is known, or in other cases concealing the granting of a dispensation and the "straightening out" of a marriage, because the invalidity is not known or one party is a cleric or religious. If death does not ensue, the parties should at least conduct themselves so as to repair any scandal.

When the condition of danger of death allows, the usual liturgical rite of marriage is employed. Otherwise, the pastor puts to each party the question of consent and then declares the bond contracted. Dispensations granted in the external forum are to be reported promptly and with sufficient explanations to the local Ordinary and record of the marriage or of a convalidation made in the marriage and baptismal registers.[317] In dispensing it should be stated by what authority the favor is granted and for specific impediment.

3. *Assisting priest of c.* 1098, 2º

If it is impossible, without serious inconvenience, to have or to

---

316. Cf. c. 199. Some hold it to be probable that a priest with general delegation for all marriages in a parish or with delegation to assist at a particular marriage enjoys the powers to dispense in the circumstances of cc. 1044-1045, within the parish limits only and when recourse to the pastor or local Ordinary is impossible. This priest, at any rate, may act as the priest of c. 1098, 2º or as the confessor. Cf. also Cod. Or. c. 34, 1.

317. c. 1046. This canon contains obligations of themselves serious. The "promptly" means three days, unless a just cause excuses.

approach a pastor or an Ordinary or a delegate who would be authorized to assist at marriage, in danger of death, if there is at hand
another priest who can assist, he must be summoned and, together
with the witnesses, assist at the marriage.[318] This assistance is for
the lawfulness and not the validity of the marriage.

This assisting priest enjoys the faculties of dispensation as in the
case of the pastor but only regarding those at whose marriage he
assists. He may not delegate this power. He normally should first
seek to obtain delegation to assist at the marriage, unless he prudently judges this to be seriously inconvenient. Only in an extraordinary circumstance should he dispense from witnesses. He is
bound to report the dispensations and register the marriage.

4. Confessor

When it is impossible to reach any of those qualified to assist
at a marriage who are mentioned above, the confessor enjoys the
same faculties of dispensation from the canonical form and from
impediments, but only as affecting the internal forum and in the
course of a sacramental confession. No record or registration is
made. The confessor in these circumstances is every priest empowered
to hear the confession of penitents in danger of death.[319] It is not
necessary that the confession be sacramentally valid or that absolution
is imparted. Because he is limited to the internal sacramental forum,
it is doubted whether he can dispense from public impediments; it is
probable that he can do so as regards their effect in conscience.
The penitent is to be urged to approach, if possible, the pastor or
qualified priest in the external forum for rectification of the marriage
in that forum.

The confessor cannot dispense from the obligation of consent.
When he judges it prudent to dispense in the internal forum from
the canonical form, he must have the penitent renew marital consent
and notify his partner that consent must be renewed by both parties.
This he may allow the penitents to do privately and secretly, i.e.,

---

318. c. 1098, 2⁰. Cod. Or. c. 89, 2⁰ states that the available priest is to be
a Catholic priest.
319. Cf. c. 882.

externally but without the canonical form and without others know-
ing about it. If the requisite circumstances are present and he judges
it to be prudently expedient, the confessor may urge that he be
approached outside the sacramental forum and act as the assisting
priest of canon 1098, 2°.

Assistance at or convalidation of a marriage in danger of death
should be approached with great caution. In an urgency of the condition of danger of death the preparation of the soul of the dying
person by right dispositions for the sacraments is paramount. A
promise to do what is necessary to straighten out the invalid marriage
situation would suffice. Dispensation would be given from impediments and from the canonical form (if indicated), absolution imparted from sins and censures, marital consent asked for and received or renewed.

G. *Case of urgency*

1. *Law*

Local Ordinaries can dispense their own subjects wherever they
may dwell and all those actually dwelling in their territory, provided that scandal is avoided and that the usual declaration and
promise of the Catholic party are given if a dispensation is granted
from disparity of worship or mixed religion, from each and every
impediment of ecclesiastical law, whether public or occult, even
multiple, except the sacred priesthood and affinity in the direct line
after a marriage has been consummated, as often as an impediment
is discovered when everything is already prepared for the marriage
and it cannot, without probable danger of grave harm, be deferred
until a dispensation is obtained from the Holy See. This faculty is
also operative for the convalidation of a marriage already contracted, if there is the same danger in delay and time is not sufficient
for recourse to the Holy See. In the very same circumstances the
pastor, a priest who assists at marriage in conformity with canon
1098, 2°, and a confessor enjoy the *same faculty, but only for occult
cases* in which not even the local Ordinary can be reached, or not
without the danger of violation of a secret.[320]

---

320. c. 1045, 1-3.

2. *Pastor*

a. *valid exercise.* There must be the impossibility of recourse in the time remaining even to the local Ordinary who is competent to dispense with the faculties he possesses in the case. The period of delay in approaching the Holy See is longer, some few weeks.[321] Thus there must be sufficient cause to judge that the marriage is imperative and cannot be delayed for the time required to obtain the necessary dispensations or faculties. It is more probable that there is no faculty given in a case of urgency to dispense from the canonical form, as the canon makes no mention of it. The faculty enjoyed is only for *occult cases*, even though the impediment may be public by nature;[322] also when even the local Ordinary cannot be contacted without danger of violation of a secret, not only of a sacramental or confessional secret but also of any true secret which the parties may lawfully refrain from revealing. The pastor may delegate this faculty.

There must be a discovery of an impediment after the preparations for the marriage have been made (*"omnia sunt parata ad nuptias"*) ; it need not be that the impediment was altogether unknown but that it was brought to the pastor's attention after all the preparations were made,[323] even deliberately. The preparations that have been completed refer to the completion of the canonical prematrimonial requirements and not necessarily that all the secular or material preparations have been completed. In the circumstances it must be that the wedding must take place before a reply from an authority can be received. Coupled with this circumstance must be the presence of danger of grave harm or serious consequences resulting from such a delay, which danger or fear of it need be only at least probable in the prudent judgment of the pastor,[324] such as scandal, ill-repute due to pregnancy, financial loss, etc. If the probable danger of serious harm is not present, the preparations alone are not sufficient for dispensing. The same circumstances and danger must prevail regarding a convalidation.

321. Cf. n. 313 above. Even though the Apostolic Delegate has faculties, the power of the local Ordinary to dispense is not restricted.
322. PCI 28 dec. 1927.
323. PCI 1 mart. 1921.
324. Cf. Rota 25 maii. 1925.

b. *lawful exercise.* The pastor must employ his faculty in such a way as to avoid scandal. Dispensations are registered in accordance with the forum.

3. *Assisting priest of canon 1098, 2°, and the confessor*

The same conditions for validity and lawfulness apply in their respective fora. Detecting a public impediment, the confessor should arrange to have the case taken outside the sacramental forum, even if the impediment is presently occult but it is foreseen it will be divulged.

XVI. *Validation of an invalid marriage*

Validation is the process whereby an apparent marriage which is actually invalid is rendered valid in conscience and in the sight of the Church. There must have been some formality or species of a marriage contract entered into, even though it was ineffective; otherwise there would not be an invalid marriage but mere concubinage. The apparent marriage may have been invalid because at least one of the parties did not give true consent, or the canonical form was not observed, or a diriment impediment prevented the contract from being valid. Not all invalid marriages can be subsequently rendered valid. Validation may be effected either by a renewal of consent under certain conditions (simple validation) or by a dispensation from the renewal of consent (radical sanation). Other designations are given to the process of validation, such as convalidation, revalidation, rectifying, fixing up, straightening out.

A. *Simple validation*

1. *Presence of a removable diriment impediment*

The marriage is invalid because at the time it was contracted they were bound by a diriment impediment and thus unable to exchange valid consent. Even though the impediment has ceased to exist (e.g., nonage) or has been dispensed, the law requires that for the validity of the marriage consent be renewed. The fact that consent was originally exchanged (even in good faith, ignorance, etc.) and not revoked does not excuse from this obligation.[325] The renewal must be a new act of the will directed to the marriage which is known to have been invalid from the beginning.[326] The juridical effects begin from the moment of the renewal of consent and for the future.

If the impediment is public, after dispensation both parties must renew consent in the form prescribed by law,[327] so that the validation might be publicly known and scandal avoided. Usually the essentials of the juridic form are observed, with a dispensation from the banns and without the nuptial blessing or the blessing of the ring. In case the public impediment is actually not known to others, the marriage should take place with all due secrecy; but the fact must be made known if scandal has to be removed. Registration is made in the usual registers.

If the impediment is occult and known to both parties, after dispensation it suffices that both parties give a new consent privately and secretly.[328] Thus, in the external forum the marriage is considered valid and disclosure of invalidity by a public renewal would be apt to raise scandal. Although the parties may express their mutual consent (which need not be simultaneous) without others being aware and without pastor and witnesses, it is recommendable to exchange consent before a priest and in the usual formula. Consent may be renewed by other signs than by words as long as they are external and the parties mutually realize what is being signified. If one party refuses to make the renewal, a radical sanation may be in order.

If the impediment is occult and known only to one party, after dispensation it suffices for this party to renew consent privately and secretly, provided that the consent of the other party perseveres.[329]

325. c. 1133. Cod. Or. c. 122.
326. c. 1134. Cod. Or. c. 123.
327. c. 1135, 1. Cod. Or. c. 124, 1.
328. Ibid., 2. Cod. Or. ibid., 2.
329. Ibid., 3. Cod. Or., ibid., 3.

The party aware of the nullity may renew consent implicitly, e.g., by carnal intercourse with marital affection, but it is recommendable that the confessor or priest elicit from this party an explicit expression of consent.

If the impediment is occult and unknown to both parties, they should be told so that they might live chastely until validation is effected, or at least one party should be acquainted with the fact so that consent might be renewed. If even this is not possible without foreseeable danger developing, such as material sins becoming formal, desertion with serious danger to the spouse or the children, etc., they may be left in good faith until a dispensation is obtained or a radical sanation effected. The case in which the marriage cannot be validated is considered below, together with the precautions to be noted respecting every invalid marriage.

2. Lack of consent

A marriage that is invalid because of a defect of consent is validated if the party who did not consent now supplies it, provided that the consent given by the other party perseveres. If both parties are cognizant of the lack of consent, it is better that both renew consent. If the defect of consent was merely internal, it is sufficient that consent be now given interiorly, e.g., if unknown to others a wholly simulated consent was given. If the defect of consent was also external (attestable by two witnesses willing and able to testify), it is necessary also to manifest consent externally either in the form prescribed by law, if the defect was public, or in some private and secret manner, if it was occult.[330]

3. Defect of form

A marriage that is invalid because of a defect of the canonical form can be validated only by a renewal of consent in the prescribed form.[331] If one party will not appear for the new celebration

330. c. 1136, 1-3. Cod. Or. c. 125, 1-3.
331. c. 1137. Cod. Or. c. 126.

either personally or by proxy, or if there would be proportionate danger or scandal in manifesting the nullity, a dispensation from the form or a radical sanation may be petitioned.

B. *Radical sanation*

1. *Nature and effect*

Radical sanation (*sanatio in radice*) is a retroactive or retrospective validation, a healing in the root, i.e., a healing of the consent, since this latter is the root and basis of marriage. It is the act by which a marriage is validated effecting, besides a dispensation from or a cessation of the impediment, a dispensation from the law requiring renewal of consent, as well as a retroactive reinstatement by a fiction of the law, of the canonical effects of marriage,[332] and dating from the moment when the marital consent was truly but invalidly given.

The validation (and the sacrament, if the parties are baptized) is effected as of the moment when the favor is granted; but its retroactive effect (but not the sacrament) is understood to date from the beginning of the marriage, unless some restriction is expressly stated in the rescript. Dispensation from the law of renewal of consent can be granted even if one or both parties are unaware of the favor.[333] Radical sanation is perfect if both parties are dispensed from renewal of consent and there is retroaction of canonical effects to the beginning; otherwise it is imperfect if any element is lacking. The principal retroactive effect is to make legitimate and not merely legitimated children, if they were born after the consent given by the parents to the marriage which the radical sanation now validates. Radical sanation can be granted after the death of one of the parties but only for canonical effects and not the bond itself. If the terms of a rescript of radical sanation should require renewal of consent, the nature and retroactive power of the act are not thereby changed.

2. *Required conditions*

"Any marriage entered into with the consent of both which was

---

332. c. 1138, 1. Cod. Or. c. 127, 1.
333. Ibid., 2-3. Cod. Or., ibid., 2-3.

naturally sufficient but juridically insufficient because of an ecclesiastical impediment or because of defect of canonical form can be radically sanated, provided the consent perseveres. But the Church does not sanate a marriage contracted with an impediment of the natural or the divine law, even if later the impediment ceases, not even from the moment of the cessation of the impediment, although it can, and for special reasons has.[334] If there is a lack of consent in both parties or in one party, the marriage cannot be radically sanated, whether the consent was lacking from the beginning or, if originally given, was later revoked. But if the consent was lacking in the beginning but was later given, the sanation can be granted from the moment when the consent was given.[335] Consent is considered to exist until it is positively revoked, even though the parties knew they could not contract a valid marriage originally, or they intend to separate or have already separated, or one party refuses to renew consent according to the canonical form. The character of consent is judged by what was factually done, not by what would have been done if knowledge, only later acquired, was possessed at the time.

Besides an impediment that is dispensable and a true consent that is perduring, there must also be a serious justifying cause for a radical sanation,—a situation that does not allow of the more normal process of simple validation. Thus, if neither party can be informed of the invalidity without serious harm arising, e.g., due to lack of proper jurisdiction in the assisting priest, or because the marriage would break up with great injury resulting to the children, or if a non-Catholic spouse will not renew consent according to the canonical form, reason exists to petition a radical sanation. The reason for the sanation must be in addition to that for dispensing an impediment. The clauses of the rescript received must be exactly executed.

---

334. c. 1139, 1-2. Cod. Or. c. 128, 1-2. Cf. case of cessation of ligamen, sanation granted (S. C. Sac. 9 feb. 1957). The S.C.D.F. may grant a radical sanation in certain special cases when the Catholic party is clearly repentant but the other party is opposed to the Catholic Baptism of future offspring.
335. c. 1140, 1-2. Cod. Or. c. 129, 1-2.

3. Competent authority

A radical sanation can be granted only by the Holy See.[336] However, local Ordinaries are empowered to grant a radical sanation, provided consent perdures, for marriages invalid because of an impediment of minor grade or because of defect of form, even in the case of mixed marriages or the impediment of disparity of cult, provided, in the latter cases, that the prescriptions of law and the restrictions of the Holy See are observed.[337]

The U.S.A. Ordinaries by their quinquennial faculties can grant a radical sanation, under certain conditions, for marriages (of their own subjects anywhere and of others in their territory) attempted before a civil officer or a non-Catholic minister, where the impediment existed of mixed religion or disparity of worship, and for marriages invalidly contracted due to an impediment of major or minor grade, except the impediments arising from the priesthood and affinity in the direct line when the marriage has been consummated.

C. Cautions

1. Every pastor and priest in the external forum and every confessor in the internal forum is aware that, besides the norms of the common law and the regulations and procedures of a particular diocese, extreme caution and prudence must be employed in matters of marital validation. Haste in validating an invalid marriage sometimes worsens an already bad situation; on the other hand, any factual approval or acceptance of an unlawful union supplies the material for scandal. In these cases, which are often complex and

---

336. c. 1141. Cod. Or. c. 130, 1. By their quinquennial faculties (S.C.E.O. 16 maii 1957), outside their patriarchates Metropolitans and other local Ordinaries (except Vicars General) of the Oriental rites, who have no superior below the Holy See, can radically sanate the mixed marriages of their subjects which are invalidly celebrated for lack of form, even if the non-Catholic party refuses to give the guarantees, so long as the Catholic party has duly given them and it is morally certain the entire progeny will be educated as Catholics.

337. Motu proprio **Pastorale Munus**, nos. 21-22; **Matrimonia Mixta**, n. 16; **De Episcoporum Munus**, IX, 16-18.

difficult, the common good must be safeguarded, even at the sacrifice of individuals.

2. When an invalid union is discovered it is lawful to dissimulate or to omit to enlighten and to warn the parties only 1) when there is good faith on the part of both parties in that neither is aware of the invalidity, 2) when others are ignorant of the invalidity so that scandal will not arise, 3) when there is a proportionately grave reason for permitting a material sin, which is still an evil. Under these *certain* conditions such a reason would be present if the marriage is *incurably null* and the parties, although in good faith, probably would not have the courage to make the heroic sacrifice of separation, especially if there are children or financial or other problems.

3. In some cases the better procedure is separation with a subsequent declaration of nullity. Such instances would exist when the parties certainly are unsuited to each other, or where the Catholic party does not wish to validate the marriage or where validation is not possible in the circumstances, or when divorce has taken place.

4. If the nullity of the marriage is unknown to both parties, and unknown also to others, and it is prudently judged that they can be beneficially warned of their condition, they should be told and required to separate from bed and to live in such a way that all proximate danger or occasion of sin is removed. Petition made to the local Ordinary for temporary permission to live as brother and sister may be in order. If there is an indispensable impediment, however, the circumstances may recommend the procedures of 1 or 2 above or of the brother and sister arrangement as described below. If it is judged that only one party could be profitably informed, but the nullity is incurable, the same approach would be used. If there is a dispensable impediment, the party can be informed after the dispensation has been obtained (in order to avoid formal occasion of sin) and simple validation take place or a radical sanation sought for sufficient reason without knowledge of the parties.

5. If the nullity of a marriage is publicly known, then for the avoidance of continued scandal the parties must separate until everything is arranged for the validation. If the nullity is canonically

public but factually not known and there is sufficient cause militating against separation, the local Ordinary should be petitioned for a brother-sister arrangement. If the parties desire validation but are not willing to separate to the extent required to avoid the proximate occasion of sin until the marriage is rectified, the local Ordinary should be consulted. If, however, the marriage is incurably null or should not in prudence be validated, separation should take place and a decree of nullity obtained.

6. If invalidity is known only to one party and not to the other and not to others, either separation must take place and a decree of nullity obtained or a brother-sister arrangement sought, if the marriage is incurably invalid. If the marriage can be validated and ought to be, the party cognizant of the invalidity must neither seek nor render the marital debt, whether or not the other party can be profitably informed of the invalidity until validation is effected.

7. When a marriage problem is discovered by the priest in either form, or presented to him, he must act with all deliberate prudence avoiding haste in attempting to validate or precipitateness in informing the parties of the invalidity. No more than a promise to do what he can to help and to investigate the case should be given to the parties, but no hope of satisfactory solution until all the facts and circumstances have been assembled and carefully examined. Simple validation is the normal process to be pursued, with radical sanation as the last resort.

8. When validation is not possible at all, or when it cannot be effected until such time as all requisite data has been presented to the local curia, petition may be made to the local Ordinary for a temporary or permanent brother-sister arrangement, as the case indicates. Even though a marriage may have been entered into invalidly but cannot be canonically so established, the Church does not allow a second marriage already contracted to be validated.[338] There must be *compelling serious reasons* for allowing continued cohabitation in an invalid union, together with the *absence of danger of incontinence and scandal.* All cases of brother-sister petition which are in any way canonically public, formally or materially, or will become so, should be referred to the

338. S.C.D.F. on so-called "Good Conscience" cases, 11 apr. 1973.

local Ordinary alone for decision. Some dioceses have specific regulations and procedures. A confessor in the sacramental forum is
restricted by what he can learn of the penitent and from the penitent.
Thus, if he has any doubt concerning the public or occult character
of the problem, he ought not to permit a brother-sister arrangement
but urge that the problem be taken into the external forum. Even if
a case before the confessor is *certainly* and *completely occult* (in
which situation alone he ought to act), the danger in granting such
permission is such that the confessor is cautioned by expert authorities almost never to grant such permission in the confessional.

XVII. *Dissolution of the marriage bond*

Marriage is of its nature perpetual and indissoluble; by divine
institution what God has joined together no man may dissolve.
There is no human power or authority which is capable or qualified
to dissolve a valid marital bond; this is the prerogative of the divine
author and the restorer of the institution of marriage. This authority
has been communicated by Christ to his Church in a restricted degree,
i.e., with regard to certain types of valid bond and under specific
conditions.

A. *Sacramental and consummated marriage*

"A valid sacramental and consummated marriage (*ratum et consummatum*) cannot be dissolved by any human power or for any
cause except death."[339] History proves that the Roman Pontiffs have
always been conscious of this impossibility, even in face of the direst
consequences. This intrinsic and extrinsic indissolubility is thus of
divine law. This is certain teaching, as marriage is taught to be
indissoluble even in a case of adultery, and consequently for lesser
cause.[340] The Church will never grant a dispensation in a marriage
case where there is a possibility of its existence as a sacramental

---

339. c. 1118. Cod. Or. c. 107.
340. Florence, Denz.-Schön. 1327; Trent, Denz.-Schön. 1805, 1807; Pius
     XI, ency. **Casti Connubii**. Cf. Vatican II, Const. **Gaudium et Spes**,
     n. 48; Decree **Apostolicam Actuositatem**, n. 11.

and consummated union. Although a consummated marriage is naturally perfect in its firmness inasmuch as it actually achieves the primary end of marital union, it is especially perfect as a sacred sign of Christ's union with his Church.[341]

B *Sacramental but unconsummated marriage*

1. *Fact*

Unconsummated marriage between baptized persons or between a baptized person and one not baptized is dissolved both by the law itself upon solemn religious profession and by dispensation granted by the Holy See for a just cause at the petition of both parties or of one party even though the other is unwilling.[342]

2. *Solemn religious profession*

The Church has recognized the greater bond which exists between man and God through solemn religious profession over the force of a union between man and woman united to each other by consent alone in a marriage which is not yet consummated.[343] She

341. **Summa Theol., Suppl.,** q. 61. a. 2, ad 1: "Before consummation marriage signifies the union of Christ with the soul by grace, which is dissolved by a contrary spiritual disposition, namely, mortal sin. But after consummation it signifies the union of Christ with the Church, as regards the assumption of human nature into the unity of Person, which union is altogether indissoluble." **Ibid.,** q. 67, a. 2, ad 3: "Although indissolubility belongs to the second intention of marriage as fulfilling an office of nature, it belongs to its first intention as a sacrament of the Church. Hence, from the moment it was made a sacrament of the Church, as long as it remains such it cannot be a matter of dispensation, except perhaps by the second kind of dispensation" (or miraculous dispensation).

342. c. 1119. Cod. Or. c. 108.

343. Trent, Denz-Schön. 1806. **Summa Theol., Suppl.,** q. 61, a. 2: "Before marital intercourse there is only a spiritual bond between husband and wife, but afterwards there is a carnal bond between them. Wherefore, just as after marital intercourse marriage is dissolved by carnal death, so by entering religion the bond which exists before the consummation of the marriage is dissolved, because religious life is a kind of spiritual death, whereby a man dies to the world and lives to God." For the fulness of Apostolic power by which the Church acts, cf. n. 347 below.

has declared that this solemn religious profession upon taking place dissolves a valid marriage whether with a baptized or an unbaptized partner (through a dispensation from disparity of worship or through conversion), on condition that it has not been consummated. It is exclusively the *solemn* religious *profession*, which embraces a vow of perfect chastity, which enjoys this power of dissolution; no simple vow nor also the vow solemnized in the reception of sacred orders dissolves a valid marriage.[344] A record of the solemn profession and the dissolution of the marriage bond must be entered in the parish registers.

Since a married person cannot validly be received into a novitiate while the marital bond exists, a dispensation must be obtained from the Holy See.[345] At the same time a further petition may request a shortening of the time before solemn religious profession in order to free the spouse remaining in the world for contracting a subsequent marriage. This latter spouse may petition a dissolution of a sacramental (if both are baptized) but unconsummated marriage. In either case, the non-consummation of the marriage must be satisfactorily proved. The testimony of the free state of the party remaining in the world to contract a subsequent marriage must always contain proof of nonconsummation and of solemn profession effected.

3. *Papal dispensation*

a. *power*

It is "Catholic doctrine"[346] that the Church can dissolve an un-

344. The Jesuit simple vow annuls only a marriage which is celebrated after the vow is taken.
345. c. 542, 1⁰.
346. Cf. S. C. Sac. 7 maii 1923; S. Off. 12 iun. 1942; Pius VII (Brief, 8 nov. 1803) Denz-Schön. 2705-2706; Pius IX Syllabus, Prop. 67, Denz-Schön. 2967; Pius XII, **Allocution to the Rota** (3 oct. 1941): "It is superfluous . . . yet it is not inappropriate to repeat that sacramental marriage which has been consummated is indissoluble by the law of God, so that it cannot be dissolved by any human power (c. 1118); whereas other marriages, though they are intrinsically indissoluble, have not absolute extrinsic indissolubility, but, granted certain necessary prerequisites (We are speaking, as you know, of cases which are relatively rare) can be dissolved, not only in virtue of the Pauline privilege, but also by the Roman Pontiff in virtue of his ministerial power."

consummated marriage in which at least one party is baptized. The Roman Pontiffs have for centuries employed their fulness of Apostolic power, i.e., their ministerial or vicarious power,[347] in dissolving such unions, and such constant and general discipline of the Church is regarded as pertaining to the indirect object of infallibility. However, the Holy See does not act in such cases unless there is certified proof that the marriage was really not consummated and that there is a just cause for granting the dispensation. Such dispensation is sparingly granted as an extraordinary remedy to provide for the salvation of souls.

b. *proof of non-consummation*

The manner of proof of this fact is carefully regulated by the local Ordinary, normally by competently supervised inspection and the testimony of appropriate witnesses. The woman in the case should never be advised to consult a physician before the case has been submitted to the episcopal curia for consideration and instructions, as this may complicate later findings. The consummation is taken in the canonical sense of true and natural intercourse after the celebration of valid marriage; thus offspring may have been produced before marriage by illicit relations or even after marriage by means of fecundation that canonically cannot be considered certainly as consummation. The consummation of marriage is always presumed until adequate proof is presented to the contrary; non-consummation is usually most difficult of certification, especially if the woman has remarried. A forced or an unconsciously performed conjugal act is nevertheless true consummation. A case is seriously prejudiced and even its continuance as a case jeopardized where it appears that there has been an avoidance of consummation through the practice of onanism or birth prevention.

347. Mt. 16:19: "And I will give to thee the keys of the kingdom of heaven; and whatsoever thou shalt bind on earth shall be bound in heaven, and whatsoever thou shalt loose on earth shall be loosed in heaven." 28:20: "And behold I am with you all through the days that are coming, until the consummation of the world."

c. *causes*

Frequently a just cause for dispensation is probable impotency, where it cannot be sufficiently determined whether or not the defect antedated the celebration of the marriage, or whether or not it is perpetual. In such cases a second marriage is often forbidden without leave of the Holy See. Other causes are similar to the following examples: the spiritual welfare of one or both parties after separation following an unconsummated marriage, which may include civil divorce and especially another civil marriage; the legitimation of offspring involved in the previous example;[348] voluntary and too protracted a delay of one spouse in consummating the marriage; extraordinary and implacable conflicts between the spouses; crime which especially results in a long prison term; the claim, which is not sufficiently proved, that the marriage is null through fear or defective consent, together with certainty of non-consummation; disease, especially that which impedes the use of marriage; probable great scandal or family quarrels that will develop.

d. *cautions*

Since the marriage in question is a valid union, and often sacramental, the efforts of the priest in both fora must be to try to reconcile the parties, to remove the difficulty or ameliorate the problem, especially when the spouses continue to live together and where there are children, even employing the aid of a reputable Catholic physician or expert. If the efforts appear unpromising or even harmful, consideration then can be given to a possible dissolution. This is more indicated when the union has hopelessly foundered and when in addition civil proceedings have been initiated.

The priest or confessor suspecting the elements of a non-consummation case should not enlighten the parties of a possibility of dissolution. Discreet questioning, preferably outside the confessional, will tend to bring out pertinent factors in the case. Assertions and

---

348. Legitimation of offspring which took place by an unconsummated marriage contracted after the birth is not affected by the dispensation.

remarks made by the spouses and others at a time when they are not aware of the value and utility of the information are weighty. All information should be carefully recorded. A dispensation is not necessarily granted only in view of another bond to be contracted. It is effective when granted and not upon the entrance into another union. The dispensation is to be noted in the matrimonial and baptismal registers. The case is a chancery or tribunal case and is only pursued under proper instructions.

Since a case of this kind is usually quite involved and the matters it concerns are often not easily susceptible of proof, greatest forethought should precede sponsorship of this type of case. The dispensation is strictly a favor from the Holy See and one to which the parties can lay no claim. The avoidance of any scandal or a consequence of disrespect for the Church or the sanctity of marriage is always to be kept in mind.

C. *Pauline privilege case*

1. *Privilege*

"But to those who are married, not I, but the Lord commands that a wife is not to depart from her husband, and if she departs, that she is to remain unmarried or be reconciled to her husband. And let not a husband put away his wife. For to the rest I say, not the Lord: If any brother has an unbelieving wife and she consents to live with him, let him not put her away. And if a woman has an unbelieving husband and he consents to live with her, let her not put away her husband. . . . But if the unbeliever departs, let him depart. For a brother or sister is not under bondage in such cases, but God has called us to peace."[349]

The law of indissolubility is relaxed in a marriage which has been contracted by *two unbelievers,* that is *unbaptized* parties, if on the conversion of one to the Christian faith through *Baptism* the other remaining unbaptized consents to live together either *not at all* or *not peaceably,* inasmuch as the convert can enter a new marriage upon which marriage the preceding marriage, even though consum-

349. 1 Cor 7: 10-16.

mated, is *ipso facto* dissolved. St. Paul recognized two situations attendant upon conversion. In one instance the unbaptized or unbelieving partner agrees to live in peace with the new convert and thus conversion is no cause for the breakup of the marriage but rather an anticipated benefit for the unconverted spouse and present or future children. On the other hand, many prospective converts would be restrained from embracing the faith on account of the marital difficulties that would result. Thus, if the unbeliever refuses to live together or at least in peace, thereby departing in the language of St. Paul, the convert is not bound to restrain him or to entice him back to a restoration of the marital union. Ancient teaching and practice, and the legislation of the Church have confirmed this privilege, which was promulgated by St. Paul under divine inspiration.

2. *Conditions*

a. *conversion*

There must be a true and *valid* marriage contracted when *both* parties are *unbaptized*.[350] When there are several wives or when there have been several marriages, there must be an investigation from the beginning to determine which is the first lawful wife. One spouse must be *converted* to the Christian faith.[351] The privilege does not apply when both parties become baptized at the same time, nor does it apply to a baptized party who contracted marriage with an unbaptized with a dispensation from disparity of worship.[352] The spouse who has been converted from unbelief must not have lapsed again into unbelief or atheism and must be still married to an *unbaptized* partner. The conversion must be through a certainly established Baptism of *water*, thus excluding catechumens.[353] If both

---

350. c. 1120, 1. Cod. Or. c. 109, 1.
351. Normally it is conversion to the Catholic faith, but the Church may allow the privilege to the baptized convert in a non-Catholic sect in order to free him to marry a Catholic party (cf. S. Off. 6 maii 1959).
352. c. 1120, 2. Likewise, it does not apply to a baptized non-Catholic who marries an unbaptized person.
353. S. Off. 13 mart. 1901; S.C.P.F. 16 ian. 1803.

spouses should become baptized, even unbeknown to each other, there is no Pauline case. The privilege also does not apply to two doubtfully baptized non-Catholics; recourse to the Holy See must be made in the case of a doubtfully baptized non-Catholic and an unbaptized spouse.[354] The convert spouse without forfeiting the privilege may have lived for some time after conversion and baptism in marital union with the unbaptized spouse, even consummating the marriage again.[355]

b. *departure*

The valid cause for the application of the Pauline privilege is the unjust "departure" (physical or moral) of the unbaptized party.[356]

Physical desertion on the part of the unbeliever after the Baptism of the convert which takes place for any reason at all is a cause for applying the privilege, *as long as the convert has provided no just and reasonable cause for such departure,*[357] e.g., by adultery. The departure may be either *involuntary*, such as slavery, capture, imprisonment, perpetual insanity of the unbaptized party, etc., which prevent cohabitation, or *voluntary*, such as a refusal of the unbeliever to cohabit or to move to another dwelling place, the contracting of a second marriage which the unbaptized party refuses to or cannot abandon, departure out of hatred of the Christian faith, disappearance in order to avoid the interpellations, etc.[358]

Moral departure or desertion takes place when the unbaptized party refuses to cohabit peacefully with the convert without offense to the Creator. Moral desertion is present when danger to the convert of perversion by the unbaptized spouse is present, such as impelling the convert to give up the Catholic faith, or to commit a serious sin, or to impede the convert from practicing the faith or observing the

---

354. S. Off. 11 iul. 1866; 10 iun. 1937.
355. c. 1124. Cod. Or. c. 113.
356. If the unbaptized party retracts his departure the marriage may be dissolved by c. 1127.
357. Cf. c. 1123.
358. S. Off. 12 iun. 1850; 22 nov. 1871; 8 iul. 1891; S.C.P.F. 5 mart. 1787.

laws of God or the Church or from educating present or future children in the faith.[359] Likewise, when there is offense to the Creator given by the unbaptized party, such as habitual blasphemy, constant ridicule of the Catholic religion and practices, a life of concubinage or habitual adultery. Also, when conjugal servitude is laid upon the convert inasmuch as the common life is made odious and morally intolerable by quarrels, fights, etc., without just cause, by a dissolute manner of life, criminal pursuits, etc. The motive for the departure may be other than the conversion itself of the baptized convert, as long as no just and reasonable cause after Baptism was provided by the latter and conjugal life in practice is impossible.[360]

c. interpellations

Before *validly* contracting a new marriage the convert must ask the questions: 1) whether the unbaptized spouse is also willing to be converted and to receive Baptism, and 2) if not, whether the unbaptized party is willing to dwell peaceably with the convert without offense to the Creator.

The divine law requires proof of the departure of the unconverted spouse if the departure cannot be otherwise made evident;[361] the normal means of certification required for validity of the use of the Pauline privilege are the interpellations. The law of interpellations binds *all* the baptized *always*, unless dispensed.

Only the Holy See can dispense from the law of interpellations,[362] and thus those who become baptized in a non-Catholic communion are unable to apply the Pauline privilege without making the interpellations or without a dispensation from the same. Dispensation may be sought because of the impossibility of locating the unbaptized party, of grave danger resulting to the convert or others in making the interpellations, etc. The interpellations are to be regularly made after the conversion and Baptism of the Catholic party and before that of the unbaptized spouse. However, the local Ordinary

359. S. Off. 5 aug. 1795; 5 mart. 1816; 11 iul. 1866; 14 dec. 1848.
360. Ibid., 5 mart. 1787; 4 iul. 1855; 11 iul. 1866.
361. c. 1121, 1. Cod. Or. cc. 110-112 cover the procedure of interpellations. Cf. S. Off. 12 iun. 1850.
362. c. 1121, 2.

may permit, for a serious reason, that the interpellation of the unbaptized party be made before the Baptism of the party being converted to the faith. Also, for a serious reason, he may dispense from
the interpellations before the Baptism of the converted party, provided, in the latter case, that the proof he had from at least a summary and extrajudicial process that the interpellations cannot be
made or would be useless.[363]

It is sufficient that the interpellations be made once, but out
of charity they may be made more than once. They may be made
in the summary judicial form, i.e., before the Ordinary of the convert or his delegate, which is very seldom done; or in the summary
extrajudicial form, i.e., an authorized delegate of the Ordinary
making contact either in person or by official letter, which is the
usual form; or in a private form, i.e., privately by the convert
party,—which interpellations are valid albeit to be prcved in the
external forum, and lawful if authorized by the local Ordinary.[364]

If the interrogated unbaptized party answers both questions in
the negative, departure is verified and the Pauline privilege is applicable. If the answers to both questions are in the affirmative, there
is no departure and the privilege is not applicable. If the answer to
the first question only is in the affirmative and in the negative to
the second *without a just reason* being given, the unbaptized party
is considered to be insincere and thus to have departed, allowing
the application of the privilege.

If the first question is answered in the negative but the second
in the affirmative, there is no departure, unless the unbaptized party
later ceases to dwell in peace with the convert. If there is doubt
regarding the seriousness or sincerity of the answers, the Holy See
should be consulted.[365] If the unbaptized party refuses to answer
the questions at all or within the appointed time, the refusal or
silence can be judged a negative reply.[366] A negative reply may be
explicit or implicit.

363. Motu proprio **Pastorale Munus**, no. 23.
364. c. 1122. S. Off. 12 iun. 1850.
365. S. Off. 29 nov. 1882; 8 iul. 1891; 26 apr. 1899.
366. c. 1122, 1.

3. *Use of the privilege*

The convert party does not lose the right to use the Pauline privilege if the unbaptized spouse again departs after a reconciliation and resumption of marital life after Baptism, even with renewed consummation.[367] New interpellations may be made to verify the departure. Although the convert is not obliged to use his right to dissolution of marriage by the Pauline privilege, he is obliged at least to effect a suspension of the common life if this is the only means of avoiding grave danger of perversion for himself of the offspring. If, after the Baptism of one spouse marital life is continued and the other spouse also receives or seriously intends to receive Baptism, the right to a second marriage by the Pauline privilege is lost.

4. *Effect of the privilege*

The bond of the former marriage which was contracted in unbelief is dissolved *only* at the time when the baptized party contracts a new marriage *validly*.[368] Thus the unbaptized party is bound by the impediment of bond (*ligamen*) until the convert has validly contracted a new bond. The new marriage of the convert must be contracted with a *Catholic* party. Due to the impediments of mixed religion and (in this case) of disparity of worship, a Catholic never has the unrestricted right to marriage with a non-Catholic, nor does the Pauline privilege concede this right.[369]

In summary form it can be stated that the *right* to the Pauline privilege, i.e., to interpellate, is acquired at the time of the Baptism of the convert; the *cause* for its use is the unjust departure of the unbaptized spouse; the *use* of the privilege is not of obligation nor does it cease by non-use; the *effect* of the privilege, i.e., the dissolution of the natural bond contracted when both parties were unbap-

---

367. Cf. cc. 1123; 1124. Cod. Or. 112; 113.
368. c. 1126. Cod. Or. c. 115.
369. Cod. Or. c. 112 expressly mentions a new marriage "**cum persona catholica**." S.C.D.F. 24 iul. 1970 states that henceforth the "favor of the faith" or conversion of the other party must be verified.

cized, is had upon the valid contracting of the second marriage.

5. Cautions

Before admitting a prospective convert to instructions, and certainly before any Baptism, an investigation must be made by the pastor or priest to determine the canonical and civil marital status of the party. A complete course or period of instructions in the Catholic faith as well as a sufficient time in the practice of the faith is a normal requirement (which may be more precisely determined by local regulation). It is a most prudent caution (if not otherwise prescribed) for the pastor or priest not to baptize a convert in a possible Pauline privilege case (especially a divorced person) before approbation by the local Ordinary or curia verifies the presence of all necessary requisites for the use of the privilege.

A prospective convert who is under instructions, being in this case already validly married, must not keep company with another person, or, if marriage has been attempted a second time, must separate from this new partner. The Catholic must be strongly admonished about his obligations and the dangers involved. If separation is not possible in the circumstances, a petition for a temporary brother-sister arrangement may be made. It should be noted that any intercourse engaged in by the baptized party after Baptism (being adultery), unless condoned, affords the unconverted spouse cause for just departure and renders the Pauline privilege inapplicable. If the party wishing to enter the Church has been baptized in a sect subsequent to the original marriage, conditional Baptism will follow the norms of prudence mentioned above for approbation before the interpellations are sought. Where there has been an attempted marriage with a baptized party, the impediment of crime is to be investigated and dispensation sought. Oftentimes factors in a Pauline privilege case may change the situation into another category of dissolution in favor of the faith (Petrine privilege) or into a sacramental unconsummated marriage case. Likewise it is not a Pauline privilege as such if the prospective convert is the unbaptized party wishing to marry a Catholic and if the original spouse of the prospective convert was subsequently baptized in a sect. In every case, all danger of scandal must be avoided. The pastor or priest is not to inform a convert of the possibility of a dissolution, Pauline or otherwise, until all the facts are in, or promise any favorable outcome, since such cases often consume much time and investigation.

The Pauline privilege case usually requires such documentation as the following: the formal petition, the certificates of marriage and divorce (if obtained), affidavits or testimonies from the convert and the non-convert parties and from their witnesses to prove the non-baptism at the time of the marriage and that the convert was not responsible for the departure, the certificate of Baptism if received after the marriage, the answer to the interpellations or the dispensation from them.

D. *Petrine privilege cases*

All cases of marriage which are not clearly dissoluble under the terms of the Pauline privilege must then, to be dissoluble, come under the *vicarious and ministerial* or instrumental power, the fullness of Apostolic power, committed to Peter and his successors.[370] Whenever there is question of the Baptism of one of the spouses, the marriage becomes subject to the Church. All instances in which a valid marriage is dissoluble for the purpose of allowing one party either to embrace the Catholic faith or to preserve the same are called "privilege of the faith" or "favor of the faith" cases. This obviously pertains to the Pauline privilege. However, other situations have developed in which valid bonds have been dissolved in favor of the faith and which derive their dissolubility from the supreme vicarious power of the Roman Pontiffs. Authors and the Code itself do not always employ the generic terms "privilege of the faith" and "favor of the faith" in the same way, referring sometimes to the Pauline privilege and at other times to non-Pauline cases and even to both together. For practical purposes the following cases, since they are not, or at least not clearly, contained under the Pauline privilege, are listed under the so-called Petrine privilege. Like the Pauline, the Petrine privilege is a favor and not a right, and thus

370. Cf. no. 347 above.

the Church may impose certain regulations for the granting of the favor—which in every case means the dissolution of a natural bond or non-sacramental marriage.

1. *Apostolic Constitutions*

Certain papal provisions which were once made for particular places have been extended by the Code to other regions also in the same circumstances.[371] Local diocesan curias are not usually apt to consider a case solely on the basis of the Constitutions but rather on some other grounds.

a. *"Altitudo" of Paul III.*

This provision (June 1, 1537) concerns a polygamous convert[372] who does not remember which of his wives he married first, i.e., with whom he first gave true marital consent. In this case he is permitted to retain whichever one he chooses. There are no inter-pellations required. If the convert remembers the wife he first law-fully married, he must retain her and dismiss the others. The poly-gamy may be successive as well as simultaneous.[373] The person he chooses may even be in the third degree of consanguinity, which is thus dispensed by the Constitution. Even if another spouse desires to receive Baptism and the one chosen does not, the convert may still choose the latter. If the one chosen is unbaptized, there is implicitly granted a dispensation from disparity of worship.[374] Al-though the guarantees (*cautiones*) are to be made *ad cautelam*, there must at least be absent any danger of sinning for the convert party and a firm resolve to provide for the Catholic education of the children and the conversion of the unbaptized spouse.[375] Renewal

---

371. c. 1125. Cod. Or. c. 114. c. 1127 can be applied to the Constitutions. Such marriages and the faculty employed must be inscribed in the proper registers.
372. Included also is a polyandrous convert (S. Off. 5 sept. 1855).
373. S.C.P.F. 14 ian. 1806.
374. S. Off. 30 iun. 1937.
375. If the unbaptized party is a Jew or a Mohammedan, there must also be absent any danger of ritual circumcision or other religious rite or invocation.

of matrimonial consent in the usual form is always made, at least *ad cautelam*. This Constitution is hardly application in countries like the U.S.A. where civil ceremonies and records usually can identify the first spouse.

b. *"Romani Pontificis"* of Pius V.

This Constitution (Aug. 2, 1571) deals with polygamists, whether simultaneous or successive, i.e., who have exchanged marital consent with more than one person. It permits them upon conversion to choose any one of their wives who has been or who is willing to be baptized and to retain her to the exclusion of the others, even though she was not the first one who was lawfully married. The reason required is the very great difficulty for the convert to be separated from the chosen partner with whom he is living and who is willing also to locate the first wife. There are no interpellations.[377] The wife chosen should be baptized previous to the renewal of marital consent; this latter renewal must be made in the canonical form.[378] The Constitution does not include any dispensation from consanguinity in the third degree. If, however, the first wife spontaneously declares that she is willing to be baptized or has already been baptized, recourse should be had to the Holy See; it has been indicated that this Constitution applies also in such a case.[379]

c. *"Populis"* of Gregory XIII

In the case (Jan. 25, 1385) of anyone, whether polygamist or not, who has contracted marriage in unbelief, faculties are granted for both fora to dispense from the interpellations when it appears from a summary and extrajudicial process either that it is impossible (physically or morally) to interpellate the absent party according to law, or that the latter has failed to reply within the stated time, even though it afterwards becomes known that the former unbap-

376. S. Off. 5 sept. 1855; S.C.P.F. 14 iun. 1806.
377. S.C.P.F., 1924.
378. S. Off. 30 iun. 1937.
379. Ibid., 19 apr. 1952.

tized spouse was prevented from declaring his will or even was converted and baptized before the second marriage took place. Dispensation from the interpellations is not *ipso iure* from the Constitution
but is granted to local Ordinaries, pastors, and Jesuit confessors
approved in the place (and all missionaries having the general care
of souls, according to some) to be exercised only that the convert
party might enter into marriage with a Catholic. The new marriage
must be in the canonical form. As in *"Altitudo"* and *"Romani Ponti-
ficis"* the other canonical procedures in common with a Pauline case
are to be followed.

2. *Doubtful cases*

The Code states: "In a case of doubt, the privilege of the faith
enjoys the favor of the law."[380] In other words, a certain juridic pre-
ference is granted to contract a new marriage with a Catholic in
every case where such a union would result *in favor of the* (Catholic)
faith, and where, notwithstanding insoluble doubts, it is at least
certain that the former marriage can be *dissolved* by the ministerial
or vicarious power of the Apostolic See. This privilege is applicable
when any doubt arises as to whether all the conditions requisite for
the Pauline privilege or the Constitutions or the dissolution of some
type of natural bond are fulfilled. However, if the good of the faith
of the convert party does not require the dissolution, then the norm
of validity of a previous marriage[381] is maintained, i.e., that a
marriage is presumed to be valid and that a doubt is to be solved
in favor of the validity of a marriage until the contrary is established.

When the Baptisms of both parties to a consummated marriage are
in doubt the favor of the faith privilege does not apply. Reserved
to the Holy See are cases in which the Baptism of a non-Catholic
party in a marriage with an unbaptized person is involved in an
insoluble doubt.[382] Recourse is indicated in practice when the Catholic Baptism in a case is doubtful. No impediments to the new marriage, whether certain or doubtful, are removed by this privilege

380. c. 1127. Cod. Or. c. 116.
381. c. 1014.
382. S. Off. 10 iun. 1937.

but rather by the prescribed modes of dispensation. Likewise, there can be no sanation or suppliance of consent, but consent must be renewed by the parties themselves in the canonical form.

The doubt respecting the status of the original marriage must be one that is proved to be morally insoluble after diligent investigation, study and consultation have been made,[383] i.e., when moral certainty cannot be attained. The doubt may respect the existence of a marriage contracted in unbelief or its validity, the verification of the conditions for a Pauline privilege, the fact or validity of the Baptism of one party only, the person or identity of the first spouse in a polygamous union, the dissolution of a marriage contracted in unbelief, the sufficiency of the reasons for a departure, the sincerity of a reply to the interrogations or the adequacy of the reasons for dispensing from them, etc.

In certain cases—so-called "*aut-aut*" cases—the insoluble doubt or doubts may present a dilemma each horn of which opens an entirely distinct avenue of dissolution. Such a case may or may not involve the Pauline privilege or the Constitutions. The doubt regards which authority is to be operated under in the situation as a source for possible dissolution. However, in every case, no matter what the possibilities or the elements involved, the existing bond must be from any point of view chosen clearly dissoluble by the power of the Apostolic See.

3. *Other natural bond cases*

All things being equal, a marriage entered into between an unbaptized party and a baptized non-Catholic may be dissolved upon the desire of the unbaptized party to embrace the Catholic faith and to marry (or validate a union with) a Catholic, the non-Catholic party having already remarried after civil divorce.[384]

---

383. Ibid., 19 maii 1892.
384. Cf. ibid., 5 nov. 1924, upon petition of the diocesan curia of **Helena**, Montana, U.S.A., between an unbaptized man and a baptized Anglican woman. Divorce followed the original marriage, the Anglican remarried and the unbaptized man subsequently sought admission

Dissolution of the natural bond is possible likewise in a marriage between a baptized non-Catholic and an unbaptized partner when the non-Catholic party, subsequent to the breakup of the union, now wishes to embrace the faith and marry (or validate a union with) a Catholic person.[385]

Marriage contracted with a dispensation from disparity of worship between a Catholic party and an unbaptized person may be dissolved, upon the breakup of the first marriage, to allow the Catholic spouse (or even the unbaptized party after coming into the Church) to The current norms of the diocese and of the Holy See in all marry anew a Catholic party.[386] The current norms of the diocese and of the Holy See in all natural bond or privilege of the faith cases should always first be ascertained.

4. *Requirements*

Privilege of the faith cases that come under the Petrine privilege follow most of the procedures and observe the cautions already noted for Pauline privilege cases, such as securing adequate proofs, witnesses and testimonies or affidavits, promises not to keep company or live as husband and wife, instructions and delay of Baptism. As with a Pauline case, the regulations and procedures laid down by the Ordinary and his curia must be observed. Since it is a privilege or favor that is being sought, there is no *right* to *demand* even a consideration of the case by the Church and thus the latter may

to the Church and the favor of marriage with a Catholic woman. The Holy See has subsequently granted dissolutions of this type.

385. Cf. **ibid.**, 10 iul. 1924. The Holy See has subsequently granted dissolutions of this type. It has also dissolved such a union in order that the non-Catholic party, even without entering the Church but with the usual requirements, might validate a union with a Catholic party (**ibid.**, 3 aug. 1949; 3 iun. 1960).

386. **Ibid.**, 18 iul. 1947; 2 feb. 1955; 8 aug. 1955 in the **Fresno** cases, i.e., dissolutions granted upon petition of the diocesan curia of Monterey-Fresno, Calif., U.S.A.; also in the **Dedza** case, granted to the diocesan curia of Dedza in Nyasaland, Africa.

New norms of the Holy See (S.C.D.F., Instruction 6 dec. 1973) govern the solution of marriage cases in favor of the faith.

establish certain requirements as conditions for accepting a case and pursuing its course. Petrine privilege cases must be sent to the Holy See who judges the facts, especially the proof of non-baptism. In a successful case the dissolution of the first marriage takes place when the rescript is granted and its conditions fulfilled. A usual condition is that the unbaptized party is to be baptized before the second marriage is contracted.

The pastor or priest handling a case must make an informal investigation to ascertain if there is truly a case present and that the proper certifications can be satisfactorily secured before submitting a case to the local curia. Sound judgment must be made that the unbaptized party is not using entrance into the Church as a means of removing the impediment of bond (*ligamen*) to a prospective union with a Catholic. True sincerity is present usually if the party wishes to enter the Church even though there is given no likelihood (even an unlikelihood) that a new marriage can take place. A case is prejudiced if marriage is attempted nevertheless during the course of instructions or while the case is being considered by the competent authorities. There must be a grave reason for petitioning the favor of dissolution and the absence of scandal or amazement resulting.

XVIII. *Separation of spouses*

A. *Notion of Separation*

Marriage is defined as "living together in undivided partnership." Thus, married couples are obliged to preserve the common bond of conjugal cohabitation unless a justifying reason excuses them.[387] Normally conjugal life requires and obliges to the habitual sharing of bed, board, and home (*communio tori, mensae et cohabitationis*) for the full attainment of the purposes of marriage. Severance of

---

387. c. 1128. "If anyone says that the Church is in error when she decides that for many reasons husband and wife may separate from bed and board or from cohabitation for a definite period of time or even indefinitely, let him be anathema." Trent, Denz.-Schön., 1808.

this conjugal life, saving the bond itself, is called imperfect divorce or *separation*. Separation is total or complete if it includes the three-fold sharing; it is partial if it is from bed alone (mutual consent to abstinence from intercourse is not pertinent to this context). The common law of the Church refers only to complete separation.

Complete separation is either of itself *perpetual*, and then there is no obligation to resume the common life, or *temporary* only, which of itself must cease upon the cessation of its cause. The principal and practically only cause for perpetual separation is the adultery of one party. Mutual consent to complete and perpetual separation is seldom permissible because of the danger of incontinence and scandal. Only the Holy See may authorize this in the case of couples desiring a higher life of perfection.

B. *Perpetual separation*

1. *Cause*

Either party by reason of adultery on the part of the other has the right, though the marriage bond remains intact, to terminate the community life even permanently, unless he consented to the crime, or was the cause of it, or condoned it expressly or tacitly, or himself committed the same crime. There is a tacit condonation if the innocent party, after learning of the adultery, of his own accord receives the other with conjugal affection; condonation is presumed unless the injured party within six months expels or deserts the adulterer, or brings a legal action against him.[388]

2. *Requisites*

The crime of adultery must be a) *formal* or committed with a free and deliberate will and not through any force, fraud or ignorance; b) *consummated* or effected by perfect copulation and not merely attempted or begun by kisses, touches, embraces, etc.; consummated sodomy, bestiality, etc., are equivalent to adultery;[389]

388. c. 1129.
389. Cf. Rota decision, 29 nov. 1960.

c) *morally certain*, at least by sufficient signs or presumptions which leave no room for prudent doubt; d) committed *after Baptism*, since the sacrament totally wipes away the crime; e) *unapproved*, in that consent to the crime has not been given expressly or tacitly, e.g., by not preventing it when this could be done without great inconvenience or difficulty; f) *unprovoked* or caused directly and proximately, e.g., by frequent *unjust* refusal of the marital debt, by desertion, failure to provide, etc.; g) *uncondoned*, once the crime has become known, e.g., condoned by a request for or by a free rendering of the marriage debt, or by the continuance of a peaceful marital life with display of affection; h) *uncompensated*, in that the other party does not commit a similar crime.

3. *Authority*

The innocent party *may* terminate the conjugal life either in pursuance of an ecclesiastical decree upon proof of the fact or on his own private authority, provided that the crime is certain and public, i.e., either commonly known or committed in such circumstances as easily to give rise to such knowledge, or even if it is occult when serious inconvenience or hardship would result. Outside of cases of direct argument, such as admission of guilt, witnesses, etc., the authority of the external forum, i.e., the local Ordinary, should always be involved. A doubtful right to separate is to be submitted to the judgment of the local Ordinary.

"We forbid all married persons to go to civil tribunals in order to obtain separation from bed and board, unless they have previously consulted ecclesiastical authority. If anyone should attempt this, let him know that he has offended gravely and that he is to be punished according to judgment of the bishop."[390]

4. *Effect*

The innocent party who has departed lawfully, whether in pursuance of a judicial decree or on his own authority, is never bound to admit the adulterous party again to conjugal life; but he may

390. III Baltimore (1884), no. 126.

either receive or recall the party (who is to return), unless the latter has in the meantime with his (the innocent party's) consent embraced a state of life inconsistent with marriage,[391] such as religious vows or sacred orders. Other effects of separation are the same as mentioned below for temporary separation.

C. *Temporary separation*

1. *Causes*

The reasons mentioned in the common law[392] which would justify separation of spouses for a time are not taxative or exhaustive but exemplificative or categories of causes. Thus the delinquent spouse gives reason by: a) *joining a non-Catholic sect,* which involves a formal adscription to some sect[393] (spiritual adultery), but not if one spouse is a non-Catholic before the marriage took place; b) *educating the children as non-Catholics,* which is directly against the *bonum prolis* and a kind of spiritual adultery; c) *living a criminal and ignominious life,* which is to be understood as an habitual state or condition, such as a drunkard, jailbird, homosexual, etc.; d) *causing serious spiritual or bodily danger to the other spouse,* which danger to the *soul* would be continual or frequent provocation to serious sin, e.g., stealing, adultery, prostitution, (according to many) conjugal onanism, and to the *body* would be serious hatred, serious threats, disease such as is contagious in the use of marriage (e.g., syphilis) or presents an immediate danger (e.g., violent dementia), but not other diseases which rather should be occasions for solace and aid than separation; e) *cruelty,* such as beatings, serious and frequent quarrels, contumelies, squandering of the family funds, denial of sustenance, etc.

2. *Authority*

These and other causes of similar nature are so many lawful

391. c. 1130.
392. c. 1131, 1.
393. Including an atheistic sect (PCI 30 iul. 1934).

reasons for the other party to depart, on the authority of the local Ordinary, or even on his own authority, if the grievances are certain and there is danger in delay.[394] Separation must be practically the only way to avoid sin in these cases, especially in the use of marital relations.

3. Effect

In every case when the cause for the separation has ceased to exist, the common marital life is to be restored; but if the separation was decreed by the local Ordinary for a definite or an indefinite period, the innocent party is not bound to the common life unless by another decree of the Ordinary or upon expiration of the period. When separation is effected, the children are to be educated under the care of the innocent party, or, if one of the parties is a non-Catholic, under the care of the Catholic party, unless in either case the local Ordinary decrees otherwise for the good of the children themselves, always without prejudice to their Catholic education.[395] By a lawful separation granted by sentence of an ecclesiastical judge or by a decree of the local Ordinary, whether for an indefinite time or perpetual, a wife acquires her own proper domicile.[396] The woman and the children have a right to continued support. The civil law must be taken into consideration in each case, as it is not always the same as canon law.

D. Cautions

Cases of separation should normally be referred to the local Ordinary, or to the diocesan separation court where this exists. Particular diocesan law or regulations may specify further requirements in this matter. If the parties have already separated with or without recourse to civil authority and without ecclesiastical authorization the obligation need not be insisted upon nor the parties disturbed, if they are in good faith and no benefit can be expected from

394. c. 1131, 1.
395. Ibid., 2; 1132.
396. c. 93, 2; PCI 14 iul. 1922.

the admonition and if no great scandal exists. Civil separation or separate maintenance (or even civil divorce) may be necessary in a particular case in order to secure certain civil effects for the injured party. Such a process may be instituted only with the permission of the local Ordinary. The civil laws and the civil rights of parties as they exist in each State or civil jurisdiction are to be consulted, at least for the protection of the innocent party and the children. Pastors and confessors should take reasonable caution in separation cases to avoid the danger of a civil suit for alienation of affections being brought against them.

XIX *Civil divorce and marriage*

It is never permitted Christians to seek a perfect civil divorce for the purpose of entering a new marriage while still bound by the impediment of previous marriage bond (*ligamen*). For the purpose of settling certain civil effects it may be permitted—because necessary—that Catholics seek a separation or partial divorce, or even a complete divorce, provided that ecclesiastical permission to separate for a canonical cause has been obtained, that there is serious difficulty from which they expect to be freed by seeking such civil divorce, and that there is no other way to remove the hardship or disadvantage.[397] Civil divorce proceedings may be authorized in an individual case as long as it is clear that this is only for maintaining civil effects and to safeguard a party from injury, e.g., to regulate substantial property rights. Sometimes where a dissolution of a previous marriage bond has been granted by competent ecclesiastical authority it will be necessary to seek permission to secure a civil divorce in order that a second marriage in the Church become also recognized in civil law.

Since the marriage cases of Catholics depend solely upon ecclesiastical authority, the permission of the local Ordinary (or the diocesan divorce court) is necessary in order to invoke the civil law. The effects desired from the civil law are gained in some civil jurisdictions by a decree of separate maintenance or separation; conse-

397. The S. Poenit. by referring to approved authors (30 iul. 1892) seemed indirectly to approve this common teaching.

quently the ecclesiastical permission to go to civil court will be given only to this extent and not for a complete or perfect civil divorce.

When civil law requires it, it is not forbidden parties to present themselves before a non-Catholic minister acting only as a civil officer, merely for the purpose of performing the civil act of marriage for the sake of the civil effects.[398] However, American civil law everywhere recognizes pastors and qualified ministers of religion as authorized to officiate at marriages which are thus valid in civil law. Some civil jurisdictions require particular formalities, such as registration as an officiating minister, residence, etc., as well as witnessing of the marriage license. There is hardly ever an occasion for parties to a marriage to present themselves to a civil officer or justice of the peace, and still less to go before a non-Catholic minister, in order to secure the civil effects of their marriage. A case could arise— and a merely civil ceremony permitted by the local Ordinary—whereby the original valid marriage, meanwhile dissolved by a civil divorce in the sight of the State, is to be resumed, and thus a new civil ceremony is in order for its civil effects. Although there is no penalty in the common law for attempting marriage before a civil officer or a justice of the peace, a local prohibition may be in effect.[399]

XX. *Legitimation of offspring*

A. *Notion of legitimation*

Children are called legitimate or illegitimate inasmuch as the parents from whom they spring are validly joined in marriage or not. Illegitimate children are called *natural*, if no impediment existed which would have prevented their parents from validly contracting marriage; *spurious*, if it is otherwise; *sacrilegious*, if at least one of the parents is bound by solemn profession or by a sacred order;

---

398. c. 1063, 3.
399. Cf. III Baltimore, n. 124, which excommunicates one who dares to attempt marriage after obtaining a civil divorce or one who merely attempts marriage with a divorced person.

adulterine, if one of the parents is already validly married; *incestuous,* if the parents are related within the forbidden collateral degrees of consanguinity or affinity; *nefarious,* if within the forbidden degrees of the direct line. *Legitimacy* is a juridical quality conferred on a child born in wedlock; it produces definite effects in law based upon the natural dignity deriving from the natural law. *Legitimation* is an institution of positive law or a concession of a lawful superior which attributes to a child born out of wedlock at least some, if not all, of the juridical effects of legitimacy; being one of the inseparable effects of marriage, it pertains exclusively to an ecclesiastical tribunal. Permission should be secured in order to approach the civil court for the merely civil effects.

B. *Law*

Those children are legitimate who are conceived in or born of a valid or of a putative marriage, unless at the time of conception the use of the marriage previously contracted was forbidden on account of solemn religious profession or of the reception of a sacred order.[400] Foundlings are usually to be regarded as legitimate unless their illegitimacy has been proved (legitimation *ad cautelam* may be advisable in a case of promotion to Orders). The father is he who is shown to be such by the existence of a recognized marriage, unless the contrary is proved by sufficient evidence. They are presumed to be legitimate who were born at least six months after the day on which the marriage was celebrated or within ten months from the day on which conjugal relations were suspended.[401]

By the subsequent valid or putative marriage of the parents, whether it is a validation or the original contract, even if it is not consummated, the offspring is legitimated or made legitimate, provided the parents were qualified to contract a valid marriage with each other at the time either of the child's conception or of the

400. c. 1114; cf. Cod. Or. c. 103.
401. c. 1115; cf. Cod. Or. c. 104.
402. c. 1116. Cod. Or. c. 105. However, the subsequent marriage of the parents does not have the effect of legitimating a child begotten by them while they were bound by the impediment of age or of disparity

pregnancy or of the child's birth.[402] Legitimation by means of a dispensation from an invalidating impediment does not apply when the children are sacrilegious or adulterine.[403] The fact of the subsequent marriage of the parents is to be added in the margin of the baptismal register of the children who are recorded there as of unknown father or of unknown parents or of parents not joined in wedlock.[404] Notification of the celebration of the marriage is to be sent to the place of Baptism.

Children legitimated by a subsequent marriage are to be considered, as regards canonical effects, as the equivalent of legitimate children, unless the contrary is expressly provided.[405] Children legitimated by subsequent marriage may be admitted to the seminary.[406] Solemn profession removes the irregularity of defect of birth but not the illegitimacy itself.[407] A particular rescript from the Holy See may effect legitimation, as does a radical sanation.[408]

XXI. Conjugal act: right and obligation

A. Right

The procreation of offspring in marriage is achievable by the conjugal act; thus a prime obligation in marriage is the proper use of this act. As a fulfilment of exercise of the marital contract it is an obligation contained in the duty of marital fidelity (bonum fidei). In the fullest sense the conjugal act refers to marital intercourse which is of itself apt for generation. In the wider sense of including

of worship, which impediment, however, has ceased at the time of the marriage (PCI 6 dec. 1930).
403. c. 1051.
404. c. 777, 2.
405. c. 1117. Cod. Or. c. 106. For the exceptions cf. cc. 232, 2, 1º; 320, 2; 331, 1, 1º; 504; also cc. 984, 1º; 1363, 1-2.
406. PCI 13 iul. 1930. The local Ordinary may admit illegitimate sons, except adulterine and sacrilegious, if they possess the qualifications for admission into the seminary (Motu proprio **Pastorale Munus**, no. 31).
407. c. 984, 1.
408. c. 1138.

also the various actions which are accessory to conjugal intercourse which is to take place or which has been performed, it is sometimes called the use of marriage (*usus matrimonii*).

The right and duty of marital intercourse is both a natural institution and of divine law, and its fulfilment or observance may also be meritorious.[409] Marital love is uniquely expressed and perfected through the marital act, which within marriage is noble, worthy,[410] and meritorious when under the influence of charity.[411]

B. *Obligation to render the debt*

Each spouse has from the very beginning of marriage the equal right and duty with respect to the acts proper to conjugal life.[412] There is an obligation binding in strict and commutative justice to render the marriage debt when it is justly requested. The object

409. I Cor. 7:3-5. "Marriage, in every way, must be held in honor and the marriage bed kept free from stain; over fornication and adultery, God will call us to account" (Heb 13:4).

410. Pius XI, ency. **Casti connubii**; Vat. II, Const., **Gaudium et Spes**, no. 49.

411. Summa Theol., Suppl., q. 41, a. 4: "For if the motive of the marriage act be a virtue, whether of justice that they may render the debt, or of religion that they may beget children for the worship of God, it is meritorious (corp.). . . . The root of merit, as regards the essential reward, is charity itself; but as regards an accidental reward, the reason for merit consists in the difficulty of an act; and thus the marriage act is not meritorious except in the first way (ad 1). . . . The difficulty required for merit of the accidental reward is a difficulty of labor, but the difficulty required for the essential reward is the difficulty of observing the mean, and this is the difficulty in the marriage act." (cf. **Sed contra**). "The shamefulness of concupiscence that always accompanies the marriage act is a shamefulness not of guilt but of punishment inflicted for the first sin, inasmuch as the lower powers and the members do not obey reason (ibid., a. 3, ad 3) . . . . And since the marriage act, by reason of the corruption of concupiscence has the appearance of an inordinate act, it is wholly excused by the marriage blessing so as not to be sin (ad 4). . . . The excess of passions that corrupts virtue not only hinders the act of reason but also destroys the order of reason. The intensity of pleasure in the marriage act does not do this, since, although for the moment man is not being directed, he was previously directed by his reason" (ad 6).

412. c. 1111.

and end of the marital contract is something serious; the right to the body of one's spouse is precisely what is transferred in marriage and to deny its exercise or fulfilment is a serious vexation to the petitioner. There is thus a serious obligation to accede to a request that is made seriously, reasonably, and lawfully, whether expressly or tacitly. It admits of lightness of matter, and therefore it seems to be no great injury to refuse on one or another occasion, especially if the request is frequent or remiss. However, there may be an obligation at least in charity if otherwise the petitioner would be in danger of incontinence, such as pollution, or of some other great harm. If a spouse only grudgingly accedes to a request or makes intercourse too unpleasant, too difficult or too infrequent, there is an implicit denial. To cause oneself to become sterile is a violation of the right to the use of marriage and against justice.

C. *Obligation to request the debt*

Although a spouse has a strict right to the conjugal act, he has not a strict obligation in justice to request it, as he is free to exercise his right or not. There are times, however, when charity or some other virtue will require that the debt be requested. Such occasions arise when one partner is perceived to be in danger of incontinence, or out of a sense of shame will not make the request, or when it is useful to prevent dissension or to foster marital love and affection. It is the husband who normally makes an explicit request, whereas the wife requests implicitly, e.g., by showing certain signs of affection. The spouses by mutual and free consent may lawfully abstain from the act temporarily for some physical or spiritual benefit. Perpetual abstinence would be rare and only for a very serious cause.

D. *Limitations*

The right to the marital debt (and the correlative obligation to render it) is not unlimited. The area in which the right is inoperative is often difficult of precise determination because there are often physical, moral or spiritual conditions of individuals involved and even the necessity of medical advice. A graver cause must exist to deny the debt absolutely than to restrict it or to put it off for a period. Examples of causes recognized as sufficient justification to deny the debt are: a) if one spouse is guilty of adultery (likewise sodomy or bestiality) such as suffices for a cause for separation, or if a spouse has given sufficient cause for legitimate separation from bed and board; b) if one partner is affected by loss of reason or perfect drunkenness, etc., as long as the condition endures unless it becomes expedient to render the debt in order to avoid serious harm or hardship, such as beatings, incontinence, etc.; if both spouses should become insane, intercourse is unlawful because of the inability properly to procreate and educate offspring; likewise when only one spouse becomes insane, especially the mother, if there is danger to the offspring; c) if the request is immoderate or too frequent, as this can be harmful, especially to the man; intercourse more than two or three times a night even in early married life is considered immoderate and unlawful but not if it is not more than once a week, especially early in marriage; d) if immoral means are used, such as onanistic or sodomistic intercouse, or unlawful circumstances attend the act, such as others being present or liable to be scandalized; e) a *certain* impotency or inability to copulate (not merely an inability to generate) which renders the use of marriage unlawful and which has arisen subsequently to the marriage, since any probable hope of accomplishing true intercourse safeguards the use of the right.

Difficulties which can arise and which are intrinsic to marriage are not of themselves sufficient cause to deny the debt, such as the large number of children already born, past experience of a difficult pregnancy or birth, fear of another miscarriage, etc. The serious danger or hardship to either party or to the offspring must be also extrinsic to the marriage, as in the cases of serious illness, grave danger of abortion, serious heart trouble, probably communication of a contagious disease or of infection especially from frequent intercourse, a certain and grave danger of death in a new pregnancy (which danger should be certified from several prudent and expert medical and moral sources), the weeks immediately following childbirth, failure of a husband to provide for the present children, etc.

E. *Lawfulness*

1. *Conjugal act itself*

Conjugal intercourse as instituted and designed by God for the propagation of the human race is lawful when apt for generation and in accordance with the *bonum prolis* and the *bonum fidei*.[413] If performed for the proper purpose and in due circumstances, it is an act of the virtue of conjugal chastity and can be meritorious. Whatever takes place among spouses which is in consonance with the purpose of marriage and thus favors generation is thereby free from all sin. Whatever is opposed and positively impedes generation is always a serious sin. Whatever takes place between spouses and which is outside the purpose of marriage, neither favoring nor impeding it, of itself never exceeds more than slight sin. Meanwhile, if the attainment of the generation of offspring is impossible, the fostering of mutual love and the alleviation of concupiscence also supply a norm of morality.

2. *The intention of the spouse*

The intention of the spouse in performing the act of intercourse must be for a good purpose which is conformable to the end of the act itself. Positively to exclude the generation of children in marriage, to intend to take measures to impede its achievement is a serious sin. To intend explicitly another purpose of marriage and only to abstract from the generative element is lawful, since implicitly the latter is included. However, it is an inordinate use of a lawful thing and outside the purpose of marriage to intend principally and solely the pleasure of the act so that the generation of offspring is positively excluded or postponed (in the intention) ; this is at least slight sin.[414]

413. Cf. Gn 1:28; 1 Cor 7:3; c. 1081, 2.
414. Innocent XI (S. Off. 4 mart. 1679) condemned the proposition: "opus conjugii ob solam voluptatem exercitum omni penitus caret culpa ac defectu veniali." Denz.-Schön. 2109. Cf. also **Summa Theol.**, Suppl., q. 49, aa. 4-6.

A desire which is merely inefficacious—that conception will not take place—because of a condition of poverty of resources, infirmity or some other honest reason, is not sinful, as long as no unlawful means are employed to prevent conception and the act itself is apt to generate. It is serious sin for a spouse to engage in intercourse with an adulterous desire, i.e., to act under the consideration that another than the spouse is present or to desire to have intercourse with that person and consent to such a desire. To think of one's spouse as possessing the beauty or other features of someone else is not sinful, at least seriously, but it is dangerous because risking consent to adulterous thoughts or desires.

Intercourse is lawful even though it is foreseen that an unprovoked abortion or miscarriage will result later, since this is accidental to the good purpose of the act. It is also lawful for those who are sterile or who are advanced in years to engage in intercourse, as long as they can perform the act itself or enjoy the hope of doing so. Likewise if the seed is lost before or during copulation, since generation is accidental to the human action performed.

3. *Circumstances*

The natural position for intercourse is of itself obligatory. The parties face each other with the man taking the superior position stretching his body over that of the woman (*incubus*), while the woman assumes the usual supine position (*succuba*). It is sinful to change the natural position without any justification, but not seriously sinful, if the act performed is still apt to generate. It is lawful and not sinful for a sufficient reason to assume other than the natural position, e.g., during advanced pregnancy, because of some difficulty or a condition of frigidity, illness, obesity, etc., even if accidentally some seed is thereby lost. The couple will be justified in assuming any position which is most effective for them at any particular time.

It is of grave obligation that the act be performed in a secret place lest scandal be given. If the requisite privacy is perchance invaded, intercourse may be terminated immediately, even though seed is accidentally lost outside the vagina. Parents who live in straightened housing circumstances should be especially vigilant with regard to the presence of children, even though below the age of reason.

There is no prohibition of time regarding the conjugal act, even before approaching Holy Communion, although in an individual case abstinence at certain times may be advisable. When serious harm would result, the action would be unlawful. It is lawful but not advisable to copulate during the menstrual period. Danger of harm is always present in the few weeks after a birth and thus the action is unlawful in the measure of the harm involved. During a condition of pregnancy moderate use is always indicated, but it is unlawful to use the right when there is a danger of abortion or of harm to the child or mother resulting.

4. Accessory acts

Whatever is necessary or useful for complete copulation between spouses is in itself always lawful. Actions which do not constitute but are somewhat more or less connected with the act of intercourse, although seriously sinful for the unmarried, are not sinful at all or at least not seriously so for the married, since of their nature they are ordered to the marital act. These are the acts of lovemaking or love play. This requires that there develop an individual adjustment in marital relations, which must be learned and acquired principally through experience in married life, as it is not instinctive or automatic. The accessory acts, as well as the conjugal act itself, should be expressions of mutual conjugal love and not merely sexual releases or physically satisfying activities. They require an appreciation of differences of sex and personality, demand patience, tact and cooperation, and suppose a giving of the whole self or personality in a shared love with all that each can contribue to its fulfilment in moderation and the virtuous control of selfish exploitation or of the defect of perfunctory performance of a duty. The man, who is usually more quickly aroused sexually and more aware in this area, should extend and prolong his lovemaking so that the spouse, who is normally less sexually excitable and aware but more desirous and appreciative of expressions of love and affection, can attain her full measure of lawful satisfaction at about the same time. Mutual respect and love, and a sense of delicacy will carry the couple through the normal experience of adjustment in marital relations regarding what is mutually useful, and satisfying.

As long as there is no danger and intention of losing seed outside of marital intercourse, all imperfect venereal acts of lovemaking, whether mutual or solitary, are lawful, such as looks, touches, embraces, kisses, conversations, and other sexually stimulating acts. Spouses should refrain from truly obscene actions, such as rectal penetration, application of the mouth or tongue to the genitals, etc,. because these frequently present a danger of pollution, cause a lessening of conjugal shame, and make it easier for a slight sin to become serious. Merely to touch or to penetrate the rectum (mouth or other part) without danger of pollution, or to begin intercourse in such manner with the intention of consummating or completing it in the vagina, is probably not more than a slight sin; it is no sin at all if it is a necessary means in the individual case and with sufficient reason is undertaken to secure the lawful exercise of marital rights.

Although the woman is not obliged to do so, she may immediately after her husband's ejaculation in the vagina or immediately after his withdrawal upon ejaculation obtain her own complete satisfaction through her own or her spouse's efforts performed by means of touches or in some other manner. This is considered to be the natural complement of the conjugal act and to possess a moral union with the male insemination. It is commonly held that the woman may not do this if the husband withdraws in an onanistic manner, since the woman's satisfaction is then not obtained to complete true copulation but rather directly intended to procure pollution or orgasm. It is controverted but in practice there is no serious sin if a woman seeks her own complete satisfaction before the ejaculation of the husband but at least after the latter's penetration of the vagina. There would be no sin at all if there were good reason for doing so. However, the husband cannot complete his own act if the woman should withdraw or terminate the intercourse before insemination has been effected, since this would be pollution.

Morose delectation (and also desires) enjoyed with respect to intercourse with one's own spouse, regarding acts performed in the past or to be accomplished in the future, is no sin at all, or at most a slight sin, as long as there is no danger of pollution taking place or it does not regard seriously forbidden actions. Whatever is libidinous and opposed to the generation of offspring is seriously unlawful even for the married. Voluntary pollution had outside of marital intercourse, as well as whatever can induce the proximate danger of it, either in the man or the woman, is serious sin against chastity and also against commutative justice.[415] Likewise seriously sinful is any sodomitic or rectal intercourse, i.e., insemination in the rectal orifice, which is an unnatural sin and against conjugal fidelity. Regardless of the good intentions of the woman, vaginal lotions may not be used immediately after intercourse has taken place and insemination accomplished, since conception is thereby rendered impossible or unlikely. They may be used only if truly requisite for health; however, it is commonly taught that at least two or three hours must elapse (even longer if they are to be used for a lighter reason), and some twelve hours must have passed before applying a uterine lotion. It is required and suffices in confession that the sinner declare that he is married when confessing these sins.

5. *Cautions*

A confessor or a priest in the external forum must beware of hasty and minute questions concerning the various ways of accomplishing intercourse and of lawful or unlawful actions between spouses, since they are not always necessary for the integrity of confession or the effectiveness of counselling by the priest and may give rise to scandal. Questioned on such matters he should reply as briefly as possible and by the general principles of moral theology instead of descending to particulars and details. The instruction that is needed in a particular case may indicate that the penitent or spouse be

415. The S. Poenit. (2 sept. 1904) has stated that a confessor is to be denounced who instructs a penitent that wives do not sin who desire to have pollution as such out of love for an absent husband, or who promote such a pollution by touches as though performed by the absent husband, or who experience such a pollution in their desire for the absent husband.

referred to someone else who is prudent and expert or experienced in such matters.[416]

XXII. *Conjugal act*: *abuses*

A. *Artificial insemination*

1. *Notion*

Artificial insemination or fecundation is the injection by art of the male seed into the uterus of a woman and which takes place outside of perfect copulation. Artificial insemination of a woman by donor insemination, i.e., with the seed of a third party, even though it is done with the consent of the husband, is intrinsically evil, since the offspring is had in marriage but not *of* the marriage.[417] This type is not further considered here, but only the process in which the husband is the donor.

When there is not a substitution for or a replacement of the natural act of intercourse but merely an artificial aid to its achievement this may be called in a wide sense artificial insemination. Thus, it may be necessary or very useful in a certain case before intercourse takes place for the vagina of the woman to be dilated by means of an instrument in order, during the normal performance of coition, better to retain the male member and its ejaculate and thus provide for its reaching the uterus. Likewise, in another situation, after the spouses have achieved perfect intercourse in the normal manner in the vagina, a physician with the aid of a syringe or instrument injects into the uterus the seed already ejaculated into the vagina, without extracting it from the latter, so that fecundation, which otherwise would not have taken place, follows.

Artificial insemination in the proper and strict sense is accomplished in several ways. 1) During normal intercourse the husband withdraws at the point of climax and ejaculates the seed into some receptacle whereupon a physician collects it in an instrument and

416. Cf. S. Off., Instruction, 16 mai. 1943.
417. Pius XII, **Allocution to the Fourth International Congress of Catholic Doctors**, 29 sept. 1949; **Allocution to the Italian Catholic Union of Midwives**, 29 oct. 1951; **Allocution to the Second World Congress of Fertility and Sterility** (19 mai. 1956).

then or later injects it into the vagina or even the uterus. Similarly, the man may ejaculate into a condom during intercourse in order to provide seed for the physician's action.[418] 2) By a solitary pollution procured outside of intercourse, whether by voluntary masturbation or involuntary nocturnal emission, the husband deposits seed in a receptacle for a subsequent injection. 3) A physician draws off seed immediately from the testicles (epididymis or seminal vesicles) by means of a surgical puncture (aspiration of seed) and subsequently artificially injects it into the woman.

2. Morality

In the case of artificial insemination taken in the wide sense, natural and perfect intercourse is accomplished between the spouses; rather than opposing or frustrating nature its purposes in a natural manner may be more effectively aided.[419] For sufficient reason a woman may cooperate in this practice.

Artificial insemination in the proper sense is contrary to the order of nature and intrinsically evil. Any other method of transmission of seed between spouses, even though biologically possible, than conjugal intercourse in the usual manner is not permitted by nature and thus is unlawful, unjustifiable, and immoral.[420] A woman must resist in the same manner as required in the case of condomistic intercourse. A marriage is not considered to be consummated in this way, as there is no true conjugal act.

The malice of artificial insemination has been made clear by the Teaching Authority of the Church.[421]

B. Copula dimidiata

1. Notion

Intercourse is called *copula dimidiata* when there is only a

---

418. The same condition results from the husband depositing seed not in the vagina but at or about its mouth and which is then introduced by the physician's action.
419. Pius XII to Catholic Doctors, **loc. cit.**
420. **Ibid.**
421. S. Off. 24 mart. 1897; Pius XII, cf. no. 417 above; John XXIII, ency. **Mater et Magistra**, Denz-Schön., 3953; Paul VI, ency. **Humanae Vitae**, 25 iul. 1968, no. 14. Cf. also Pius XII as quoted.

very slight penetration of the vagina, at best a half or third, and nothing impedes further penetration. This, then, differs from the case when the seed is deposited merely at the orifice or between the labia,

2. *Morality*

The practice of this imperfect penetration without sufficient justification is at least a slight sin. It is not the perfection of the union of two in one flesh. It would be seriously sinful if the idea and intention in undertaking such a practice was totally to impede generation. Even though nothing is done to impede generation itself, a fear of procreating offspring, a desire to render conception more difficult or less likely are insufficient justifications and cause the practice to be venially sinful. A proportionate cause is present if a woman cannot bear full penetration because of some defect or infirmity in the genital organs or the pain caused thereby, or because of a form of vaginism which affects her at the time, etc.

A confessor may not encourage or permit this practice as a remedy against some form of onanism, since sin may not be encouraged. Scandal is more apt to arise in the area of sex morality than in any other and such a practice easily leads to a diminution of offspring and the practice of birth prevention. A confessor may not state something to be lawful, which is unlawful.[422]

C. *Amplexus reservatus*

1. *Notion*

The practice consists in coition which takes place with the intention of abstaining from insemination either within or outside of the vagina. The parties have developed sufficient control over the sexual functions that both can restrain their orgasm (*continentia amorosa*). The promoters of *amplexus reservatus* (also called *copula inchoata* or *reservata*) have recommended it as freeing the spouses to enjoy the physical pleasure of the conjugal act and of achieving the secondary ends of marriage, especially when there is need to restrict the bearing of children such as in a danger of a further

422. S. Off. 23 no. 1922 to the Bishop of Haarlem, Holland.

pregnancy and when abstinence (*continentia ascetica*) is too difficult and the use of the sterile periods insecure.

2. *Morality*

It cannot be held that *amplexus reservatus* is simply lawful, unob-
jectionable from the viewpoint of Christian morality and law and
recommendable for all.[423]

Even though this practice is not unassailable, it is not fully clear
that it is immoral in itself. Some hold that it is in itself, by reason
of its object, not immoral; only the purpose for which it is practiced or the circumstances in which it takes place will make it
immoral. As long as it is done by mutual consent, for a good purpose not opposed to the generation of offspring and for present
motives which are proportionately serious to risk the danger of
pollution, e.g., health, poverty, etc., it is an incomplete venereal action
permitted to spouses. It is conceded that this practice cannot be
indiscriminately recommended because of the tendency to indulge in
pleasure alone, the ever-present ease of pollution and the temptation
to practice onanism and forget the natural duty of marriage. Others
label *amplexus reservatus* simply and of itself unlawful and immoral,
at least slightly. The essential order to generation is lacking from
the intention of restraining insemination and the dangers noted above
cannot be divorced from this practice.

As a practice or system of conjugal relations *amplexus reservatus*
is not clearly proved to be immoral in itself. However, because of
the moral dangers noted above and the lessening of the true Christian
outlook on marital life which readily result from the purposes and
the pleasure involved, justification for it in an individual case would
usually be most difficult, such as the absence of the proximate dangers
listed, the right purpose, grave cause, founded expectancy of restraint from seeking mere pleasure.

D. *Conjugal onanism: natural onanism*

1. *Notion*

Conjugal onanism in general is vaginal copulation sought in such

423. S. Off. 30 iun. 1952.

a way as positively to impede generation which cannot result, although there is a flow of seed. In the proper and strict sense conjugal onanism is achieved by a human action alone, i.e., by withdrawal, without the use of artificial means or devices, and thus it is a natural onanism.[424]

2. Morality

a. malice

Onanism and every other manner of intercourse whereby the natural order to generation established by God is destroyed is intrinsically against nature and thus gravely evil, directly also against the good of fidelity. The way is opened up to many evil effects, such as injury to bodily health, nervous and emotional disturbances, especially on the part of the woman in whom also concupiscence is not satiated but rather increased through temptation to seek carnal pleasure elsewhere; discord, deceitfulness, and loss of a sense of respect and piety ensue; family life is affected since children strengthen the bond between spouses, and the children themselves benefit by being reared together. Sometimes onanistic parents suffer in the children they do have or, on the other hand, later in life when they find that it is impossible to have offspring. Catholic teaching has been explicit on the malice of onanism.[425]

b. cooperation

Cooperation is the giving of help to another for the performance

424. Cf. Gn 38:9.
425. S. Off., 21 maii 1851: "Q. What theological note is to be attached to the following propositions? 1o For upright reasons spouses are allowed to make use of marriage in the manner of Onan. 2o It is probable that this use of marriage is not prohibited by the natural law. 3o It is never expedient to question spouses of both sexes about this matter, even if it is prudently feared that the spouses, man or woman, would abuse marriage. Ad 1o. The proposition is scandalous, erroneous, and contrary to the natural law of marriage. Ad 2o. The proposition is scandalous, erroneous, and elsewhere implicitly condemned by Innocent XI in proposition 49a. Ad 3o. The proposition as it stands, is false, too lax, and dangerous in practice." Ibid., 19 apr. 1853: "Q. Is the imperfect use of marriage, whether onanistically or condomistically accomplished, as in the case, lawful? R. Negative.

of an act, or to act with another. Cooperation is *physical,* when by a physical action one helps another to perform an external action; it is *moral,* when influence is brought to bear upon the action by command, counsel, exhortation, confirmation, etc. (In the case of onanism the principal cooperation is physical, by the voluntary supplying of the necessary physical means of intercourse whereby the abuse is occasioned.) *Formal* cooperation is knowingly and willingly giving help in the performance of another's action inasmuch as this has a determined morality. Cooperation is *material* when there is a physical participation in the action of another without any intention of participating in and without any participating in its morality.

A spouse is under no obligation to render the debt to an onanistic partner, as the marriage contract did not surrender the right to the body for practices which frustrate the purpose of marriage. *Formal* cooperation in onanism is never permitted and is equally a serious sin, since it includes the approval of the sin of another or it wishes or intends the sin committed by another. It is a sin against chastity and against charity by scandal. The cooperation may be explicit by agreeing to the onanistic action or directly inducing it, or implicit by knowingly giving cause for it or indirectly inducing it by insistent complaints about the number of children, the difficulties of pregnancy or birth, etc., so that the husband takes the opportunity to practice onanistic intercourse.

Material cooperation in onanism may be lawful under due conditions, as long as the action is not intrinsically evil. The conditions

For it is intrinsically evil." Pius XII to Midwives (29 oct. 1951): "In his encyclical **Casti connubii** . . . Pius XI . . . solemnly related the basic law of the conjugal act and conjugal relations. 'Every attempt on the part of the married couple during the conjugal act or during the development of its natural consequences to deprive it of its inherent power and to hinder the procreation of a new life is immoral. No "indication" or need can change an action that is intrinsically immoral into an action that is moral and lawful.' This prescription holds good today just as much as it did yesterday. It will hold tomorrow and always, for it is not a mere precept of human right but an expression of a natural and divine law." Paul VI, ency. Humanae Vitae, 25 iul. 1968: "The Church, calling men back to the observance of the norms of the natural law, as it is interpreted by her constant doctrine, teaches that **each and every marriage act must remain open to the transmission of life.**"

are: a) there must be a proportionately serious cause, since the woman (or a man cooperator) is bound out of charity to impede the sin of another. The certain fear of discord or strife, of adultery on the man's part, of incontinence on the part of the woman, the serious difficulty for the woman of otherwise constantly abstaining from the conjugal act are examples of sufficient cause for material cooperation, since the woman has a strict right to place the action of intercourse. b) the cooperation must be only passive, in that the woman in no way gives consent to or approval of the onanistic intent or action of the spouse. The woman may feel and enjoy the sensible pleasure attached to the act and even be pleased at its result which is the failure to generate (which, however, is easily a dangerous frame of mind in the circumstances), but she must firmly detest the unlawful means used and be prepared to bear and to do all she can to eliminate the sinful methods. She may not show external repugnance to the sinful action and have internal consent, since all sin must be internally detested. Passive cooperation in onanism for a just and serious cause allows the woman the internal and external acts which would be lawful for her if intercourse were performed in the right way. The action of natural onanism is lawful in the beginning and performed in the natural manner; its evil comes from the intention of the onanist and from the withdrawal with loss of seed outside the vagina, and thus there is nothing intrinsically evil on the part of the action itself of intercourse until interrupted and frustrated. c) the onanistic spouse must be prudently warned and admonished of the proper manner of performing natural intercourse as often as, and up to the point when, there is a founded hope that the warning will be beneficial,[426] since charity obliges to this attempt. The wife is not bound to do this on every occasion, but on the other hand on admonition may be omitted entirely if it is prudently judged that it will be of no avail, since no one is bound to the useless; charity more than one occasion, as long as there is hope of correction. The would not bind the woman to her own grave disadvantage to impede the sin on only her husband's part.[427] The action of a confessor with

426. S. Poenit. 27 maii 1847.
427. S. Poenit. 23 apr. 1822; **ibid.**, 1 feb. 1823; **ibid.**, 3 apr. 1916; Pius XI,

penitents involved in withdrawal is considered under artificial onanism.

E. *Conjugal onanism*: *artificial onanism*

1. *Notion*

Conjugal onanism whereby generation is positively impeded by the use of artificial means or devices is called artificial onanism (onanism in the improper sense, also called neo-Malthusianism, anti-conceptionism, contraception, birth control, etc.). In this practice or method the man uses condoms, sheaths, caps, rubbers or safes, etc., either over the whole penis or only the glans penis; the woman during intercourse employs diaphragms (pessaries), jellies, caps, suppositories, sponges, tampons, false vaginas, foam, etc., inserted into the vagina to close off the mouth of the uterus to the entrance of the male sperm. Connected with artificial onanism but consequent to intercourse is the use of vaginal lotions, powders, antiseptic douches, etc., to expel or destroy the seed after it has been properly placed in the vagina. The morality of this latter practice has been considered above.

2. *Morality*

a. *malice*

Artificial onanism is a serious sin[428] whose malice is greater than that of withdrawal, since artificial means are employed to frustrate nature. The act in itself is wrong or vitiated from its very beginning, even outside the intention, since generation is precluded and becomes impossible. It is a serious sin against chastity and charity.

> ency. **Casti connubii** (31 dec. 1930): "Holy Church knows well that not infrequently one of the parties permits sin rather than commits it, when for a really serious cause a perversion of the right order is reluctantly tolerated. In such a case, there is no sin, provided that, mindful of the law of charity, one does not neglect to seek to dissuade and to deter the partner from sin."

428. Cf. no. 425 above.

b. *cooperation*

Formal cooperation in condomistic intercourse or artificial onanism is never permitted. (Cooperation in sodomistic intercourse is judged by the same norms.) *Material* cooperation in artificial onanism, since it is intrinsically wrong and evil in its beginnings, cannot be permitted in the sense that the woman can ever assume a passive attitude i.e., omit positive resistance, except when overcome by force or subjected to the fear of a very great evil. She is always obliged to offer continuous and active resistance to such an onanistic husband as a virgin is obliged to resist by force one who attacks her virtue.[429] Only when oppressed by force or faced with the gravest actual danger, e.g., loss of life, can she cease to offer positive resistance (and provided there is no proximate fear of consent to the intrinsically evil intercourse or of willingly having any part in it). Threats of adultery, cruelty, desertion, divorce, or perversion of the Catholic religious education of the children, etc., are serious dangers but not the very grave actual dangers listed by the theologians, such as serious beatings or woundings, the inability to offer further resistance, etc., as sufficient to cease positive resistance to intercourse which, e.g., uses a contraceptive device.[430] A woman must positively resist the introduction into her vagina of a sponge or of some such instrument able to impede the seed from reaching the uterus (like the insertion of douches, powders, etc.),

---

429. S. Off. 19 apr. 1853: "Doubt I. Is the imperfect use of marriage, either onanistically or condomistically, as in the case, lawful? R. Negative. It is intrinsically evil. Doubt II. Can a wife be knowingly passive in condomistic intercourse? R. Negative. For it would be an involvement in something intrinsically unlawful." S. Poenit. 3 iun. 1916: Q. 1. Is a woman held to positive resistance in the case in which to practice onanism the husband wishes to use an instrument? 2. If the answer is negative, do reasons equally serious as for natural onanism (without an instrument) suffice to justify passive resistance on the part of the woman, or rather are very grave reasons entirely necessary? 3. So that this whole matter might be developed and taught in a safer manner must a man using such instrument be truly compared to an oppressor: to whom then the woman must oppose that resistance which a virgin puts up to an attacker? R. Ad I: Affirmative. Ad 2: Provided for in the first reply. Ad 3: Affirmative."

430. S. Poenit. 3 apr. 1916.

nor may she do these things by herself, since it would be active cooperation in an act ordained to an evil end. There can be no cooperation in the occlusion of the vagina, and the use of a false vagina is intrinsically evil from the beginning, since the seed is not received in the due place or *vas debitum*. If the woman, against the husband's will, uses an occlusive pessary or some other birth control instrument or device to impede generation, the husband can in no way cooperate. He must exert his marital authority to forbid such action and, as far as possible, to remove and destroy the artifacts.

If from the beginning of intercourse the woman uses a cervical cap or some such device or bung to stop up the cervical canal, and if the seed is received in this as in an envelope, such action is morally equivalent to condomistic intercourse. If the seed, however, is deposited in the natural vagina but its further progress to the uterus is cut off by such means, it is not clear and definitely agreed, that this (although sinful) is intrinsically wrong from the beginning and thus that cooperation by the husband entirely forbidden. Since the definition of true intercourse does not contain the mouth of the uterus as an essential element, and since the artificial occlusion of the uterus temporarily is likened to the condition resulting during pregnancy or the permanent condition induced by total hysterectomy, doubt exists in the case as to the intrinsic evil of intercourse from the beginning. Thus in practice the husband may not be held to more than the conditions laid down for material cooperation in natural onanism.

c. *confessional treatment*

Penitents are to be seriously admonished to abstain from onanism in the future, when they spontaneously confess it as a sin and are conscious of its serious malice.[431] By fatherly and opportune instruction and advice they should be brought to a firm resolve here and now to desist from the practice in the future, to do what they can to eliminate the temptation, in particular by destroying all contraceptive devices possessed, and to have confidence in God's wise Providence, especially in face of an increasing family. More often penitents who bring up the matter or who ask questions have some

431. Pius XI, ency. **Casti connubii**; S. Off. 21 apr. 1955.

realization of its sinfulness. When onanism has been mutually agreed to, neither partner is disposed for absolution without a serious promise to cease, without a basis for hope of correction; they are habitual sinners and the confessor should follow the norms in such cases and with pastoral purpose. In a case only of cooperation, if the onanism cannot be prevented, the penitent should be disposed to cooperate only materially under the proper conditions. A man is to be more severely dealt with in this case than a woman, since he can more easily avoid this than the woman can. On the other hand, a woman is more apt to consent to partial or total continence. However, a woman should be questioned by the confessor whether she directly or indirectly induced the practice of onanism.

With all onanists there must be a warning given of the sin and instruction about its serious malice, even if there appears to be no probable hope of success in dissuading the penitent, and even if the penitent claims that he is not convinced of the evil of the practice or of the Church's teaching in this matter. In practice the questioning would be omitted only in the extraordinary case of a dying penitent who may be left in good faith, and there is no good to be gained by enlightening him and no future occasion of the sin or danger to the common good that is prudently judged. The common good of souls in a society permeated with the abuse of birth prevention requires that this practice be not allowed even to those who may perhaps be in good faith, and the confessor's silence can be a scandal to the faithful; rumor of indulgence, of connivance at or apparent approval of this practice is destructive of good morals. A confessor who exhausts the other means of dissuading a party from the practice of onanism to no avail cannot advise withdrawal as a lesser evil (due to the scandal involved), but he may discreetly insinuate the notion of periodic continence, as noted below. If the penitent will promise to refrain from the forbidden practice at least until a subsequent confession, absolution may be given.

If the confessor has basis for suspecting the presence of the sin of onanism, although the penitent has not accused himself of it, he must regularly question in a prudent and discreet manner, in terms which are general but yet sufficient to ascertain the facts. There must be a cause (either on the part of the individual or widespread conditions in a locality) for suspecting the presence of the sin, since it is wrong to interrogate even married penitents indiscriminately and confession is made difficult and even scandalous.[432]

What is said above applies to illicit actions and methods of birth prevention and regulation.

XXIII. Conjugal act: periodic continence and regulation of birth

A. Periodic continence

1. Physical aspect

Medical research has discovered a periodic rythm of fertility and sterility in the menstrual cycle of the woman. In the normal monthly cycle of menstruation the period of fertility or conception is eight days; the remaining days of the cycle, the sterile period, comprise a period of days before and a number of days following the first day of menstruation. Thus in every normal cycle there is a tidal movement characterized by a period of infertility or sterility, one of fertility, and a further space of infertility. The verification of this commonly recognized rhythmic cycle varies in practice in the concrete case with different individuals and in changed circumstances. Leeway has to be allowed for an absence of a constant cycle-length. For this reason, in any acceptable system followed to ascertain the rhythm of the periods, accurate observance of the requirements, great restraint and perseverance is required of the spouses, and there should be consultation of competent medical judgment.

By isolating the days (the ovulation period) in her own cycle during which intercourse would likely result in conception, a woman can determine or forecast on which days she is unlikely to become pregnant. Various means are employed to obtain this knowledge: charting the pattern of ovulation changes, body temperature or basal temperature readings, test tape method, etc.

The rhythm system, the system of periodic continence, or the "safe" period (i.e., safe from incidence of conception), requires an appreciation of individual biological and psychological factors that can vary in individuals and of the fact that with every method em-

---

432. S. Poenit. 10 mart. 1886.

ployed to compute the cycle of fertile and unfertile periods there is not always absolute reliability.

2. *Moral aspect*

As regards the conjugal act spouses are free to choose whatever time they wish to use their marital right or also to abstain by mutual consent. Thus they are not obliged to perform this act only during the fertile period, neither are they obliged to refrain during the sterile period.[433] God has endowed the nature of woman with both periods. Deliberately to limit the use of marital relations exclusively to the sterile periods in order to avoid conception (i.e., to practice periodic continence or rhythm) is, according to the common teaching of theologians, morally lawful *in actual practice* if there is mutual consent, sufficient reason, and due safeguards against attendant dangers. It is also common teaching that this practice of family limitation without good and sufficient reason involves a degree of moral fault. This fault certainly could be grave if serious injustice is done or there exists grave danger of incontinence, divorce, serious family discord, etc.

The two conditions required for the use of rhythm are: 1) mutual consent or willingness of the spouses to practice rhythm, lest the right be violated of one spouse reasonably requesting the debt; 2) their ability properly to observe periodic continence of the absence of danger of incontinence due to the practice, since it is not permitted to enter into a proximate occasion of sin. In addition to the conditions for use, there must also be sufficient justification or cause for adopting the rhythm plan.[434]

Spouses who are justified in practicing periodic continence fulfill the other purposes of marriage, viz., mutual love and fidelity and the

433. Pius XI, ency. **Casti connubii:** "Nor are those considered as acting against nature who in the married state use their right in the proper manner, although on account of natural reasons either of time or of certain defects new life cannot be brought forth. For in matrimony as well as in the use of the matrimonial rights there are also secondary ends, such as mutual aid, the cultivation of mutual love, and the quieting of concupiscence, which husband and wife are not forbidden to intend as long as they are subordinated to the primary end and as long as the intrinsic nature of the act is preserved."

434. Pius XII, Address to the Italian Catholic Union of Midwives (29 oct. 1951): (36) "There are serious motives, such as those often men-

alleviation of concupiscence. Unlike onanism, there is no physical hindrance or frustration places against the normal process of conception. On the other hand, to limit intercourse of set purpose to the sterile or unfertile periods in order to avoid conception—and to do so without sufficient justification—is certainly not without sin, granted the positive obligation upon couples to procreate.[435]

B. Regulation of births

In the responsible approach to the regulation of births by spouses with sufficient reason to space out births[436] there are norms by which any action or method is to be judged: 1) each and every marriage act must remain open to the transmission of life;[437] 2) the direct interruption of the generative process already begun and, above all, directly willed and procured abortion, even if for therapeutic reasons, are to be absolutely excluded as licit means of regulating births;[438] direct sterilization, whether temporary or perpetual, whether of the man or of the woman, is excluded;[439] similarly excluded is every action which either in anticipation of the conjugal act, or in its accomplishment, or in the development of its natural consequences,

tioned in the so-called medical, eugenic, economic and social 'indications,' that can exempt for a long time, perhaps even the whole duration of the marriage, from the positive and obligatory carrying out of the act. From this it follows that observing the unfertile periods alone can be lawful only under a moral aspect."

435. Pius XII, loc. cit. (29-35, 39-41); no. 10: "In relation to physical, economic, psychological, and social conditions, responsible parenthood is exercised, either by the deliberate and generous decision to raise a numerous family, or by the decision, made for serious motives, and with due respect for the moral law, to avoid for the time being, or even for an indefinite period, a new birth." Paul VI, ency. Humanae Vitae, no. 16: "If, then, there are serious motives to space out births, which derive from the physical and psychological conditions of husband and wife, or from external conditions, the Church teaches that it is then licit to take into account the natural rythms immanent in the generative functions, for the use of marriage in the infecund periods only, and in this way to regulate birth without offending the moral principles which have been recalled earlier."
436. Cf. previous note.
437. Paul VI, ency. Humanae Vitae, nos. 11-12.
438. Ibid., no. 14.
439. Ibid.

proposes, whether as an end or as a means, to render procreation impossible.[440]

Responsible parenthood is an obligation which is always serious and which is to be exercised with respect for the order established by God.[441] Moreover, the use of therapeutic means truly necessary to cure diseases of the organism, even if an impediment to procreation, which may be foreseen, is not unlawful, provided such an impediment is not, for whatever motive, directly willed[442]

XXIV. *Duties of spouses*

A. *To each other*

Married couples owe each other mutual love,[443] mutual help and solace,[444] and a common life or cohabitation.[445] These are obligations which are of themselves serious but allow of lightness of matter, and in certain circumstances and for proportionate causes do not oblige in whole or in part. It would be a sin against charity for one spouse to hold the other in contempt or hatred, or to sadden or anger the other with injurious words or deeds; likewise to deprive the other in any way of those things which are necessary for a decent maintenance of life and respectable condition. They are bound to preserve conjugal fidelity both internally and externally, and to render mutual aid in the carrying out of their respective duties and functions, in bearing the burdens of marriage, especially in times of adversity. Unless a legitimate reason excuses, they are to dwell together and share the same domestic or family life. The wife retains the domicile of her husband and is bound to follow the husband wherever he fixes his residence, unless reasonably excused.

In the society of the family the husband is the head and the woman has been given to him as helpmate and associate, thus owing him due reverence and obedience in all good and lawful things. Husband and wife are absolutely equal as persons with consequent equal

440. **Ibid.**
441. **Ibid.**, no. 16; **Gaudium et Spes**, no. 50.
442. **Humanae Vitae**, no. 15.
443. Cf. Mt 19:5; Ep 5:25; Tt 2:4; 1 Tm 2:15; Col 3:18.
444. Cf. Gn. 2:18.
445. Cf. Mt 19:5; Gn 2:24; Ep 5:31; c. 1128.

rights; also with respect to the marriage contract. But they have different roles to fulfill in the procreation and education of offspring, which roles are interdependent rather than unequal. In these functional differences the headship of the husband is more in terms of the common good of the family unit. He must protect and provide, and in this function he is aided by the wife, just as the wife is aided in her role of maintaining a comfortable home and of supervising the daily rearing of the children. The relationship is a partnership and companionship with each contributing according to ability the best performance of their respective roles for the common welfare, physical, material, spiritual. Patience, forbearance, kindly consideration and even at times substitution in another's role are the hallmarks of conjugal love and fidelity. Both must edify by example and correct by counsel and friendly persuasion. The common goods or fortune as well as individual possessions must not be dissipated or injured, nor domestic peace and comfort disturbed by word or action or negligence.[446]

B. *To their children*

Parents have the serious duties of teaching their children what is necessary for them,[447] to correct them when necessary or expedient,[448] and to give them good example. The fatherly power or authority (*patria potestas*) over the offspring, which by nature belongs to the father and subordinately to the mother, requires that provision be made for the well-being and rearing of the children. Civil authority may further detail this obligation in regard to its extent and responsibility affecting the public good. It should also supply public aids for the parents in fulfilling their duties and should safeguard the children from parental neglect, but it may not supply for or supplant parental authority or rights. Ecclesiastical authority

---

446. Cf. 1 Cor 11:3; Gn 2:18; Col 3:18. Cf. Leo XIII, ency. **Arcanum divinae sapientiae**; Pius XI, ency. **Casti connubii**; Vat. II, **Gaudium et Spes**, nos. 49-50; **Apostolicam Actuositatem**, no. 11; Paul VI, ency. **Humanae Vitae**, no. 9.
447. Cf. Dt 11:19; Ec 7:25; Pr 22:6. Cf. Vat. II. **Gaudium et Spes**, no. 52.
448. Cf. Pr 13:13-14, 24; Ep 6:4; Col 3:21.

may further specify the spiritual obligations of the parents toward their children.

The parental duty to care for their children (even illegitimate) so that they might take their proper place as individuals, as citizens of the community, and as sons of God and members of the Church is a serious office. They must provide for the physical, mental, and spiritual life and development of the offspring, certainly until the attainment of maturity and self-sufficiency. They are to provide for the future reasonable opportunity of the children to live decently, as children are not for the enrichment of the parents but vice versa.[449] In their choice of state of life, children are free and independent of their parents, although the parents should in all piety and prudence be consulted and their advice respected. According to their capacity and experience parents are bound to counsel their children about their future; they sin if they force a state of life upon them or if without sufficient cause bring about the abandonment of their choice.

---

449. Cf. 2 Cor 12:14; cc. 1113, 1372; **Summa Theol.**, II-II, q. 101 a. 2, ad 2.